# Letters to Mollie
## from Her Mormon Past
## 1860 – 1912

Also by Gary C. Vitale:

*Practical Approaches for the Actor and Director*
*Practical Principles for Public Speaking*

# Letters to Mollie

## *from Her Mormon Past*

## 1860 – 1912

## Gary C. Vitale

Mill Creek Press
Springfield, Illinois

First printing 2003

Although the author and publisher have exhaustively researched all sources to ensure the accuracy and completeness of the information contained in this book, we assume no responsibility for errors, inaccuracies, omissions, or inconsistencies. Any slight to people or organizations is unintentional.

Library of Congress Control Number: 2003101400

ISBN 0-9727438-0-4

Printed in the United States of America

o Jean

s should be forever.

# Errata

Page 11:   The birth date of Adaline Works should be April 1, 1809.

Page 18:   The age of Abigail "Nabby" (Marks) Works at the time of her death, January 28, 1846, should be 64, not 75.

Page 21:   The death date of Aunt Adaline (Works) Bonney should be February 10, 1857, not 1859.

Miriam "Mollie" (Works) McNutt
1844 – 1920

# Contents

# ILLUSTRATIONS

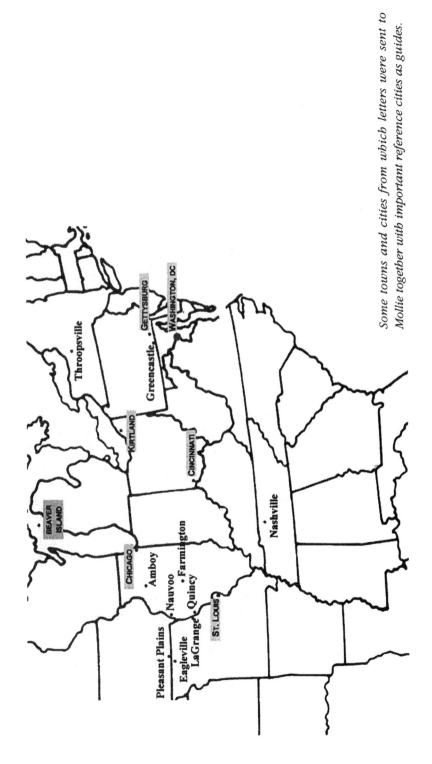

*Some towns and cities from which letters were sent to Mollie together with important reference cities as guides.*

**Ebenezer Robinson** *(1816-1891). Baptized by the Prophet, Joseph Smith, Jr., and married to Angeline Works by Smith, Ebenezer was a staunch Mormon, but balked at "spiritual wifery." He set the type for THE BOOK OF MORMON, 2ND EDITION, and arranged for the printing of the 3rd edition. With Don Carlos Smith, he edited Nauvoo's newspaper, TIMES AND SEASONS. When Brigham Young won out over Sidney Rigdon after Smith's death, Ebenezer edited the Rigdon faction's newspaper, LATTER-DAY SAINTS MESSENGER AND ADVOCATE, and when Rigdonites tried to establish a Zion in Pennsylvania, he founded Greencastle's CONOCOCHEAGUE HERALD (now the ECHO-PILOT.) He broke with the RLDS in 1886. With John and David Whitmer, he founded the Church of Christ. The autobiographical account of his Mormon experiences were being serialized in yet another of his newspapers, THE RETURN, when he died.*

**Angeline Eliza (Works) Robinson** *(1814-1880). Sister of Miriam (Works) Young, Brigham's first wife, Angeline, with her parents, Asa and Abigail (Marks) Works, were Mormons very early in New York. In Ohio, she married Ebenezer Robinson, gave money for the Kirtland Temple, and, with her parents and younger brothers, suffered in Missouri before settling with Ebenezer in Nauvoo, Illinois. With Ebenezer, she followed the Rigdon faction to Pennsylvania and there gave birth to her only child, Grace. Plagued with unnamed illnesses much of her life, she enlisted her nieces as hired girls: the Rockwells, Adliza first, then Deborah Ann; and finally Mollie, the orphaned daughter of her brother Asa Daniel Works.*

# INTRODUCTION

## 🌸 Finding the letters

In late summer, many years ago, I went with my wife and her parents to Fall Creek (Illinois) township and the McNutt family farmhouse. New tenants were moving in, and some decisions had to be made about various family items that had made their way to the attic of the 1849 farmhouse, a farmhouse whose land deed had been signed by President James Monroe. In an old trunk in that attic, we found letters—letters more than 140 years old.

Some of them were in envelopes; some without. Most of the valuable stamps had been torn or cut off. Shredded remains had been used as nests for mice, but a surprising number of the letters were intact. With only a little interest, we looked at some, dusted off others, and put all into a convenient shoebox while we decided whether a hatstand was worth wrestling down a narrow staircase.

For two years the letters stayed in shoeboxes on a closet shelf. Then one February day, when the world seemed an endless grey, we opened the box and slowly began reading directly from a century we had only heard about before. The writing on many of the pages was very clear, a result of good ink and better paper. Soon, reading the letters and transcribing them into typewritten copy became a pleasant winter pastime. But transcription required not just deciphering the words on the pages, but knowing who was being written about, who was being written to, and what was being referred to. Research followed, and the result of that research is this volume.

The letters were written to Miriam (Works) McNutt, called "Mollie." She was the niece and namesake of Miriam (Works) Young, the first wife of Mormon leader Brigham Young. She was my wife's great grandmother. Many of the letters were written by her cousins, almost every one a follower of Joseph Smith, Jr., the founder of the Mormon religion. The bulk of them were written between 1860 and 1869, during and immediately after the Civil War and during the early formative days of the Reorganized Church of Jesus Christ of Latter Day Saints. Of the letters that survived, 111 are reprinted here. Most are from that time in Mollie's life just before and after her marriage. Some later letters, from the 1880s on, are included because they explain what happened to people who wrote to her during those eventful 1860s.

The letters come from three primary places: Pleasant Plains (now, Pleasanton), a small town in extreme south central Iowa; Eagleville, Missouri, a town immediately over the border from Pleasant Plains; and LaGrange, Missouri, a former bustling steamboat stop on the Mississippi River, eight miles north of Quincy, Illinois. Although there are postmarks on the letters from St. Joseph, Missouri, and Farmington, Illinois, for instance, they occur because the people in these three primary towns travelled for a short time to other places and wrote from there. The other places from which Mollie received letters were the forts, camps, or post hospitals that were the mailing addresses of her cousins and friends in the Union army.

Mollie received these letters because in the fall of 1862 she left Pleasant Plains and travelled to Payson, Fall Creek township, near Quincy, Illinois, to begin a new life away from her Mormon[1] heritage. She and her brother, Perry, had been orphans since she was eight and he, five. He had stayed in Illinois while Mollie had been taken to Iowa to live and work for an aunt. Aunt and uncle were Mormon, and, with them, Mollie found herself in the Mormon community of Decatur County, Iowa. There she grew to young adulthood. At sixteen she decided to find her brother and return to Illinois.

While she modestly made a life of her own, her friends and cousins wrote to her. Without a true home that she could remember, the letters she received became precious to her. She kept them even after she married. Sometimes she would hide them under rugs in her farmhouse. Few of her husband's relatives remembered her childhood friends, and Mollie, who had never been Mormon and felt a certain embarrassment about the more scandalous aspects of the religion, rarely talked about her very early life. She died in 1920. In the trunk she had brought with her from Iowa were the letters.

## 🌸 Editing the letters

Nothing in the letters has been deleted in this publication of them.[2] They are as they have survived. This includes their sometimes elaborate formal salutations, openings, and closings. From the earliest (1860) letters to the latest (1912), the language of the letters becomes more modern, even telegraphic. All of the idiosyncrasies of a letter writer's style are preserved.

Spelling has been standardized to make the letters easier to read. The cue for this editorial decision was taken from the writers themselves, many of whom begged Mollie to "excuse bad spelling and writing and make all well." In an age when spelling was far from uniform, it is hardly surprising that a letter writer might spell "unis," without capitalization, when she meant "Eunice." To save today's reader having to struggle through such spellings and to free the letters of an unwholesome peppering of footnotes, all spelling has been "made well."

Punctuation and capitalization have been added where there were none in some of the letters. Often, letter writers made no distinction between the end of one sentence and the beginning of another—no period, no capital letter. In some cases, this resulted in ambiguous meanings. Research resolved most quandaries as to whether a prepositional phrase such as "in the spring" or an adverbial clause such as "when I saw you last" belonged at the beginning of the next sentence or at the end of the last sentence.

Paragraphing, a clarification device unknown to most of the letter writers, was done simply in the edited versions. A new topic deserved a new paragraph, even if it was a one sentence paragraph. The letter writers, after all, were closer to a tradition in which sentences were sometimes written perpendicularly across others in order to save paper and postage. A reader had to extract meaning from a grid of words as if it were hidden behind a cross-wire fence. Though none of Mollie's letter writers practiced this older tradition, very few of them used paragraphs, and some pages of the actual letters are hemmed with tinier and tinier words that are stitched to an edge in a somewhat desperate effort to save another piece of paper.

Where the full name of the person who is written about is known, the name is written directly into the letter. For instance, where Louisa Booth actually wrote, "Olive and I went to meeting up to your

Uncle's to meeting and I give Grace the letter you sent to her..."
bracketed names identifying the people referred to allow the reader a
better understanding of the passage, so that, in the edited version, it
reads, "Olive [Booth] and I went to meeting up to your Uncle
[Ebenezer Robinson]'s to meeting and I give Grace [Robinson] the
letter you sent to her..."3

Finally, the letters were put into a standard format. The dateline
was usually in the upper right of the first page of most of the letters,
so all of the letters were standardized in this way. Most letters
separated the salutation from the body of the letter, so that, too,
became standard. Where pictorial material was added to the letters
(an outline of a strawberry to impress Mollie with its size, the stick
figure of a man, etc.) notes in brackets indicate where in the letter
these occur. Sometimes there were extraneous additions to the letters:
a name and address of someone, the lyrics of the national anthem.
These were transcribed with the letter as well to show that the letters,
after they were received, were sometimes reused. In fact, the rare
letter *from* rather than to Mollie has survived because it was written
on the back of a letter written to her.

## 🌺 Background of the letters

Because it is necessary to read the letters with Mollie's memory,
not ours, a CHRONOLOGY OF PAST EVENTS precedes the letters. This
chronology is a concise list of events in the Asa Works family as it
was affected by the Mormon movement. Asa Works, Mollie's paternal
grandfather, and the first father-in-law of Brigham Young, began as a
fifer in the Revolutionary War in Massachusetts and was buried in
Nauvoo, Illinois, just before the Mormons abandoned that stronghold.
Although the beginnings of the Reorganized Church of Jesus Christ of
Latter Day Saints and the Civil War affected Mollie most, without
some notion of her past, we cannot begin to understand the actions
of those adults who influenced her early life. The CHRONOLOGY OF PAST
EVENTS gives a bare outline of that past.

In 1842, Mollie's parents were married in Adams County, Illinois.
Until that time, her father had gone with his parents as they moved
from Aurelius town, Cayuga County, New York (near Auburn), to
Kirtland, Ohio, and on to Far West, Missouri, following the migrations

of the early Mormon church. In Far West (near present-day Independence), the persecution of the Mormon settlements by the Missouri mobs and the infamous executive order by Governor Lilburn Boggs to "exterminate" the Mormons eventually drove the sect to Illinois. The people of Adams County were moved by the atrocities the Mormons suffered in Missouri, such as the killing of 42 people that came to be known as the Haun's Mill massacre. The Illinoisians welcomed the retreating Mormons to Quincy and the surrounding countryside in the winter of 1839.

With the help of his son-in-law Ebenezer Robinson, Asa Works, his wife, and his two youngest sons settled in a country home outside the city of Quincy. Soon, however, the Robinsons moved north to Nauvoo, the city the Mormons were building on the Mississipppi riverfront in a grand way. The Workses, except for Mollie's father, Asa Daniel (now in his early twenties) moved with the Robinsons. On January 23, 1842, Asa Daniel Works married Deborah Malcolm, a young woman who had come from New Jersey with her sister, Rachel (Malcolm) Stewart. The couple moved to the new city of Millville (now Marblehead), Illinois, south of Quincy. Like many other towns on the banks of the upper Mississippi River, Millville was full of people hoping to prosper as a favorite port of call for steamboats.

Besides farming, Asa taught school. His small family did not have luxuries: two horses, two cows, three hogs, and a wagon. In contrast, Deborah's brother-in-law Samuel Stewart, had five head of cattle and hogs, and other goods and chattel, $100 more of taxable property than Asa had. Inside the Works' cabin, Deborah had tables and chairs, bedsteads, a stove, pots and pans, and a desk coffee mill. Asa had carpentry tools, plows, a lot of hogback, and a lot of beef—enough to last the family through the year. There was one cradle.[4]

Miriam Works was the first child of Asa and Deborah's to live (a son, Leander, had died earlier). "Miriam," meaning "thick, strong," was the name of the biblical prophetess who was the sister of Moses and whom God punished for speaking against him. Her name's tradition did not fit Mollie, for she was small, thin, and by all accounts meek. Her name came to her from her father's sister, Miriam (Works) Young, Brigham's wife, and could be traced to her great grandmother, Miriam Marks, the mother of Abigail (Marks) Works, her father's mother. Often, the nickname, "Mollie," was given to girls whose first names were "Mary," "Maryann," "Marian," "Mariam," or "Miriam." Mollie, as the letters prove, was called by all of these names.

If they were unsure what to call her, her friends and relatives were not likely to forget her birthday. She was born on the exact day that Hyrum and Joseph Smith, Jr., were killed in Carthage, Illinois—June 27, 1844. On that fateful day, firebells and churchbells aroused the people of Quincy—not to Mollie's birth, of course—but to the possibility that the dreaded Nauvoo Legion would be marching to avenge The Prophet's death. Hundreds from Hancock County, where Nauvoo was the largest city, abandoned their homes and farms and streamed south to Quincy, fearing Mormon reprisals. The next morning, when it was obvious there were to be no reprisals, they returned sheepishly to their homes. From the day of her birth to at least the day of her marriage, Mollie's life would be affected most by the forces that were unleashed by the visions of the Mormon Prophet from Palmyra.

As it was in the year of Mollie's birth, the Mississippi River, in 1851, flooded until it was "...like a vast sea from bluff to bluff." Families on "the bottoms" were drowned out and had to move to Quincy or other high ground.[5] Food prices were rising: Beef was 8 cents a pound, and mutton was 7 cents. A cholera epidemic was beginning. The winter of 1851 – 52 was very cold. Whatever the cause, cholera or cold, Asa Daniel Works died on January 18, 1852. His wife, Deborah, was very ill. She had moved the family—Mollie and Perry—in with her sister, Rachel. Perhaps because she felt herself dying, Deborah made her brother-in-law, Samuel Stewart, administrator of her estate. It was during this time that Mollie's most vivid childhood memory, seeing her aunt Rachel packing up the Works' goods and provisions— "stealing" them—burned itself into the mind of the seven-year-old. Three months later, her mother Deborah was dead, and the two orphans were given over to the guardianship of Samuel Stewart, who signed the official document by making an "X" for his name.

Mollie did not stay long with the Stewarts. When her aunt Adaline (Works) Bonney came from Quincy, Illinois, in the first week of September, 1852, Mollie gladly went with her. The Bonneys: Amasa and Adaline, but not their son, Joseph, decided to move north to a community of believers who had gone west as far as Iowa after abandoning Nauvoo. The community was in Decatur County, near an area called Nine Eagles. Already there were such recognizable families as the George Moreys, the John Keowns, the Alfred Moffets, the Austin Cowles, and the Ebenezer Robinsons. The Amasa Bonneys, with Mollie in tow, joined them.

In Decatur County, Mollie grew from a girl to a young woman. While she did so, the adults she lived with, who could neither accept the leadership of Brigham Young, nor forget the religious exaltation of their early Mormon experience, worked to fashion a church, a religion, that they believed would be true to the best of what the Prophet from Palmyra had left them. They finally settled on Joseph Smith III, the son of the Prophet, as a leader. But the young man was not ready to wear his mantle until 1860.

In the meantime, schooling continued, and in Decatur County, Mollie was taught in the Moffet Schoolhouse. There she made friends with young people like Helen and Eunice Morey, Henry Cowles, George Keown, Sallie Monk, Bob Booth, and her own cousin, Gracie Robinson. In the many letters that she would receive, these were the names that would stir her memories.

Then, in February, 1859, her aunt Adaline died. Amasa Bonney decided to return to New York. Once again, Mollie was without a home. A cousin, Deborah Ann (Rockwell) Morey, who was a housewife before she was fifteen, had been recently given the added burden of caring for her brother's child. Mollie, the eager worker, moved in with the Moreys. When David Morey decided to move to Illinois in 1860, Mollie worked and lived in her aunt Angeline (Works) Robinson's home.

Ever since she was old enough to pull a stool up to a sink to stand on while she "did up the work" (washed and wiped dishes), she was earning her stay with her labor. It did not matter that her young cousin, Gracie Robinson, always seemed to have a "hurry call" that took her to the outhouse right after meals, Mollie worked and she learned from her aunt Angeline.

But as she grew older, she began to feel the pressures of her situation. She had not yet been baptized in Brush Creek by George Morey, head of the Little River Branch of the Reorganized Church of Latter Day Saints. So many had been baptized in Brush Creek that it was known as "Mormon Pool." She was also coming to an age when she should be married. Although the greater demands of the Civil War were felt later, already young men in Decatur County had enlisted and were leaving. And what of her brother, Perry? Where was he? Was he in the army? She had not seen or heard from him since she had so willingly left Illinois for Iowa.

This is Mollie's situation when she writes her first letter to her cousin Joe Bonney, who was living in LaGrange, Missouri. Joe's response is the earliest letter to Mollie that survives, and it begins the central part of this book, the letters in chronological order. Before each letter is a brief explanation of some of the people and events that Mollie would be familiar with. Through letters that span the years, Grace Robinson grows from an exuberant schoolgirl to the saddened matron who must, in one week, bury both her baby and her mother. At the same time, Amulek Boothe passes from a carefree young man to a religious convert, a soldier, a father, and finally a work-stiffened old farmer—all the while seeming to nurture a love for Mollie that was only a little beyond what cousins should show one another. These are only two of the stories that come alive by reading the letters.

## 🌸 Researching the letters

To work such magic, many minds and much charity was needed. Thanks go to the staffs of research facilities such as the Illinois Historical Library, the Illinois State Archives, the St. Louis Public Library, Auburn (New York) Historical Society, Case-Western Reserve Library, Newberry Library, Graceland College Library—especially its DuRose Room—and the archives of the Reorganized Church of Jesus Christ of Latter Day Saints and the genealogical library of the Church of Jesus Christ of Latter Day Saints.

There were unexpected and most generous sources of help from individual genealogists such as Mrs. Nancy Gerlock, a descendant of Deborah Ann Morey, and Mrs. Mary Hemphill, a descendant of James Marks Works. Charlotte Wright provided information on the Boothe family; and Betty June Johnson on Pleasant Plains and the Cowles family.

Inestimable are the kindnesses of McNutt family members, Mollie's grandsons George A. McNutt and Robert G. McNutt, who provided the letters themselves, many of the photographs, and encouragement through the years. A long memory and willingness to share that memory made the contributions of Miriam (McNutt) Echols, another of Mollie's grandchildren and the last, so far, to bear her name, especially valuable. Some valuable private genealogy work was done by Mrs. Nell Simpson, a descendant of Iola (Bonney) Sellers. Out of a barn in Canton, Missouri, where they had been stored after her death, her notes, jumbled in a cardboard box, were given over to me.

The sources of information for the book are roughly divided into three categories. First, there are public sources such as censuses, deeds, records of wills, lists of soldiers, and other official documents. Then there are the common sources such as newspapers; the approved history of the Reorganized Church of Jesus Christ of Latter Day Saints; the applicable county histories; the biographies of the renowned and near-renowned; Civil War almanacs, old medical books; old song books; privately published family histories, such as those on the Gurleys and Rockwells; and the works of other scholars studying various aspects of the Mormon movement. Finally, there are private sources. The series of letters from James E. McNutt to Mollie, his mother, as he went west to Utah in the 1890s; the bit of information from a family remembrance about how Deborah Morey dressed a wound or what made John Keown angry; the tape-recorded interviews of Manly Amulek Boothe, Lew Moffet, Austin Cowles, and Miriam Echols; the pages of the Robinson family bible; and James Alexander McNutt's accounting ledger.

From these three types of sources and patience and time and the generosity of others who shared their knowledge, the letters began to become understandable. With the untiring hard work and expertise of my good friend Mark Pence, the manuscript was designed and prepared for printing. The people of the letters began to emerge from their pages—human beings, not just names; lives, not just dates. With this publication is the hope that, in the imaginations of its readers, these very real people will live again.

Gary C. Vitale
Springfield, Illinois
December, 2002

NOTES

1. Though members of the Reorganized Church of Jesus Christ of Latter Day Saints do not now like to be referred to as Mormons, during those early days, as the letters attest, they did identify themselves with that term. Since 1999 they prefer to be called the Community of Christ, though they still recognize Reorganized Church of Jesus Christ of Latter Day Saints (RLDS) as an official designation.

2. Being more respecters of paper than words, the farmhouse mice have been rather strict redactors, sometimes excising whole pages. Wherever logic could replace the missing words, they have been replaced; otherwise, missing portions are noted in the letters as they occur.

3. Note that the extra "to meeting" was not deleted, nor was "give" corrected to "gave." All this, to preserve the flavor of Louisa's language.

4. Estate Records of Asa D. Works, Adams County, Illinois, filed January 21, 1852.

5. *History of Adams County, Illinois 1879* (Chicago: Murray, Williamson, and Phelps, 1879) p. 424-5.

# CHRONOLOGY OF PAST EVENTS

## LEADING TO THE WRITING OF THE LETTERS

(Names of letter writers are boldfaced.)

| | |
|---|---|
| 1801 | Asa and Abigail (Marks) Works, Mollie's paternal grandparents, are married. Their sons and daughters, whose birthdates follow, include Mollie's father as well as her aunts and uncles, those who raised her, taught her, and provided her homes. |
| 1802 | Joseph Tunnicliff Works, first child of Asa and Abigail Works, is born near Cooperstown, N.Y. After his first wife dies, he will leave his two children with her relatives and marry in Ohio. |
| 1804 | Abigail Works is born in Aurelius, N.Y. She will be the mother of **George** and **Deborah Rockwell**, two of Mollie's cousins who became important letter writers. |
| June 7, 1806 | Miriam Works is born in Aurelius, N.Y. She is Miriam ("Mollie's") namesake and will marry Brigham Young and bear his first children, Elizabeth and Vilate. |
| 1809 | Adaline Works is born in Aurelius, N. Y. She will be the first of Mollie's paternal aunts to offer her a home, and she will become the mother of **Joseph Bonney**, Mollie's cousin and lifelong correspondent. |

June 23, 1811    Parthenia Works is born in Aurelius, N.Y. She will become the mother of **Angeline** and **Amulek Boothe**, two more of Mollie's cousins who become letter writers and friends.

August 22, 1814   Angeline Works is born in Aurelius, N.Y. She will be most influential in raising Mollie, and she will become the mother of **Grace Robinson**, Mollie's cousin, a lifelong letter writer, and later the mother of Mollie's daughter-in-law.

May 19, 1815    Jerusha Works is born in Aurelius, N.Y. She will become the mother of **Charles Worden**, Mollie's cousin and a Civil War soldier.

May 25, 1816    Ebenezer Robinson is born in Floyd, N.Y. He will marry Angeline Works and father **Grace Robinson**. His work in the Mormon Church includes editing and publishing several Mormon newspapers and an edition of the *Book of Mormon*. He gave Mollie a home.

1819        Asa Daniel Works is born in Aurelius, N.Y. He will marry Deborah Malcolm and father Mollie and **Perry Works**.

October 5, 1821   James Marks Works, the youngest of Mollie's uncles, is born in Aurelius, N.Y. He is in Nauvoo, Ill., at its end, and he will live in Brigham Young's home in Salt Lake City, Ut.

October 8, 1824   In Port Byron, N.Y., Brigham Young, he a glazier, brickmaker, and Methodist at the time, marries Miriam Works, Mollie's aunt.

1826        Deborah Malcolm is born in New Jersey. She will come to Illinois with her sister, Rachel, and become Mollie's mother.

| | |
|---|---|
| March 27, 1827 | Near Hill Cumorah, N.Y., Joseph Smith, Jr., says he is visited by the Angel Moroni and is taught from the golden plates of the *Book of Mormon*. |
| April 6, 1830 | In Peter Whitmer's farmhouse near Fayette, N.Y., the Church of Christ, with the Bible and the *Book of Mormon* as its scripture, is legally established. Many of the Workses become early Mormons. |
| February 1, 1831 | In Kirtland, O., Joseph Smith, Jr., is welcomed by Sidney Rigdon's Campbellite congregation which has converted to Mormonism. |
| March 26, 1831 | Cousin **Angeline**, eldest child of Lorenzo Dow and Parthenia (Works) Boothe, is born in Cayuga County, N.Y. |
| September 6, 1832 | In Throopsville, N.Y., aunt Jerusha Works marries the widower John Worden, while her sister Angeline Works is a witness. |
| September 8, 1832 | Aunt Miriam (Works) Young dies in Mendon, N.Y. |
| July 23, 1833 | In Kirtland, O., cornerstones are laid for the first Mormon temple. Mormons move to Kirtland. |
| November 12, 1833 | In Rochester, N.Y., cousin **Joseph**, second son of Amasa and Adaline (Works) Bonney is born. |
| April 4, 1834 | Cousin **George**, fourth child of David and Abigail (Works) Rockwell, is born in Geauga County, O. |

| October 16, 1835 | Joseph Smith, Jr., baptizes Ebenezer Robinson in the Chagrin River near Kirtland, O. |
| December 13, 1835 | Angeline Works, Mollie's aunt and teacher, weds Ebenezer Robinson in Kirtland, O., Joseph Smith, Jr., performs the ceremony. |
| March 27, 1836 | Kirtland Temple is dedicated in the rain; Sidney Rigdon gives a dedicatory speech; George Morey, who will later influence where Mollie will live, is one of the doorkeepers. |
| May 26, 1836 | Cousin **Amulek**, third child of Lorenzo and Parthenia (Works) Boothe and writer of 15 letters, is born in Geauga County, O. |
| 1836 | Sidney Rigdon convinces church leaders that its name should be the Church of Christ of Latter-day Saints since the end times were at hand; Church founder David Whitmer insists the full name of Christ be included. |
| December, 1836 | Angeline Robinson and Amasa Bonney, among others, buy shares in the Kirtland (Anti) Bank(ing) Society, an unchartered Church bank that goes bankrupt. |
| | Ebenezer Robinson helps set type for *Book of Mormon*, second edition. |
| Spring, 1837 | Financial Panic of 1837 hits. |
| April 17, 1837 | Ebenezer and Angeline Robinson leave for Far West, near present-day Independence, Mo. the Zion, or gatheringplace, for Mormons. |
| May 1, 1837 | Asa Works and his family leave Aurelius, N.Y., for Kirtland, O., and then Far West, Mo. |

| | |
|---|---|
| January 12, 1838 | Joseph Smith, Jr., and Sidney Rigdon flee Kirtland, O., for Far West, Mo. |
| July 4, 1838 | At Far West, a second Mormon temple is begun; a belligerent speech against Mormon persecutors by Sidney Rigdon angers non-Mormons. |
| August 6, 1838 | Mormons voting in a block sway a sheriff's election; a mob attacks; Mormons are wounded. |
| August 30, 1838 | Missouri Gov. Lilburn Boggs orders Maj. Gen. David Rice Atchison to raise 400 armed and equipped militia for action against the Mormons. |
| October, 1838 | A mob kills 30 Mormons at Haun's Mill, Shoal Creek, Mo. |
| October 25, 1838 | Armed Mormons, including George Morey, rout a Missouri mob at Crooked Creek, Mo. |
| October 26, 1838 | In a letter, Missouri Gov. Boggs orders the extermination of Mormons. |
| October 30, 1838 | Mormon Crooked Creek warriors, including George Morey, flee north to Iowa, through the Pleasant Plains area, later a home to Mollie and many of her letter writers. |
| November 1, 1838 | Far West Mormons surrender to Missouri militia; many Mormons, including Ebenezer Robinson, are taken prisoner. |
| April 15, 1839 | Bailed or escaped Mormon prisoners find refuge in and around Quincy, Ill. |

| | |
|---|---|
| April 25, 1839 | Church committee selects the former Commerce, Ill., renamed Nauvoo, in Hancock County, as the new Mormon gatheringplace. |
| | Ebenezer Robinson sends for his wife, her parents and their youngest sons to come from Far West, Mo., to Illinois. |
| May, 1839 | The Robinsons and Asa and Abigail Works are living in a loghouse on the banks of the Mississippi River in Nauvoo, Ill; Asa Daniel Works, 20, soon to be Mollie's father, stays near Quincy in Adams County, Ill. |
| July, 1839 | Ebenezer Robinson and Don Carlos Smith, brother of the Prophet, begin printing *Times and Seasons*, first Nauvoo newspaper. |
| March 30, 1841 | In Danbury, Conn., cousin **Deborah Ann**, the seventh child of aunt Abigail (Works) and uncle David Rockwell is born. She will live in Geauga County, O. |
| April, 1841 | In Nauvoo, the Robinson printing business is so successful he builds brick home and office. |
| January 23, 1842 | Asa Daniel Works and Deborah Malcolm, Mollie's parents, are married by Rev. Elijah Reed in Millville, Ill., near Quincy. |
| January 28, 1842 | Joseph Smith says God wants the Church to own *Times and Seasons*, Nauvoo's newspaper. |
| February 4, 1842 | Ebenezer Robinson sells printing business and home/office to Joseph Smith, Jr.; Robinsons are forced to take up temporary lodging with their good neighbor, Aaron Johnson. |
| March 9, 1842 | Asa and Abigail Works, Mollie's grandparents, receive a patriarchial blessing from Hyrum Smith, the Prophet's brother, in Nauvoo. |

| | |
|---|---|
| May, 1842 | Ebenezer Robinson builds a row of 11 rental tenements on Kimball Street next to his friend Austin Cowles' property in Nauvoo. Renters include Lorenzo and Parthenia Boothe, parents of cousins **Amulek** and **Angeline**, and Amasa and Adaline Bonney, parents of **Joe**. |
| October, 1842 | Countering newspaper reports, the Robinsons and others sign affidavits that only the marriage ceremony in the Mormon *Doctrine and Covenants* was known to them. |
| July 12, 1843 | Joseph Smith reveals his doctrine of spiritual wives (religious polygamy) to church leaders; Austin Cowles, father of Elvira, one of Smith's wives, resigns from the Nauvoo High Council. |
| July 31, 1843 | Robinsons leave for the eastern states on a Mormon mission, Angeline stopping in Ohio because of the death of her sister, Abigail (Works) Rockwell, mother of cousins **George** and **Deborah**. |
| October 18, 1843 | Mollie's grandfather, Asa Works, 78, with help from neighbor Aaron Johnson, applies for a Revolutionary War pension for his service at Battle of Monmouth; his pension is denied. |
| December, 1843 | In Nauvoo, Ebenezer and Angeline Robinson are taught the doctrine of spiritual wives by Hyrum Smith, brother of Joseph. |
| May, 1844 | Joseph Smith, Jr., announces his candidacy for President of U.S. |
| June 7, 1844 | First and only issue of *Nauvoo Expositor* is published, exposing details of how young women are enticed into becoming spiritual wives. |

| | |
|---|---|
| June 10, 1844 | *Nauvoo Expositor* press and copies are destroyed; editors flee to Carthage, Ill. |
| June 18, 1844 | The Ebenezer Robinsons and Sidney Rigdons leave for Pittsburgh, Pa., campaigning for presidential candidate Joseph Smith. |
| June 24, 1844 | Joseph and Hyrum Smith, John Taylor, and Willard Richards are jailed in Carthage for their own safety. |
| June 27, 1844 | A mob "overpowers" Carthage jail guards, killing Joseph and Hyrum Smith, and wounding Taylor. Farm families, fearing a Nauvoo army, flee to Quincy, Ill., where church bells ring warnings of possible Mormon revenge. |
| | Robinsons and Rigdons arrive in Pittsburgh, campaigning for Candidate Smith. |
| | **Miriam "Mollie" Works** is born in Millville (now Marblehead), Ill. |
| August 8, 1844 | Rigdon's plan for the future of Mormon Church, including high posts for Ebenezer Robinson, George Morey, and Austin Cowles, is defeated by the oratory of Brigham Young; Rigdon returns to Pittsburgh to found his own Mormon church. Robinson publishes its newspaper, *The Latter Day Saints Messenger and Advocate*. |
| February 15, 1845 | Asa Works, 83, Revolutionary War soldier and Mollie's grandfather, dies and is buried in Nauvoo, Ill. |
| January 28, 1846 | Abigail "Nabby" (Marks) Works, 75, Mollie's grandmother, is sealed as a spiritual wife to Brigham Young, once her son-in-law. |

| February 4, 1846 | Federal troops, coming up the thawing Mississippi River to test Mormon allegiance in the matter of war with Mexico, are a strong incentive to many in Nauvoo to cross the river into Iowa, beginning the hand-cart and wagon trek west. |

March 17, 1846 — Mollie's aunt, Parthenia (Works) Boothe, wife of Lorenzo and mother of **Amulek** and **Angeline**, dies in Nauvoo.

Spring, 1846 — Rigdonite Mormons buy a farm near Greencastle, Pa., for their New Jerusalem.

May, 1846 — Robinsons move to Greencastle, Pa., Ebenezer founding its first newspaper, *Conococheague Herald.*

July 14, 1846 — Abigail (Marks) Works, Mollie's paternal grandmother, dies of cancer; her youngest, James Marks, is the only Works left in Nauvoo to bury her.

October 14, 1846 — In Millville, Ill., **Perry Works**, Mollie's brother is born.

January 2, 1847 — Lorenzo Dow Boothe, father of cousins **Amulek** and **Angeline**, drowns while crossing the frozen Des Moines River in Iowa. Two children, cousins **Amulek** and **Angeline**, remain in Iowa while the rest of the family goes on to Utah.

1848 — Adam Dennis marries Mollie's cousin **Angeline Boothe**, and they settle in northern Missouri.

December 22, 1849 — Cousin **Grace**, the only child of Angeline and Ebenezer Robinson, is born in Greencastle, Pa.

| | |
|---|---|
| 1851 | "King" James Jesse Strang, leader of Mormon Strangites on Beaver Island, Mich., begins plural wife-taking; he is immediately rejected by Zenas Gurley, Sr., and other prominent members of the sect who begin prayer vigils to find a new leader. |
| Winter, 1851-52 | Especially harsh winter; cholera in Adams County, Ill. |
| | George Morey receives a letter praising the south central Iowa region, Hamilton Township, Decatur County; the Moreys, Keowns, Trumans, and Cowles prepare to move. |
| January 18, 1852 | Asa Daniel Works, 33, Mollie's father, a schoolteacher and farmer, dies; Mollie's mother, Deborah, is ill; the family moves in with Mollie's aunt Rachel (Malcolm) and uncle Samuel Stewart. |
| January 23, 1852 | Mollie's mother, Deborah (Malcolm) Works, makes her brother-in-law Samuel Stewart legal guardian of Perry and Mollie before she dies. |
| June 12, 1852 | Zenas Gurley leads others into signing resolutions against holy polygamy, declaring 19-year-old Joseph Smith III the true leader of the Mormons. |
| September, 1852 | Amasa and Adaline (Works) Bonney take the orphaned Mollie with them to Decatur County, Ia. |
| 1854 | Ebenezer Robinson buys 160 acres in Hamilton Township, Decatur County, Ia. |
| April, 1855 | The Robinsons take their niece **Deborah Rockwell** from Geauga County, O., to Iowa. |

| November 12, 1855 | Cousin **Joseph Bonney**, son of Amasa and Adaline, marries **Sarah Abigail "Sallie" Johnson** in LaGrange, Mo. They will write many letters to Mollie. |
|---|---|
| January 1, 1856 | David Morey, 26, son of George Morey, marries **Deborah Ann Rockwell**, 14. |
| February, 1859 | Aunt Adaline (Works) Bonney dies. Her husband Amasa returns to New York; Mollie, homeless and 13, works for her cousin **Deborah (Rockwell) Morey** and their aunt Angeline (Works) Robinson. |
| 1859 | **George Rockwell**, after his wife dies, brings his two children west, leaving his oldest child with his sister, **Deborah (Rockwell) Morey**. |
| April 6, 1860 | Joseph Smith III, 27, accepts the leadership of the Reorganized Church of Jesus Christ of Latter Day Saints (RLDS). He is ordained by Zenas Gurley, Sr. and Joseph Briggs in Amboy, Ill. |
| May 6, 1860 | **Joseph Bonney** writes Mollie Letter #1 from LaGrange, Mo. |
| September, 1860 | David Morey moves his family to Illinois to be near the new church headquarters; Mollie, 16, is with her aunt and uncle Robinson in Decatur County, Ia. |
| November, 1860 | Abraham Lincoln is elected president. |
| December 9, 1860 | **Deborah Morey** writes Mollie Letter #2 from Amboy, Ill. |
| December 24, 1860 | South Carolina secedes from the Union. |

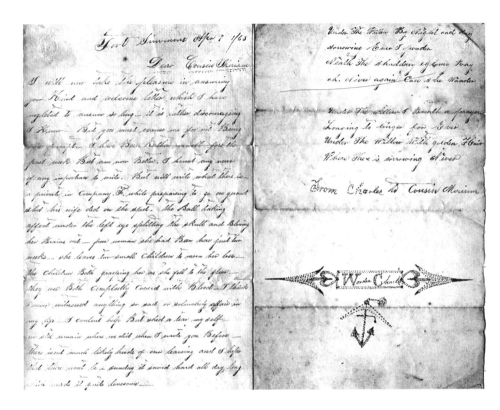

*The first page and last insert, showing song lyrics and artwork, of Letter #17 from Charles Worden, Union soldier.*

*Main Street of Pleasanton (formerly Pleasant Plains), Iowa, in 1914.*

# DREAMS OF A NEW LIFE

# 1860

## 🌸 Letter #1

This was a year of decision for Mollie. On June 27, she would be sixteen years old, and because she was an orphan, most of her life had been lived in other people's homes. In 1852, the year her mother, Deborah, died, she lived with her uncle Samuel and aunt Rachel (Malcolm) Stewart near Payson, Illinois. That same year, from nearby Quincy, her uncle Amasa and aunt Adaline (Works) Bonney had come to take her with them to extreme south central Iowa near Pleasant Plains. There the Bonneys joined relatives and friends—like the Robinsons and the Moreys—who were working to establish a new organization of the Mormon church.

The south central Iowa countryside is rich with rolling hills. It is a land the Mormons knew well. Their migration west from Nauvoo, Illinois—the famous hand cart and wagon trek—had taken them through south central Iowa on the way to Council Bluffs and, eventually, the Valley of the Great Salt Lake. As they travelled, they kept north of the dreaded Missourians, and they left provisions for others who would come after them in places like Garden Grove and Decatur County.

Since the spring of 1854 when it was laid out, Pleasant Plains (present-day Pleasanton) was a small town. It is so near to Missouri that part of a cemetery spills casually over the border without incident. Some of the earliest settlers in the area came with dreams of success: A Hungarian refugee who named a township New Buda in memory of his homeland was one of the first postmasters; Allen Scott built a horsemill for corn grinding; and many Mormons settled there, hoping to reorganize their faith into what it once was.[1] They disagreed with Brigham Young, James Jesse Strang, James Colin Brewster and other Mormon leaders who emerged after Joseph Smith was killed in 1844. Many of them had quit believing in James Jesse Strang the moment he started practicing polygamy on Beaver Island, Michigan. Some of them had come to Iowa after leaving the bankrupt Sidney Rigdon sect in Pennsylvania. All were intent on preserving what they believed to be the best of Mormonism. In April, 1860, they would choose as their leader, Joseph Smith III, the twenty-seven-year-old son of the Prophet of Palmyra. By then, Mollie was living with another aunt and uncle, Ebenezer and Angeline (Works) Robinson. The Robinsons and others were filled with hope for the newly ordained Smith and their church, the Reorganized Church of Jesus Christ of Latter Day Saints (RLDS).

But Mollie dreamt of a new life, and she felt that only her brother Perry could make it come true. Perry would be fourteen now. She had tried to write to him, addressing his letter to the Stewarts. Before her mother died, their uncle Sam Stewart had been made their legal guardian.[2] But Perry had moved away from the Stewart farm, and Mollie's first letter did not reach him. That is why she wrote to her cousin Joe Bonney in nearby LaGrange, Missouri.

Joe had not gone with his parents to Iowa. He had stayed in Missouri to marry Sarah "Sallie" Johnson and work as a sawyer in the steamboat town of LaGrange, eight miles north and across the Mississippi River from Quincy, Illinois. Joe and Sallie were just beginning their family, and their year-old daughter, Ella May, had recently died.

The oldest letter in this collection is the answer that Mollie receives from her cousin Joe about Perry's whereabouts. In it, Joe also mentions one of their other cousins, Amulek Boothe, a young bachelor across the Iowa border in north central Missouri who will be important to Mollie in reaching Illinois.

LaGrange, Missouri                    May 6, 1860

Dear Cousin,

[1]    I take this opportunity of writing you a few lines in answer to your letter. I was glad to hear from you and the rest of the folks. This is the first letter that I have got from any of you for the last 12 months. I never got a letter from Cousin Amulek [Boothe] nor Deborah [Ann Morey]'s and tell them that I should be glad to hear from them, and that I answer all the letters that I get and am always glad to hear from them and that I have often thought of writing to Amulek but didn't know where to write to, so that he would get it. Tell Amulek that I want him to write so that I will know where to write to and I will be much obliged to him.

[2]    We are all well at present and hope this may find you enjoying the same blessings. We lost our little girl [Ella May] about ten months ago. We have another one that is two months old. It only had a birthday leap year. Its name is Effa Josephine. I should like to have you come and see it. If not, I should like to come out and see you all, and will as soon as I can.

[3]    I have sold my house and am building another house, and it will keep me busy this summer. And if I can, I shall come out this fall and see you all. I have been wanting to come out for a good while, but times are so hard that I couldn't money enough to come, but am coming, as soon as I can, and see you all.

[4]    You inquired about Perry [Works]. He was well a few days ago, and I have sent for him to come and live with me so that you can have the opportunity of hearing from him often.

[5]    I haven't heard from your Uncle [Samuel] Stewart's folks lately.

[6]    This is all at present. Write soon so that we can hear from
       you all. Tell Uncle [Ebenezer Robinson] that I should like to
       have him write to me, that I wrote to him 10 or 12 months
       ago and got no answer. I want you to write soon, and I will
       answer your letter. This is all today that I think of.

       From your most affectionate cousin,
       J. E. Bonney

## ❧ Letter #2

The only other letter from 1860 is one from Mollie's cousin
Deborah Ann (Rockwell) Morey. It is written from somewhere near
Amboy, Illinois, near the new headquarters of the Reorganized
Church of Jesus Christ of Latter Day Saints. Deborah's husband,
David, a church deacon, took the family there in the fall of 1860.

Deborah's father-in-law, George Morey, was High Priest of the
Iowa Little River Branch, the local RLDS branch. He counted twenty
church members, including some of the early settlers of Pleasant
Plains.[3] He, too, was one of the first settlers in the region, bringing
with him his family and his daughters' families, the Keowns and
Trumans, to the rolling hills that he remembered as he escaped the
Missouri mobs of 1838.[4]

During "The Troubles" of 1838, Missouri governor Lilburn Boggs
had issued an order to "exterminate" the Mormons,[5] and since then
Missourians had little toleration for the sect. Nearly twenty years later,
when the Morey families began to settle just across the border in
Iowa, a posse from Missouri rode up and requested that they leave. "I
have come to stay," George Morey told them, and when they threatened to come back the next day, he said: "Fine, you will find me
here." The bullies never returned.[6]

Soon, others from failed Mormon sects were coming to the south
central Iowa region. Among these was the former Rigdonite, Ebenezer
Robinson, in whose care was a niece, young Deborah Rockwell.

Deborah's mother, Abigail (Works) Rockwell, had died when
Deborah was two. Before the Robinsons came to Iowa, they stopped
in Huntsburgh, Ohio, near the Kirtland Temple where the Rockwells
lived. In the same way that Adaline Bonney had taken Mollie,

Angeline Robinson took her niece, fourteen-year-old Deborah, with her to Iowa.[7] Living on the Robinson farm next to the Moreys, it was not long before Deborah met George Morey's oldest son, David.

On New Year's Day, 1856, a full three months shy of being fifteen, Deborah married twenty-six-year-old David Butterfield Morey. The next Christmas they buried their first child. By the time she was nineteen, Deborah had given birth to two other children, and young Mollie was helping out in her home.[8]

Deborah had much to do. Besides her own children, she also cared for a young niece, Adrianna. Deborah's brother, George Rockwell, brought his children Adrianna and Clara with him from Ohio after their mother died. As was the custom, the children of widowers—especially girls—were given to relatives until the widower remarried or the children could decide for themselves [See Letter #60, par. 3]. In Illinois, George had placed his youngest daughter, Clara, with relatives. In Iowa, George left five-year-old Adrianna with his sister Deborah. (Adrianna is called "Ada," "Ady," or "Adria" in the letters).

Although by 1861 Deborah returned to live again on the Morey farm in Iowa, this second letter of the collection, with cousin Deborah's comments about Illinois, must have been precious to Mollie, for she, too, would soon be moving back to that state.

[near Amboy, Ill.]                    Dec. 9, 1860

Dear Cousin,

[1]     I suppose you are beginning to think that I am not very
        punctual in keeping my promises. If you do, you don't miss
        it much. But however, I am going to make my word good
        once by scribbling a few lines to you.

[2]     I suppose you would like to know how I like Illinois. I can tell
        you it looks rather naked, not half as pretty as Iowa in some
        respects. But I think it is a greater country for produce.
        There! I need not to say no more about it for I am very well
        pleased so far, if we can only succeed in getting a farm.
        There is plenty of land but not many houses. I suppose we
        will have some difficulty in getting a house.

[3]     We are at present living with his [David Butterfield Morey's]
        uncle's folks and I enjoy myself very well, and they seem like
        my own folks. I don't know but we shall have to stay with
        them all winter, but we want to get to housekeeping if we
        can.

[4]     I wrote to Adam [Dennis]'s folks last week. Have you seen
        any of them? Write me all the news.

[5]     Ada [Rockwell] is going to school. She learns fast. We have
        had good health so far, and George [Myron Morey] is
        getting as fat as a little pig.

[6]     Write soon and tell me all the news. Tell Aunt [Angeline
        Robinson] to write. Give my love to her and Uncle [Ebenezer
        Robinson] and accept the same to yourself.

        From your cousin,
        Deborah Ann Morey

NOTES

1. *History of Decatur County, Iowa 1915*. (Des Moines: Nickleson
Publishers, 1915), p. 38.

2. Circuit Court Records of Adams County, Illinois 1852, Box 85.

3. *True Latter Day Saints Herald*. 1 January 1860 (Plano, Ill.) p. 21.

4. Ebenezer Robinson notes that after the Crooked Creek battle, the High
Council of Far West was reorganized due to the flight of many who were in
the battle, and John Badger filled the vacancy of George Morey. From *The
Return,* March, 1890.

5. William E. Parrish, *David Rice Atchison of Missouri: Border Politician* (Columbia, Mo.: University of Missouri, 1961), p. 24.

6. Helen Isabell Keown, Family Records, p. 2.

7. *Biographical & Historical Record of Ringgold & Decatur County,* (Chicago, Ill.: Lewis Publishing Co., 1887), p. 682.

8. Decatur County, Iowa, 1860 Census Records.

**Deborah Ann (Rockwell) Morey** *(1841-1888) and* **David Butterfield Morey** *(1830-1901). Wed on New Year's Day 1856 because, family legend has it, David thought Deborah was being overworked by her aunt Angeline Robinson, the Moreys got housekeeping help from Mollie early in their married life. But when they moved to Illinois in 1860, Mollie replaced Deborah in the Robinson house. Staunch members of RLDS, David followed his father, George, as teacher and later priest, while Deborah scolded Mollie for joining another church. In the late 1870s Deborah lost the use of her legs. She continued to mend, knit, keep accounts, bear and discipline children from her bedroom.*
[Photographs from portraits courtesy of Nancy Gerlock]

**Joseph Edward Bonney** *(1833-1918). The only child of Amasa and Adaline (Works) Bonney to reach maturity, Joe was the cousin Mollie wrote to in 1860 when she failed to reach her brother Perry. Joe did not follow his parents to Iowa when they took Mollie with them. Instead, he married Sarah "Sallie" Johnson on his 23rd birthday and worked as a sawyer in LaGrange, Missouri. When she was not working as a hired girl like Sallie's sister Emma, Mollie spent time with the Bonneys, eventually marrying George I. McNutt in their home. Later, George became a partner with Joe in a lumber business that failed. Joe's two girls, Kate and Ola, often visited the McNutt farm, as did Kate's children after she became Kate Loudermilk.*

*Part of Letter #3 from Joe and Sallie Bonney. The section of the letter here is in Sallie's hand— before she went to writing school. [See Letter #46, par. 2.]*

Dear cosin i thought i would write a few lines to you and grace. as Joseph was a writing to you. i would have writen before but i hasent to had a chance. my children is verry cross you thought my baby was big enough to do with out rocking but now there is a nother. and now i cant do any thing. i want you to write to me. and come to see me as soon as you can. bath of you. grace tell your ma and pa to come and see us. i think old Seff ought to bee hung. then we would have pedce girls i havent time to write. write soon

# A New Life Back Home
# 1862

## 🌺 Letter #3

For more than a year, Mollie did not hear from her brother, Perry. To find him, she had written a second letter to her cousin Joe Bonney. Joe's answer, the first letter in 1862, explains why she had not heard from Perry. Joe signs the letter in behalf of his wife, Sallie, who writes a short note to Mollie, teasing her about "Old Jeff," who may have been someone they knew when Mollie was living in Quincy with Joe's parents.

LaGrange, Missouri                    August 24, 1862

Dear Cousin,

[1]     I take this opportunity of writing you a few lines in answer to your letter. I thought that I would go and see Perry [Works] before I wrote to you. I was down to your uncle [Samuel Stewart]'s farm the other day. Perry was not at home. He is living at Mr. [Holman] Bowles. It is not far from your uncle's. He has been living there for some time. Your uncle said that Perry got dissatisfied and wants to stay with him, so he let him go and stay with Mr. Bowles.

[2]     Your uncle says that Perry never said much about you till since he has got old enough to realize that he had a sister. He wants to see you very much. I think that he will come up

here soon to see you. Your uncle wants you to come soon and make them a visit. The girls [Helen, Jane, and Salina Stewart] said when I was there that they [were] going to write to you right soon and perhaps you will have a letter from them before you get this.

[3]      Tell Aunt Angeline [Robinson] that we will send our picture as soon as things get settled so that we can. I want you to come down and stay with us a while. I think you have stayed up there long enough for once, and tell the rest of the folks to come down and see us.

[4]      When you write to Perry direct your letter to Payson, Adams County.

[5]      This is all that I think of at present. Write soon and tell us all the news and how you are getting along. Tell Cousin Grace [Robinson] that I will write to her soon. Give our love to all our inquiring friends.

J. E. & S. A. Bonney

To Miriam Works
Write soon.

Dear Cousin,

[6]      I thought I would write a few lines to you and Grace, as Joseph was writing to you. I would have written before, but I haven't had a chance. My children are very cross. You thought my baby [Effie Josephine] was big enough to do without rocking, but now I have another [Jessie Katie Belle], and now I can't do anything.

[7]      I want you to write to me and come to see me as soon as you can, both of you. Grace [Robinson], tell your ma and pa [Angeline and Ebenezer] to come and see us. I think Old Jeff

ought to be brung. Then we would have better girls. I haven't time to write. Write soon. Give my love to your aunt and uncle, and accept the same—both of you, Grace and Miriam.

## 🌺 Letter #4

Life in Pleasant Plains—schooling and housework—continued for Mollie. She lived and worked in her aunt Angeline and uncle Ebenezer Robinson's home. Though a niece, she was treated by Aunt Angeline as a "hired girl," just as her cousin Deborah had been before her. Salt and sugar came in blocks and had to be pounded into granules—her job. Coffee and sometimes wheat were hand-milled in the home. Bread was baked every day, and Mollie became an expert at this chore.

She had many friends. Her young cousin, Grace Robinson, was already twelve years old. David and Deborah Morey had returned from Illinois and were living in a small house on the next farm. Two of David's sisters, Helen and Eunice, were Mollie's schoolmates.

The young people did not go to school regularly. Alfred Moffet, a neighbor of the Robinsons and a one-time cobbler, cared very much about schooling for the young. He urged the building of a brick schoolhouse on his land, neighboring the Robinson's. Built from bricks made from clay out of nearby Austin Cowles' land, the school was called variously the "Moffet Schoolhouse" or the "Cowles Schoolhouse." It doubled as a meetingplace for RLDS church services.[1] Though not a member of the Reorganized Church, Mollie did attend these services as a teenager, where she was remembered as singing beautifully.

Mollie's teacher in the Moffet Schoolhouse at this time was Doc Clark, who became a romantic interest for some of the girls, especially Eunice Morey [See Letters #26, par. 4 and #68, par. 2].

The second letter in 1862, an undated one from Eunice, is likely to be one that Eunice sent to Mollie as schoolgirls often do. Eunice considered herself Mollie's special friend, not only because they shared the same name ("Miriam" was Eunice's middle name) nor because they were both born in the same year, but more importantly because they shared confidences about their futures that Mollie did not share with others. [See Letters #26 and #79].

In this short note, Eunice playfully refers to an extraordinary blackberrying party. This particular party is often remembered because its main purpose may not have been to gather blackberries but to match marriageable young ladies with young men. [See Letters #22, par. 4 and #68, par. 2].

[Pleasant Plains, Ia.]                    [in August, 1862]

**Dear Friend or Cousin,**

[1]    Your letter was duly received and perused with much pleasure. I was glad to hear that you was a-going to school. I would like to go to school with you very much if it was so I could. I have so much to do that I can't come.

[2]    I want you to take good care of Doc [Clark] for me, seeing that I can't be there to do so. I think that Doc has enough to do to talk it over with you. I want you to [?] for me the last day and kiss Doc for me, seeing that I can't be there. I would like to be there the last day to see how Doc performs, but it is so I can't be there.

[3]    I am a-going down in Missouri a-blackberrying today. Deborah [Morey] and George [Rockwell] and Martha Cowles is a-going too, and Helen [Morey] and Martha [Truman]. They are a-hurrying me, so I will have to stop writing. So, goodbye.

[4]    Please excuse bad writing and spelling. I had have not got[?] except I had been a good speller. So, no more at present. Give my love to all, and accept the same for yourself.

Eunice Morey

## 🌺 Letter #5

Mollie's brother, Perry, finally answers her in 1862, although—perhaps because of his eyes—someone else writes the letter for him.

Mollie began thinking seriously about leaving Iowa for a new life in Illinois. In the fragment of Perry's first letter he suggests a plan. Mollie's plan was to have Amulek Boothe, her cousin from across the border in Eagleville, Missouri, drive her by team to Keokuk, where rapids hindered Mississippi river traffic. There, she would meet Perry, and together they would take a steamboat to LaGrange, Missouri, where cousin Joe Bonney would meet them. Brother and sister could later go across the river to Quincy and eventually to Payson, Illinois, and the Stewart farm. An escort for Mollie was needed, not only because it was proper, but because the Civil War in Missouri made travelling alone dangerous.

Throughout 1861, Missouri swayed from staying in the Union to seceding from it and back again. The Union commanding general in St. Louis was actually a Southern sympathizer.[2] The governor refused to send the state's allotment of troops when Lincoln called for them.[3] But, secessionist meetings, like the one on April 22, 1861, in LaGrange, usually failed. A Missouri secessionist flag raised over the county courthouse in Monticello, ten miles north of LaGrange, was laughed down when many agreed that the grizzly bears on its coat of arms looked like two fat hogs rooting over a whisky barrel.[4] On the other hand, Colonel Sam Curtis had to use 400 troops from Camp Wood in Quincy, Illinois—not Missourians—to secure the Clearer and Mitchell foundry in Hannibal, Missouri. The foundry had been secretly making cannon balls for the South.[5] Missouri allegiances were split like the Union itself. Chasing pro-Southern Missouri militia in 1861, a Union soldier wrote: "We were both missionaries and musketeers. When we captured a man we talked him nearly to death; in other respects we treated him humanely. The Civil War was a battle of ideas interrupted by artillery."[6]

Later in 1861, near Keokuk, there were many skirmishes as both forces struggled to control the strategic Mississippi River. In all of this, Mollie, like others, tried simply to go on as before. For her, this meant trying to reach Illinois. On New Year's Day, 1862, railroad track in northern Missouri was torn up in seventy-five places. The Quincy and Palmyra Railroad required an oath of allegiance to the United States from all its trainmen.[7] "If you will come to Keokuk," Perry had written to her, he would meet her. But coming to Keokuk from Pleasant Plains might be the most difficult part of her trip.

[Fragment of letter written for Perry. Most probably mailed in late August, 1862.]

[1]     ...getting along. Mr. Bonney was here a day or so ago, and I did [not] get to see him, but he left word where you was a-living, and if you are a-coming down here I want you to write to me, and if you [do] come, I will come up there between [now] and winter, and I want you to write to me and tell me [how] far you live from the Mississippi river, and how I can go out where you live.

[2]     If you will come to Keokuk, I will meet you there and go home with you, and if you don't I will come up there to see you as soon as I can. I send my best respects to you all.

Perry Works

## ✿ Letter #6

Perry's second letter is in his handwriting. Mollie had guessed that he might be a bond servant for Holman Bowles, a prominent Payson landowner. Being a bond servant was an ancient way for the homeless or orphaned to apprentice to a craftsman or rich man and earn a way to a better life. But bond servitude was only a little better than outright slavery, and Perry's attitude toward it is common.

He calls his eye disease "sore eyes" (probably conjunctivitis) a disease which made his one eye itch constantly.

Mollie had asked Perry about friends and relatives who were in the army. In the first week of March of this year, one of her neighbors, Austin Cowles' boy, Henry, fought in the biggest battle in the West, the Battle of Pea Ridge. Henry had often come calling on Mollie. He was captured in the battle and ever after wore a scar at the back of his head where a Rebel sabre just missed cutting off his head. The victory at Pea Ridge secured Missouri for the Union. Confederate influence was still strong, but it was now reduced to sporadic cavalry raids.

As was common in many letters, another person (in this case, the Stewart's oldest girl, Salina, or "Lina") uses Perry's letter to write a greeting to Mollie. Perry earned Mollie's lifelong gratitude for eventually sending her the money for her trip to Illinois.

Payson, Adams Co., Ill.              September 28[?], 1862

Dear Sister,

[1]     Received your kind letter a few days ago. I was very glad to hear from you. I began to think that I was not a-going to receive a letter from you. You don't know how proud I was to hear from you. But I would rather see you. It would do more good to see you than anything on earth.

[2]     I am not bound. I am working out. I would not be bound out for anything on earth. I am staying to a man by the name of Boles [Holman Bowles].

[3]     I had a letter that I received from you to Uncle Samuel [Stewart]'s folks to read. They was very glad to hear from you. They was much surprised to hear from you. We all want to see you very bad. I would give anything in the world to see you. You don't know how proud [?] Uncle Samuel's folks would be to see you. They want you to write to them without fail, and there isn't any of Uncle Samuel's children married yet.

[4]     Cousin George [Stewart] is dead. He a-died four years ago this last May. His disease was lung fever. He was a very nice young man and was respected by all who knew him.

[5]     The young men are nearly all gone to the scene of war. Around here the young men are very scarce around here, and I think they will be scarcer yet if War don't soon come to a close, pretty soon. I have not enlisted yet and that [?] [?] all I don't. In [?] too, there isn't any of Uncle Samuel's boys gone to war yet. I don't think they will go unless they are drafted. Then they will have to go.

[6]     Uncle Samuel lives on the farm he lived on when you left Quincy. He owns that farm yet. Cousin Jane [Stewart] has grown so you wouldn't know her. She is larger than Lina [Salina Stewart].

[7]     My eyes are very sore now. They have been sore about two
        months. I am doctoring them for now. The doctor said that
        I came very near losing my right eye. Then I should have to
        go through this world with one eye. They are getting better
        now. I hope they will continue. So, I expect to start to
        Quincy in the morning to the doctor to have my eyes
        operated on again. They are better now.

[8]     Cousin Joseph Bonney was down to Uncle Samuel's this
        summer, but I did not see him. He was there and took
        dinner with them. I would love to see him and all my
        relations. I should like to see all the cousins you named in
        your letter.

[9]     I heard of Aunt Adaline [Bonney]'s death. I should like to
        have seen Aunt Adaline before she died.

[10]    If you have [the] will, come down here. I will send you
        money enough to bring you this fall. I wasn't sure you
        would get that or I would have written more.

[11]    All of Uncle Samuel's family belongs to the Christian Church
        but Charles and Samuel. We don't have any parties around
        here. Everything is very dull.

[12]    I hope we will meet each other very soon. Well, we have
        been parted a great while. I hope we may see each other
        again in Adams county.

---

[13]    Well, Cousin Mariam, Perry is here now. I take the
        opportunity of writing you a few lines to let you know that I
        have not forgotten you nor never will. You don't know how
        much pleasure it gives me to hear from you, dear cousin.
        How I should like to see you! I want you to write to me
        soon.

[14]    You supposed that we was all married, but there isn't any
        yet. I don't think we will be soon unless the War comes to a
        close. It tis a poor prospect getting married in this county,
        Cousin Mariam. Do come down here and stay all winter.

[15]     You must excuse bad writing and spelling.

[16]     Do come and see us and we will try to make you happy.
         Mother [Rachel Stewart] says she would like to see you very
         much. Helen and Jane sends their love to you, and wanted
         you to write to them. I [?] I expect you have grown out of
         my knowledge.

[17]     I must bring my letter to a close. Good-bye for this time.

         Lina Stewart
         To her Cousin Mariam Works

---

[18]     Well, sister, Lina has finished what she wanted to write. Now
         I will close by saying that I will send you money enough to
         bring you down here. Write soon as you get this letter.

         Perry Works
         to his affectionate
         Sister Mariam

## 🌺 Letter #7

In the meantime, another cousin, George Rockwell, after spending
some time in Iowa with his sister Deborah (Rockwell) Morey and
other relatives, had moved to Batavia, Illinois. His letter is numbered
with others of 1862 because it is in this year that George had a long
talk with his uncle, Ebenezer Robinson, a talk George claimed
changed his life. He writes in detail about his new home and asks
Mollie to pay special attention to Adrianna ("Ada"), his daughter, who
is now living in Iowa with his sister Deborah. [See Letter #2.]

         Batavia                    October 13 [probably 1862]

         Dear Cousin,

[1]      I now seat myself to fulfill my promise to you as to writing
         you a letter.

[2]     I am in the above place at work and have very fine times, all things considered. This is one of the pleasantest places in northern Illinois. It is in Kane co., situated on Fox River, and also the Chicago, Burlington & Quincy railroad runs through the town. There is a very fine college in the place, and one of the largest paper mills in the state. Aurora lies down the river 3 1/2 miles; Geneva, up the river 2 1/2 miles. Very fine towns, I think.

[3]     I do not intend staying long here, however. I am going to Chicago and there to remain this winter. I may come out to Iowa in November, but my stay will be short.

[4]     I wish you would once visit these parts. I know you would be delighted with it. It looks much better than I expected to find it. There is also a great call for work at farming, and wages are very hi.

[5]     I wish Amulek [Boothe] was here. You send him along, won't you?

[6]     Now, Miriam, I wish you would answer this letter as soon as you get it, and tell me how Ada [Rockwell] is getting along, and please kiss her for me. You tell me what you think she most needs, and then I can bring them. I wrote to Deborah [Morey] as soon as I got to Mr. Morey's, but I have received no answer yet.

[7]     Give my respects to Grace [Robinson], also to Aunt [Angeline], and tell Uncle [Ebenezer] I shall never forget the advice he gave me, and that I am trying to profit by it, that I am determined to live a better life, and I know by the help of God that I can, that I begin to see the way somewhat clearer, and that I am coming to have him do what he spoke of the morning I left, if he will.

[8]     Miriam, I find that there is more contentment in trying to live a Christian than I ever supposed there was. I, for one, am determined to live a [w]hole Christian. Let others do as they will.

[9]     Do you know who teaches your school this winter? I suppose you will attend and all the rest of the young ladies and will have fine times. You will please give my best respects to Hellen [Morey] and Eunice [Morey] and also to Martha Cowles. I should be much pleased to have an opportunity of attending another party as that at Mr. [Robert] Booth's. How is Olive [Booth] prospering? And finally, all the rest of the people?

[10]    You tell Ada that she may look for something nice very soon.

[11]    Oh, have you heard from your brother [Perry Works] since I left and also from Angeline Worden? Finally, tell me all the news and don't forget to write.

Yours truly with my best wishes, you know;
from your most obediant servant,
George Rockwell

## 🐾 Letter #8

Before she left for Illinois, Mollie got this next letter from cousin Joe Bonney. In it, he tells her about those who have gone to "the Valley," meaning the Valley of the Great Salt Lake, home of the rival Mormon sect, the LDS. Mollie's uncle, James Works, whom Joe mentions, was the youngest Works, six years younger than Mollie's father. But unlike any of the other children of Asa and Abigail (Marks) Works, Uncle James was a Brighamite. For a time he lived in the "Lion House," the home of many of Young's wives, doing odd jobs such as helping with the laundry by pounding clothes and carrying basketsful to be hung on a line.[8]

Joe also mentions Amulek Boothe's brother, Mosiah, another Brighamite. Although Joe doesn't think he, himself, will go to the Valley (meaning, become a Mormon) the competition between the the Josephites (RLDS) and the Brighamites (LDS) was intense, each believing they belonged to the true church. By moving away from the largely RLDS settlement of Pleasant Plains, Mollie could expect to escape this conflict.

LaGrange, Missouri　　　　　November 2, 1862

Dear Cousin,

[1]　　I make this opportunity of writing you a few lines in answer to your kind letter and was glad to hear from you and that you was well, and I am glad that you have had a letter from Perry [Works].

[2]　　I wrote a letter to Perry the other day but have got no answer from him yet. I wrote to him that I wanted to see him before he come out to see you, and I have been looking for him up, but he has not come yet.

[3]　　You wrote that Aunt [Angeline Robinson] had got a letter from Uncle James [Works] and that he thinks they are all right. I got a letter from Uncle James last year. He wanted that I should come out to the Valley [Salt Lake, Utah Territory]. But I think that I can do just as near right here as I can there. And come just as near getting to Heaven as some that is there.

[4]　　Warren Tenney [or Fenney] and his mother has gone to the Valley, and I get letters from them. They think that is the best place in town. The place may be good enough, but I don't think that is the only road to heaven.

[5]　　And I also got a letter from Mosiah Boothe. He seems cord [in accord?] with the rest of the folks. I should like to have some of my kin come to see me, but if they won't do it, I will have to do without seeing them till I get able to go and see them.

[6]　　You wanted I should come out there this fall, but I think that you had better come down here this fall. You have nobody to take along when you go, and I have an old woman and two babies to follow me. And then there would be nobody to home to pull the cow and feed the pigs and the turkeys.

[7]    You ought to be here to see the boatsful loaded with
       soldiers going down the river. We have a good view from
       our house. We are on the bluff. We can see Quincy every
       day.

[8]    Tell Cousin Amulek [Boothe] [that I] think that he might
       come down this fall and see us just as well as not. And if he
       don't want to come, to stay home, and when I come up
       there, I won't come to see him.

[9]    I wish that you would send me some of them currants that
       you tell so much about. I should like to have some of them
       to eat this winter.

[10]   This is all that I think of at present. I would have wrote
       sooner, but I have been sick for the last two weeks. Write
       soon as you get this and tell us when you are coming down
       to see us. Good-bye for the present, and don't forget to
       write soon.

       From your most affectionate cousins,
       J. E. and S. A. Bonney

## ❧ Letter #9

The last letter of 1862 is another one from Mollie's cousin, George
Rockwell. In Batavia, he listed his profession as "teacher" and lived in
a downtown boardinghouse, but his ties to his relatives in Iowa are
strong. He addresses his letter to Mollie's new home, and the letter
may have been waiting for her when she arrived in Illinois. He is
most concerned about his daughter, Adrianna, especially after
learning what happened to Deborah's newborn girl, Derexa Morey.
He uses the euphemism "vacancies" to mean "deaths."

Aurora, [Ill.]                  November 23, 1862

Cousin Miriam,

[1]      With much pleasure I seat myself to address you a few lines. I received your thrice-welcomed letter last Sabbath, and glad was I to hear that you was well, and also to hear from the relatives and friends in Iowa.

[2]      You stated in your letter that you were going to take a journey, and accordingly I will address this letter to your new home, for such I sincerely hope you may find it to be, for I know your lot has been rather hard thus far in life, and I do hope the remainder may be spent otherwise, and as you are about to be thrown into other society and probably of different instances, it will remain with you to conform yourself to their customs in order to enjoy yourself. As the old maxim goes: When you are with Romans, do as the Romans do.

[3]      You are of the age now to enjoy society now, to be happy and also to make others happy that you are called to meet with, but of one thing beware, and that is the flattering tongue, those that go about in sheep's clothing to deceive the innocent. Society is full of traps to decoy you (but Miriam,) beware of them all.

[4]      Perhaps you will not thank me for all my advice, however, but Miriam, if I had taken good advice, I should be a happy man to what I am now. But alas, I have learned, to my sorrow, some wisdom, and thereby I mean to profit now. I am trying in my weak way to lead a different life, and by the grace of God, I can do so.

[5]      Miriam, I have a great desire for your welfare, and I hope you may be prospered in all your under-takings. I shall miss you very much in my visit to Iowa. You make a vacancy which no one else can fill.

[6]     Your letter states of many others' vacancies in Iowa in family circles, and one in my sister [Deborah Morey]'s family which I was sorry to hear and which I cannot bring myself to think possible. I used to scold her in being so careless with that little one [Derexa]. I told her she would see the time she would regret it. She and David [Morey] are too careless to keep house. I never want to live as they do. They is the most reckless about that place I most ever saw anyplace, and I wish that Ada [Adrianna Rockwell] was in a different place.

[7]     You said in your letter that you thought I should have them together. I wish you would give me some advice. It bothers me very much. I expect you would say, "Marry," but I once had a stepmother, and she proved no mother at all. There is many that will make a good wife, but few a mother. The one [Clara Rockwell] that is in this state has a good home and well cared for. Will you confer on me a great favor, if you will find me one that will make me a good mother. I think they are very few.

[8]     I will not weary your patience much longer. I am stopping in Aurora with Mr. Sur Dam, working at my trade. There is some six thousand inhabitants. Work is plenty and wages good. He wants me to stay one year, but I cannot decide yet.

[9]     I will now close. You give my respects to your brother [Perry Works] and everyone. Tell your brother I should be pleased to have him write. Write soon, and don't forget your friends. Here is my love and respect to you, Cousin Miriam,

George Rockwell

P.S. Direct your letters to the above place, Kane County, Illinois.

NOTES

1. *History of Decatur County, Iowa 1915.* (Des Moines: Nickleson Publishers, 1915), p. 40.

2. Everette B. Long, *The Civil War Day By Day: An Almanac 1861 – 1865* (Garden City, N.Y.: Doubleday & Co., 1971), p. 75.

3. *Ibid,* p. 60.

4. *History of Lewis County, Missouri* (Chicago: Goodspeed Publishing, 1887), pp. 71 – 2.

5. Carl Landrum, *Quincy in the Civil War* (Quincy, Ill.: Quincy Historical Society, 1966), p. 7.

6. Long, *Civil War,* p. 7.

7. Landrum, *Quincy,* pp. 33 & 37.

8. Susa Young Gates, *The Life Story of Brigham Young* (New York: MacMillan Company, 1930), p. 323. Evidence also from: James Marks Works, Letter to Jerusha (Works) Worden, 19 January 1865.

**Phebe Louisa (Booth) Duel** *(b: 1849). The youngest daughter of Robert and Phebe (Marcelles) Booth who settled east of the Robinson farm in an area variously called El Dorado, Spring Valley, or Boothtown, one of the letters she writes is unsigned in 1863. Booth family events, including gold prospecting trips to Pike's Peak, the marriage of her sister Olive to the prominent William Clark, and a burglary of her father Robert's store were news Mollie learned from the letters through the years.* [From a tintype.]

# New Friends, Old Memories
## 1863

### 🦋 Letter #10

Though her brother Perry sent Mollie money for the trip to Illinois, it is not known whether he actually met her in Keokuk as he planned. Cousin Amulek Boothe did accompany her all the way to LaGrange, Missouri, where they were made welcome at the Bonney home. From there, Mollie went across the river to the Stewart farm.

Now in Illinois, Mollie divided her time between working as a hired girl in Payson and visiting the Joseph Bonneys in LaGrange. Her usual employer was the well-to-do Nathanial Carr. Her dislike for her aunt Rachel Stewart kept her away, as much as possible, from the Stewart farm, though it was nominally her home.

Deborah Ann Morey writes the first letter in 1863, a melancholy one full of accounts of sickness and unusual deaths. It is addressed from "9 Eagles." An area in Decatur County, near Pleasant Plains, is known as Nine Eagles. Most of Mollie's Iowa correspondents were from Decatur County. Nine Eagles, Pleasant Plains, Boothtown, Eldorado, and Spring Valley all appear as post office addresses for those in virtually the same part of the county. [See map on page ix.]

In her letter, Deborah answers Mollie's request for advice about going to school, most probably in LaGrange. Whether Mollie ever attended school there is not known.

The photographs ("likenesses") Deborah mentions may have been some that Amulek and Mollie had taken while in LaGrange or Quincy. Amulek brought the photographs of himself, Mollie, and Joe and Sallie Bonney with him when he returned to Eagleville [See

Letters #11, par. 13 and #13, par. 13]. All kinds of photography—ambrotypes, tintypes, and paper prints—were becoming very popular in the 1860s.

Deborah confidentially tells Mollie what everyone in Iowa suspected: that Amulek and Mollie would marry. Despite their being first cousins, such a marriage was not unheard of. Deborah's command about what to do with this letter indicates the hush-hush nature of what she has to say.

9 Eagles                    Jan. 26th, 1863

Dear Cousin,

[1]      I now attempt to write you a few lines in answer to your letter of December 29th. I was glad to hear that you got through your journey so pleasantly, and although I miss your society very much here, I was rejoiced to hear that you were happy in your home that is now separated from mine by many a weary mile, but, dear Cousin, imagination takes me to your side this evening and I fancy I see you, light-hearted and gay, happy in the society of new friends, while I pass my time in bewailing the past and dreading the unseen future; yet Cousin, I try to put my trust in that Supreme Being who holds the destiny of all mankind in his own hand and to say, "Thy will be done," but at times I feel to murmur at the hand of providence, yet it is wrong to feel so, and pray to be forgiven.

[2]      Well, I will change the subject, lest I weary you, and talk of something more cheery. Your friends are all well or nearly so. Jane Moffet has not been well since you left. They thought she had the dropsy of the heart, but she is getting better and they think she will get well now, and I hope she will, for she has suffered a great deal.

[3]      You recollect the Sabbath that Grace [Robinson] was baptized that Ann Peters and Horner were there. They were married the day before New Year's. She was taken sick with

a fever the 18th of January and died the 22nd. It is a heavy stroke to her husband, who went in opposition to his family when he married her. None of his people came to see her during her sickness, and none but his mother came to follow her to her narrow home and help comfort him in his sorrow.

[4]    There has been a great deal of sickness in this country since you left. James Alfrey lost their oldest child. Your teacher, Mr. Brown, was killed in one of the late battles. There is another one of Mr. May's boys died. His name was John, I believe. Perhaps you were not acquainted with him. John Clipp[inger] is a nurse in a hospital somewhere in Mo. I have forgotten the exact place. We got the news through a letter written by John Gambol.

[5]    The weather has been so bad that we haven't been able to go down to Cousin Ad[am Dennis]'s since you left.

[6]    I am well-suited with the likeness, except yours. I am very much of Amulek [Boothe]'s opinion about that, but I think that Cousin Sarah [Bonney] is very good looking and so is Joseph [Bonney]. Tell them I am proud of them. Tell Perry [Works] that I think that he was a little partial about his likeness and guess he had better send me his yet or I shall call him a bad boy. We will get ours taken as soon as we get the means and send to you and Cousin Joseph. Tell Joseph I think his babies are handsome.

[7]    If I were in your place, I would go to school even though it should deprive me of the society of a brother. Your absence will be regretted, to be sure, at the time, but the opportunity to gain knowledge passing unimproved may cause you more regret in time to come.

[8]    You will think from the blots and misspelled words that I am getting absent-minded, i expect. But perhaps I shall do better next time. Tell Cousin Joseph and Sarah to write

soon. I shall be glad to hear from them. Tell them to excuse me for not writing first for I haven't wit enough to write anymore for a while. I have answered 6 letters, with yours, and I shall have to rest a while, and perhaps I won't make so many mistakes.

[9]     David [Morey] sends his regards to you, also to our other cousins [the Bonneys]. Tell me is Joseph ever lost any children, for I thought they had 3. Tell Sarah that I think more of that roll[?] she set me than I would have 5 dollars. Give my love to all my relatives and accept the same for yourself.

From, D. A. Morey

[10]    P.S. The story was that you and somebody else [Amulek Boothe] would marry before you got far from home. How did it happen that you didn't, for what everybody says ought to be true? I think they will keep silence now for a while, don't you? Somebody asked me if you wrote whether you were going to send your likeness to a certain person or not. I told them that I had forgotten what you wrote about it but guessed you would. Will that do?

[11]    Tell me if you have heard from George [Rockwell]. The girls send and Eunice [Morey] says you must write. Read this and burn it up. For I don't want anybody to see it.

## 🌸 Letter #11

The second letter of this year marks the first of a life-long correspondence with cousin Grace Robinson, the only child of Ebenezer and Angeline (Works) Robinson, and one of Mollie's most accurate and important correspondents. Besides telling about the people in Iowa, Grace tells Mollie about their New York cousins, the Wordens, and about her Robinson relatives in Ohio. One of Gracie's cousins "hired him a substitute," a reference to the new military draft law.

The first U.S. military conscription law, in force during the Civil War, provided that a drafted man had to serve unless he could provide a substitute. Many poorer men were hired by richer ones to serve in their stead. Some men even made a business of being hired as substitutes, deserting once they were in the army, and being hired again.[1] As the tone of Gracie's letter suggests, hiring a substitute was deplored. [See Letter #21, par. 5, too.]

During the war, Mollie, like other young women, felt duty-bound to write to soldiers. Her favorite soldier was her cousin, Charles Worden, the son of John and Jerusha (Works) Worden of Throopsville, New York, near Auburn. Charles not only wrote to Mollie [See Letter #17 for a dramatic account of one his wartime experiences] he also wrote to Gracie, and he convinced his sister, Angeline, to open a correspondence with both.

February 10, 1863                    Tuesday
Nine Eagles, Decatur Co., Iowa

Dear Cousin,

[1]     I now sit down to write to you in answer to your letter which came to hand yesterday afternoon. I wrote some to Perry [Works] Sunday but have not sent it off yet, so I will send this in it.

[2]     You wanted me to tell you all the news. Well, I will endeavor so, as far as I know. Mrs. Ann Horner (who was Ann Peters) is dead. She was buried two weeks ago last Saturday. She had been married a month when she died.

[3]     Sara Ann Loose [Luce?] is married. She married a fellow by the name of Johnson. Her father is also married. He married a friged [?] girl.

[4]     You will be surprised to hear that Frank Smith is married to Nancy Dale. They have been married about a week.

[5]       Mr. [Alfred] Moffet's family are all getting better now, I believe. They have had a very hard time. Jane has been so badly bloated and had such smothering spells that for a long time she was so she could not lay down, but she has got about well now.

[6]       I received a letter from Cousin Laura Robinson not a great while ago. She said Cousin Calvin [Robinson] had been drafted, went to camp, and stayed a few weeks where he was assigned to the office of second sergeant. But he did not like it very well, so his friends "hired him a substitute." So much for him.

[7]       I was up to Margaret Snook's Saturday. They got a letter from Thomas while I was there. He was in the battle of Vicksburg but was not injured.

[8]       Margaret and I and Sallie Monk went to Geography School that evening. They have pretty good times. Mr. Wm. Barnes is the teacher. They have one every other night.

[9]       Ann and Louis Adkins go to school in town this winter.

[10]     John Crawford is now sick, so Elbert P. Swarenger (Mr. Eammell's stepbrother) is helping Mr. [James] Alfrey to teach.

[11]     I believe I told about getting a letter from Cousin Charles in my letter to Perry, but however, I will say something in yours. He wrote a very good letter and talks like a very kind-hearted fellow. He holds the office of corporal. He receives a box from home every month. If it were not for that, he says he would go somewhere and wish to die. If you write to him, direct your letter to:

Corporal Charles L. Worden
Co. I, 9th N.Y. Vol, Artillery
Washington, D.C.

[12]     Please give my respects to Cousin Joseph and Sarah
         [Bonney], and keep a good share for yourselves.

[13]     You wanted me to tell whether I thought you and Perry
         looked alike. Well, you look some alike, but not a great deal.
         I don't think that his eyes hurt his looks much. I think that
         he is as good looking as his sister is.

[14]     This is all at present. Write soon.

         Your cousin,
         Grace Robinson

## ❧ Letter #12

The third and twelfth letter in this year (Letters #12 and #21) are
written by twenty-year-old Margaret Kennedy, one of Mollie's few
Iowa correspondents who was not Mormon. Originally from
Pennsylvania, Margaret and her husband, Joe, lived on the Gregory
farm next to the Ebenezer Robinsons and Alfred Moffets. Margaret
worked for the Moffets. She provides a view of life that Mollie would
have understood, being outside the RLDS Church but within a
community dominated by it.

         Decatur Co., Iowa              Feb. 17, 1863

         Dear Friend,

[1]      With pleasure I sit down to write a few lines in answer to
         your kind and welcome letter which we received some two
         weeks ago and was happy to hear that you was well and
         also glad to hear that you was satisfied with your new
         home.

[2]      We are well at present and hope that these few lines will
         find you enjoying good health.

[3]      Well, you said for us to pack up and go and live beside you. Well, we would like to live beside Mollie very well, but we cannot go down there. We expect to start north in about two or three weeks if the roads don't get too bad.

[4]      We have had a very pleasant winter here. We have had no snow of any account. There was snow that lay on the ground two days and that was the longest. Well, there is one thing sure—we have plenty of mud.

[5]      Mr. [Ebenezer] Robinson's folks is well. Grace was here this morning. I was to Mr. [George] Morey's yesterday, and they was all well. Mr. [Alfred] Moffet's are all getting pretty well again. Adoniram [W]right is dead. He died on the 13th of January. Mr. Moffet is coming so I will not get this letter wrote today.

[6]      I will now try to write some more. It is snowing this morning. The snow is about four inches deep, and it still keeps snowing.

[7]      You wanted to know how we spent our New Year's and Christmas. Well, we spent them at home setting by the stove.

[8]      You wanted to know how Mr. Celsur [?] was getting along. Well, his dear Darling One has left him, and he has applied for a bill of divorce. He says he is a-going to have another wife. His daughter is keeping house for him now.

[9]      You will excuse me for not answering your letter sooner. I thought I would wait one week. Grace wrote last week, so I thought we need not both write at once.

[10]      I can't think of anything more to write at present, so I will close by bidding a kind adieu. I remain your friend and well-wisher,

Margaret Kennedy

## ❧ Letter #13

The writer of this letter, Angeline (Boothe) Dennis, Mollie's cousin from Eagleville, Missouri, was the oldest of the children of Lorenzo Dow and Parthenia (Works) Boothe, and Amulek's only sister. Eagleville (or, Eaglesville), where both Angeline and Amulek lived, is directly over the southern border from Pleasant Plains, Iowa. [See map on page ix.]

When Lorenzo Dow Boothe drowned by falling through the ice of the Des Moines River on January 2, 1847, most of his children (Alma, Mosiah, and Hyrum Ebenezer) followed their stepmother and other Brighamites west. Angeline, his sixteen-year-old daughter, chose to stay in the area and keep her younger brother, Amulek, eleven, with her. Even after Angeline married Adam Dennis, Amulek lived near his sister, and when Adam went to war, Amulek helped her with the farm. She helped herself, too, since she got little from her soldier husband. Mrs. Brower was a milliner in Eagleville,[2] and Angeline's letter suggests that she worked for her.

Angeline would be thirty-two a little more than a month after she wrote this letter. She had a child, Annett, fourteen, and five other children aged four to thirteen: Grace, Amelia, Susan, Caroline, and Francis ("Frank"). Her husband, Adam Dennis, was in the Union cavalry stationed near Little Rock, Arkansas.

Eaglesville, Harrison Co., Mo. February the 19, 1863

My Dear Cousin,

[1]     After the salutation of good evening, I will intrude upon your good nature by asking you to peruse a few lines from one that has not forgotten you, nor never shall, while life lasts.

[2]     The reason that I haven't written before: I thought I would wait till I could get my picture taken. I have [not] had an opportunity to have it taken since you left—you know what a hard country this is. Times are hard as ever. My husband [Adam] sent me 20 dollars last mail, the first that I have had since you left. I am...[missing fragment]

[3]    [page 2]...like it very well, but for my part I think that you have done just right. I am glad you have come to such a conclusion.

[4]    I think it is time for us all to begin to prepare for the coming of the Savior, Miriam. These are days of trials and tribulations, and if we don't live faithful and put our whole trust in God, we can't expect to escape the snares of the Wicked.

[5]    I wish, my dear cousin, that I lived close enough to you and Cousin Joseph [Bonney]'s family to come over and spend the afternoon with you. O what a happy time we would have! But fate has willed it otherwise, and if I am not allowed the privilege of seeing you, I can hear from you and that...[missing fragment]

[6]    [page 3]...before long, for I have written to him [Adam] and told him that he must write to you himself. He will try and do the best he can, I warrant you, for he thinks a great deal of his Cousin Miriam.

[7]    I tell what it is. I want to see him pretty bad. Cousin Mollie, you don't know anything about what a lonesome time I have. If it wasn't for Brother Ammu [Amulek Boothe], I don't know what I should do. I would have to do the best I could like a great many others that are left in the same fix.

[8]    Cousin Mollie, this is Sabbath evening. I have been down to Mrs. Brower's today, so I have to do my writing after night.

[9]    The most of the family are well except back colds. Francis [Dennis] is quite poorly. Phoebe J. [Dennis] is very unwell. She has had a severe spell.

[10]    Annett [Dennis] sends her love to you and the rest of her relatives. Caroline and Susan [Dennis] say tell Cousin Mariam that they are much obliged to her for their little baskets. They are going to keep them always to remember her by.

[11]     It is getting late and I want to write a few lines to Cousin Sarah [Bonney]. I will bid you a Good Night.

Forget me not.
Angie L. Dennis

My Dear Cousin Sarah,

[12]     Although we are personally strangers, you seem just as near to me as if we had grown up together from infancy, and I know from the description that Brother Ammu [Amulek Boothe] gave of you and from the looks of your picture that you are one of the best of women. I congratulate with Cousin Joseph in making his choice.

[13]     I am very much obliged to you for your picture and those pieces, and in return I will send you my pretty picture if you will promise to keep it locked up where no one can see it.

[14]     Tell Cousin J [Joseph] that I have got his picture and I am going to keep it as long as I live. Tell him it looks just as he did when I last saw him only...[last part of letter missing]

## ❧ Letter #14

In Gracie's second letter of this year, she mentions a letter to Mollie from their cousin Charles Worden [See Letter #17, par. 5] that she deliberately opened and read before forwarding it.

The deaths of soldiers recorded by Gracie are included with one who was not a soldier—Adoniram Wright, a twelve-year-old relative of Lydia (Wright) Moffet, Alfred's wife. The other young men are all soldiers from Pleasant Plains.

Again, the sore eyes that causes Arthur Broadbooks to be sent home from the army to stay at Royal Richardson's hotel is probably conjunctivitis, a disease associated with measles or an early respiratory infection. A sticky substance that burns and itches periodically oozes from the eye. Today, a drop of silver nitrate solution into the eyes of a newborn prevents the disease.

The spread of disease—especially childhood diseases—by the gathering together of many young men who had been raised in widely scattered rural communities caused as many casualties in the Civil War as did the battles.[3] The other diseases of Gracie's neighbors that she tells about may have been mild cases of smallpox, since the severer cases were often fatal. Lincoln himself was ill with varioloid, a mild smallpox, two days after delivering his Gettysburg Address this year.[4]

Gracie also reports on two who are vying for a chance to "get" the schoolhouse on the Robinson farm, another example of entrepreneurial teaching [See Letter #46, par. 2].

Gracie mentions one of the major battles, the Battle of Murfreesboro (or Stone's River), Tennessee, which began on the last day of 1862, and was interrupted by Lincoln's Emancipation Proclamation, on New Year's Day. The battle was considered a Confederate victory, but the victors failed to push their advantage.[5]

In her postscript, Gracie knew Mollie would understand that the marriage of Edward Purcell meant something to other unmarried women in Pleasant Plains [See Letter #22, par. 3].

March 8th, 1863                    Sunday
Nine Eagles, Decatur Co. Iowa

Dear Cousin Miriam,

[1]     I thought I would write a few lines to you, and I have another letter to forward to you. It came to hand last evening. I don't know what the reason that it did not come sooner, as I have had two letters from him since he wrote yours. The first one I got from him was dated the 18th of January; the last one, the 19th of February. I took the liberty to open it, not supposing you would care, and if you do, I can't help it now.

[2]     I suppose Mrs. [Margaret] Kennedy told you about the death of Adoniram Wright. We got the news the same time of the death of William Pearcey, Caroline Harmon's husband. John Broadbooks is lying very low, not expected to live, in the hospital at St. Louis. And Rufus [Broadbooks] has been quite sick in the hospital at Rolla, but is better so that he can wait on the other sick. He gets $20.00 per month for waiting on the sick.

[3]     His brother Arthur is at home. He has been in the Army, has got a discharge. He has the sore eyes, and is staying at Mr. [Royal] Richardson's. Dr. [David] Macy is doctoring him. I think he is quite a good looking Young Man, but not a geat deal better than Rufus.

[4]     I was expecting a letter from Perry [Works] and you last night but I got disappointed. I shall look for one next Saturday certain. Mr. Waldrip and Mr. Richardson were down here on a visit week before last.

[5]     Sallie Monk and Martha Waldrip want to get our school this summer, but I don't know which one will get it.

[6]     We got the news a week today of three more of my cousins being in the Army. Their names are Merritt M. Clark, William Troyer, and George Tinker. Merritt is second Lieutenant. The other two are Corporals. Two of them are Aunt Mary Tinker's sons-in-law. Cousin George was in the battle of Murfeesboro.

[7]     The cases of small-pox are all getting better. Our folks send their love to all. This is all at present. Please write soon.

Your Affectionate Cousin
Grace Robinson

P.S. Edward Purcell is married to Jane Eaton.

## ✤ Letter #15

Gracie's second March 1863 letter is addressed to LaGrange, Missouri, where Mollie often stayed. Gracie mentions Martha and Henry Cowles, the children of Austin and his second wife, Irena. Martha was seventeen, and Henry, now in the Union army, had often called on Mollie. Mollie did not care for him, though. When he came to the Robinson farm, she would hide under the bed and make Gracie answer the door.

The friendship between the Cowles and Robinsons was long-standing. Austin Cowles' hatred of the Mormon "spiritual wife" doctrine exceeded even Ebenezer's. Often derisively called "holy polygamy," it began officially in 1843 when Joseph Smith, Jr., announced the doctrine to the Nauvoo High Council. Austin immediately resigned from the Council.[6] His daughter by a first marriage, Elvira Annie Cowles, had become a "spiritual wife" of Smith's.[7]

Gracie makes sure Mollie knows that the dispute within the Little River Branch of the RLDS has been resolved through the good efforts of William W. Blair. Blair, at this time a travelling emissary for the RLDS, baptized Gracie's mother and father as well as the Moffets and Booths.[8]

Gracie's father, Ebenezer Robinson, expressed a life-long abhorence for anyone who assumed more authority than he thought was just or decent. His friends Austin Cowles and George Hinkle agreed. The dispute over authority in the Little River Branch of the RLDS began as early as October, 1860.[9] Who could baptize members of the "new organization" was especially important since some members may have had high standing in "an apostate organization" (or sect) that was no longer recognized.[10] Alfred Moffet, not High Priest George Morey, had baptized the first members of the Little River Branch, and the authenticity of this baptism was questioned by the Morey faction. The Moffets and others—including the Robinsons, Cowles, Hinkles, and Booths—withdrew from the Branch.[11] Membership fell from twenty to nine.[12]

W. W. Blair was a very effective missionary who had recently started a branch of the RLDS Church at Manti, Iowa. He was returning to Illinois when he stopped at Pleasant Plains to use his good diplomacy in the baptism dispute. As Gracie notes, George Morey, the high priest of the Little River Branch who opposed the baptism, had left early for the regular April RLDS conference and was gone when Blair resolved the matter.

The Little River Branch membership recovered after the dispute to become one of the strongest in the early RLDS Church, registering over forty members in this year alone, and among the elders was Alfred Moffett.[13] By October, High Priest George Morey would be so bold as to urge elders to minister not only in Iowa, but in "the adjoining country," including fearsome Missouri where Mormons were especially detested.[14]

Nevertheless, there continued to be tension among Little River Branch members, perhaps reflecting the tensions in the "New Organization" itself. Many thought the Saints should gather together in one place, that is, establish a Zion. In this year, a front-page article in the *True Latter Day Saints Herald*, the official newspaper of the

RLDS, stressed that "The time has not come for the Saints to gather in one place. Zion is not yet prepared..."[15] Gracie's father, Ebenezer, and his friends agreed. But some months later, on January 9, 1864, at a conference of the Little River Branch, George Morey would exhort his members to "prepare themselves for the establishment of Zion in the last days." Ebenezer Robinson rose to argue against this, calling for more faith and diligence and George Morey responded to Ebenezer. As a recorder of the meeting noted, only "the severity of the weather and depth of snow kept the congregation small," and, too, the debate.[16]

Typical of her age, Gracie seems less impressed with the disputes within the Little River Branch—even though they involved her father—than she is with William W. Blair's assistant, a young man from Manti that Blair brought with him.

Gracie also mentions Captain Brown, a Civil War veteran who was already making political speeches. He would later become an Iowa state senator.

The first mention of the Newmans and Robert Booth, Jr., trying their luck at Pike's Peak is in this letter. They would go there more than once [See Letters #16, par. 4; #18, par. 6; and #23, par. 6]. Gold was first discovered as early as 1850 near Pike's Peak, close to Denver, Colorado, but there was no "rush" until late 1858. From 1859 on, an area actually more than seventy-five miles from Pike's Peak was highly publicized. Though the famous California strike was much richer, "the Peak" attracted many Eastern fortune-hunters because it was closer. There is no evidence the Newmans ever found gold, but they did hold well-paying jobs in Colorado. [See Letter #44, par. 7].

Nothing more than what Gracie writes here is known about the spectacular affair of Old Mr. Mills.

> Nine Eagles, Decatur County, Iowa
> Tuesday March 31, 1863
>
> Dear Cousin Miriam,
>
> [1]     Your kind letter of March 21 came duly to hand last Sunday. I was glad to hear from you and that you are well for you had been sick the last time I heard from you. I wrote a letter to Cousin Perry [Works] two weeks ago and sent it to Decatur City by Mr. [Joseph] Kennedy. They moved a week last Friday.

[2] Martha Cowles was here Sunday. She got a letter from Henry [Cowles] the night before. In it was contained the sad news of the death of Rufus W. Broadbooks. He died at Rolla. His parents know nothing of his death. They got a letter from him not long ago in which he stated that he had made his will and did not expect to live long.

[3] Elder [William] Blair has been here. He started away a week today. He held three meetings while here. Jane Miller was baptized. Our folks and Mr. [Robert] Booth's and [Alfred] Moffet's joined the new organization [Reorganized Church of Jesus Christ of Latter Day Saints].

[4] There was a young man with Elder Blair by the name of Willie Redfield, aged 19 years. He is a very good looking young boy. He expects to come back here in May on his return home. He lives in Frémont Co., Iowa.

[5] We are all tolerable well at present with the exception of Mother [Angeline Robinson].

[6] Mr. [George] Morey is away now at [RLDS church] conference. He had started before Elder Blair got here. They talked some of going north this spring but I don't know whether they will or not.

[7] Captain Brown is now at home. He is going to deliver a speech at the Plaines [Pleasant Plains] next Saturday.

[8] Old Mr. Mills has been sent to jail for killing one of the Militia who was there one night last week to see the girls. This man leaves a wife and four children. He lived at Decatur City [Iowa]. It is thought that it will almost kill Mrs. Mills.

[9] I guess Cousin Deborah [Morey] has not sent an answer to your letter yet. The last time I was over there she had commenced one to you but had not finished it. She has not had a letter from George [Rockwell] since you went away. I want to know whether you have heard from him lately or not and where he is.

[10]     I am glad you have heard from Cousin Ad [Dennis], as we
         have not heard from him since you were out there. I want
         you to give me his address when you write. Olive and Louisa
         [Booth] received a letter from Annett [Dennis] a few weeks
         ago.

[11]     Moses Turpin has sold his farm to a man by the name of [D.
         R.] Ockerman. They seem to be very nice people. They have
         two sons that are young men and several girls that are
         young women.

[12]     Tell Perry that I want him to come out here this summer to
         see us very much.

[13]     Jacob Newman and Almeda are talking of starting to Pike's
         Peak in May. Robert Booth talks some of going along, but I
         guess he has about given it up now.

[14]     We have three young calves and my little black cat is as
         cross as ever. This is all that I think of at present. Our folks
         send their love to all. Please give my love to all the cousins.
         Please write soon.

         From your affectionate cousin,
         Gracie Robinson

         To Miss Miriam Works
         LaGrange, Missouri

## ❧ Letter #16

The unsigned letter of fifteen-year-old Louisa Booth, one of the
daughters of Robert and Phebe (Marcelles) Booth, is addressed from
Spring Valley, sometimes called Boothtown in honor of Louisa's
father. Apparently Louisa (most often pronounced "Loo-WISE-ah")
and her sister Olive prefer the name Spring Valley [See Letter #18].

Most of this letter confirms information in others. Rebecca is
Louisa's oldest sister, married to Charles Potter, who also tried his
luck at Pike's Peak.

Louisa teases Mollie about Mr. Sulser [Celsur?], a music teacher that the girls apparently found especially attractive. Mollie may have expressed an interest in this unknown man whose wife deserted him [See Letters #12, par. 8 and #18, par. 5]. Louisa, herself, remained single for a long time [See Letter #89, par. 9].

April the 1, A.D. 1863
Spring Valley, Decatur County, Iowa

My Dear Friend Miriam,

[1]      I embrace the present opportunity of penning you a few lines. I received yours of the 18th, and I was very glad indeed to hear from you. I began to think that you had forgotten me. I was glad to hear that you was well, and I am glad to think that you was satisfied out there.

[2]      Olive [Booth] and I went to meeting up to your uncle [Ebenezer Robinson]'s to meeting and I give Grace [Robinson] the letter you sent to her, and she said that she was glad to hear from you.

[3]      Olive is to Mr. [George] Morey's. She went up there Monday, and she is a-coming home tomorrow. She is a-going to answer your letter tomorrow. Mr. Morey has gone to Conference. He has been gone three weeks. Mr. [William] Blair has been here. He started home three weeks ago last Monday.

[4]      Almeda and Jacob is a-going to start to the Peak the first of May. Almeda sends her respects too. She says that she would like to see you before she started. All the folks has got the Pike's Peak fever. If you have to see Mr. Sulser, you will have to hurry, for all the girls is about to run away with him. He is a-teaching singing school in Mr. McCommer's schoolhouse.

[5]      Rebecca [Potter] is here today. She is a-washing. Jane Miller was baptized. Mr. Blair baptized her.

[6]     It is time to get to getting—time to go to getting supper
        and I will have to go to get supper.

[7]     I want you to be sure to answer this letter. No more at
        present, so goodby. Please answer this as soon as you
        receive this letter. And I will answer yours. Good morning.

        April Fools

## ✿ Letter #17

The next letter, which may be the one Gracie Robinson read
before forwarding to Mollie, is from their New York cousin, twenty-
year-old Charles Worden, a corporal in the Ninth Artillery of the New
York Volunteers. He was the eldest child of John and Jerusha (Works)
Worden, though his father had nine children by an earlier marriage.
Charlie's mother, Jerusha, was four years older than her brother Asa
Daniel, Mollie's father. Jerusha did not follow the Mormons west, but
she was a friend to them when they travelled back to New York, as
even Brigham Young attested to.[17]

Charles Worden spent his military tour of duty in the Washington,
D.C., area. He was quickly promoted from private to corporal, and in
1864 he was made a sergeant. The remarkable incident he relates is
repeated almost exactly in a history of the New York Volunteers.[18]

        Fort Simmons                      April 7th, 1863

        Dear Cousin Miriam,

[1]     I will now take the pleasure in answering your kind and
        welcome letter which I have neglected to answer so long. It
        is rather discouraging, I know, but you must excuse me for
        not being very prompt. I have been rather unwell for the
        past week but am now better.

[2]     I haven't any news of any importance to write but will write
        what there is.

[3]     A private in Company F, while preparing to go on guard, hit
        his wife—dead on the spot. The ball taking effect under the

left eye, splitting the skull and blowing her brains out. Poor woman, she had been here just two weeks. She leaves two small children to mourn her loss, the children both grasping her as she fell to the floor. They were both completely covered with blood. I think I never witnessed anything so sad an affair in my life. I couldn't help but shed a tear myself.

[4]  We still remain where we did when I wrote you before. There isn't much likelihood of our leaving, and I hoped that there would be. Sunday it snowed hard all day long which made it quite lonesome.

[5]  I think it was too bad that your letter was so long reaching you. It was my fault, not yours. I thought it would go safer to direct it in care of Uncle Ebenezer Robinson. But I will direct the remainder at your address.

[6]  I think that I shall go home week after next, but don't let that make any difference to you in regards to your writing to me, for my furlough is short, only a few days. I think that it is too bad to pay 25 dollars to go home [Throopsville] and then have only 10 days to visit my friends, don't you? I shall have to make short calls.

[7]  We haven't had our pay yet from the Government, but if I go home I can get my pay on my furlough at Washington. I think that you can look for my likeness in my next letter, that is, if I go home.

[8]  You seem to think that my head is all right if I am a Republican. You think right. I go in for breaking with slavery, if that is the cause of this war. And I think that it never will end until it is broke open. I think by what I can learn from the papers that they are in a pretty bad condition. I don't have mercy for them if they are. The poor women and children I have sympathy for, of course. I can't help that, for they are not to blame.

[9]     We are living high now. We have our ham but no eggs.
        They say the men fight better by feeding them good. I think
        that is reasonable. There is nothing that causes so much
        dissatisfaction in the Army as not having enough to eat.

[10]    I have heard from home. They're all as well as usual, with
        the exception of my sister Jane. She has been quite unwell
        but is now better. I trust in God that they may all live that I
        may see them all once more.

[11]    I am Corporal of the guard today—come off tomorrow at
        10 o'clock.

[12]    I wish you would have all of my cousins write to me, for I
        think that if I live to get out of this war I shall come out there
        and make you all a visit, and by their writing to me I shall
        know where to find them.

[13]    I wish you would send me your likeness and a lock of your
        hair, if you please.

[14]    I went to Washington and got my likeness taken and had
        the misfortune to lose it. I had calculated to send it to you,
        but as it is, you will have to wait until I get my pay. You shall
        have it as soon as I get my pay and can go to Washington.

[15]    This is all that I can think of this time, so you must excuse all
        mistakes and call it good. Write soon as you receive this.
        Give my love to all of my cousins and tell them to write.
        Give my respects to Joseph Bonney and all of the family.

[16]    So goodby for this time but not forever.

Truly your affectionate cousin,
Charles L. Worden

Direct your letters to:
C. L. Worden
Washington, D.C.
Co. I, 9th N.Y. V Artillery
in care of Capt. H. Hughes

## ❋ Letter #18

As several of the letters reveal, Mollie was ill in the early spring of this year [See #15, par. 1], but she was well by the time Olive Booth wrote this letter, the only one of hers to survive. Olive's relaying of Eunice Morey's insult is one of the first indications that Mollie had neglected writing Eunice [See Letters #19, par. 4 and #26].

Olive, four years older than her sister Louisa, was another of Robert and Phebe (Marcelles) Booth's children. Like Louisa, she teases Mollie about Mr. Celsur with an elaborate puzzle and a crude drawing. In the next year, at nineteen, Olive would marry William Clark, son of the founder of Clark's factory in nearby Davis City, Iowa. She remained in the Iowa area most of her life [See Letter #92, par. 5].

The Robinson Schoolhouse Olive mentions may be the same as the Moffet Schoolhouse, since it was near the Robinson farm.

Alfred Moffet's return to membership rolls of the Little River Branch marks the absolute end of the baptism dispute.

April 25, 1863   Spring Valley, Decatur Co., Iowa

Dear Absent Friend,

[1]  I seat myself to answer your kind and most welcome letter in which came to hand some time ago, and I beg pardon for not writing sooner to you. My reasons for not writing to you were because my health would not permit me to. I have been sick with the diptheria this winter, and I am not so that I have seen a well day since we have heard that you had been very sick since. Now we are there.

[2]  I saw Eunice Morey a few days ago, and she told me that when I wrote to you for me to tell you for her that the cause of your sickness were the carbuncle arising on your back. She said if you got mad at her for that, you had all the world to get pleased in. She also sent her respects to you and wished you to marry soon.

[3]  Now Miriam, I will tell you a little about her. She got Henry Cowles' likeness, and she has hers taken to send to him.

[4]     Mr. [William] Blair preaches today at 11 o'clock at the
        [Alfred] Moffet's house. He came last evening, so I
        understood. I have not saw him. We were all ready to start
        up to hear him preach, but it commenced raining so that it
        was impossible for us to go. We have heard that Mr. Moffet
        is to be baptized today.

[5]     Miriam, you said that you had picked me out a man. Well
        now, if that is the case, I shall be very much obliged to you
        for such a consideration as that, and I shall speak a good
        [word] to Mr. Sulser [Celsur?] for you in return. I always love
        to return compliments. I should like to have you send that
        man of mine out to see me before you fall in love with him.

[6]     Almeda [Newman] and family and Robert [Booth] starts for
        Pike's Peak in a few weeks. Our folks [Robert and Phebe
        Booth] are all well. Martha Waldrip teaches school at your
        uncle [Ebenezer Robinson]'s schoolhouse. She begins her
        school the first of May. Your aunt [Robinson]'s folks are all
        well the last that I heard.

[7]     Rufus Broadbooks is dead. He has passed out of this world
        and gone to a better one. He left his home and parents and
        friends to fight for his country, but now he has gone. This
        war has caused many to weep and to mourn for those lost
        friends. It has not been long since we heard the sad news of
        the death of our dear cousin F. Marcelles, and now last night
        brought the news that one of father's brothers was dead
        and gone. They both died in the army. F. was wounded and
        a-died with sickness.

[8]     Amulek [Boothe] and his sister [Angeline Dennis] was up
        here on a visit about three weeks ago. Debra [Morey]'s
        family is all well. They are a-living as are they did when you
        lived with them.

[9]     As it is Sabbath evening and is getting pretty late, I will close
        as I am expecting company. Shall bid you good-night.
        Please answer if it is worth an answer. This is from your
        friend,

        Miss Olive Booth

Direct to Miss Olive Booth
Spring Valley
Decatur Co., Iowa

[10]     Round is the ring that has no end,
says my love to you, my friend.
Just as the apple drops to the ground,
Kiss my true love as she comes around.

| and | down | have | you | |
|-----|------|------|-----|-----|
| up | as | i'll | if | |
| reads | you | it's | you | me |
| it | will | see | will | have |

Wourke this out    x x x x x x    [Here a drawing
at your leisure     x k i s s  x     of a bearded man]
                x x x x x x
                                      Sul[s]er

## ❧ Letter #19

Gracie's fourth letter of this year acknowledges Mollie's letter of April 15 in a rather formal way. (The abbreviation "inst." for "instant," meaning "of the current month," is a convention more suited to business than family letters.) Gracie may have written it tongue-in-cheek or to show off newly-learned letter writing skills. Nevertheless, her accuracy gives some idea of how speedy mail service was from LaGrange, Missouri, to Pleasant Plains, Iowa, during the war.

Fifteen-year-old Martha Jane Keown (pronounced "COW-in"), whom Gracie mentions, is the daughter of John and Mary Ann (Morey) Keown. Her mother was the eldest of George and Sylvia Morey's children. Her father was an accomplished stonecutter and worked on cutting and carving the moon and sun stones of the massive Nauvoo Temple, the centerpiece of the Mormon city of Nauvoo, Illinois. Wherever the George Moreys went, their daughters' families, the Keowns and Trumans, went too.

Thomas (called "T.J.") Brant, whom Gracie mentions, was apparently a favorite. He enlisted when he was nineteen in 1861, and then re-enlisted. From Gracie's reaction, it is no wonder that Mollie later thinks there is something between T.J. and Gracie [See #55, par. 7].

Pleasant Plain, Iowa                April 29, 1863

Respected Cousin,

[1]     I again take my pen in hand to address a few lines to you in answer to your favor of the 15th inst. which came duly to hand a few days since. It found us enjoying tolerable health with the exception of "Ma." [Angeline Robinson] Her health has been very poor all winter.

[2]     "Pa" [Ebenezer] has been at home since I wrote you last. He started away a few days ago.

[3]     Cousin George Rockwell is now at David [Morey]'s. He has been here about three weeks. He intends to start away in a few weeks. I was down there a little while yesterday afternoon and Cousin George and Eunice [Morey] and Martha Keown came pretty near home with me. George has been baptized since he came back.

[4]     Eunice wants you to write to her.

[5]     Thomas J. Brant has been at home on furlough. He started away some four weeks since. He has enlisted for three years more. I showed him your likeness and asked him if he knew it. He said "I should rather think I did." He is as full of fun as ever. The young folks had two parties for him while he was at home.

[6]     There was a very serious accident happened here last Tuesday afternoon. As Miss Isabell Fairley was riding a pony, the dogs jumped out and scairt it. It started to run, and she went to jump off and broke her leg just above the ankle. Fortunately she was within a few steps of home. Her mother and sister ran out and carried her into the house, and I went down as quick as I could. The bone was pretty near a half an inch out of her leg when I went down. They had it set, but she is not doing very well now.

[7]     I haven't had a letter from Cousin Charlie [Worden] since February. I wrote to Cousin Joseph [Bonney] some time ago but have received no answer yet. Tell Cousin Perry [Works] to write to me or I will scold him.

[8]     Well Mollie, I guess you will get tired reading this long letter so I will close. Please give my love to Perry and keep a good share for yourself. Ma wishes to be remembered to you and Perry. Please answer soon.

Affectionately, your cousin,
Gracie Robinson

## 🌺 Letter #20

The number of Amulek Boothe's letters to survive is second only to those of Grace Robinson's, and this is his first. He is one of Mollie's most faithful writers and arguably her favorite cousin. As a son of Lorenzo Dow Boothe, he is not to be confused with the Booths who lived in Decatur County, Iowa. Amulek was named for a prophet in the *Book of Mormon* who preached with another prophet, Alma, about the resurrection of Christ. One of Amulek's brothers was named "Alma." But Alma was a Brighamite, and Amulek and his sister Angeline had become members of the Reorganized Church.

Mollie's baptism as a member of the Christian Church did not please her cousin Deborah, as Amulek writes in this letter. Because of it Deborah stops writing, something noted by other letter-writers [See Letter #25, par. 4]. Though Deborah was pregnant this year [See Letter #23, par. 2] and may not have had the time or the desire to write Mollie, the issue of religious allegiance was strong, and it is clear that Deborah snubbed Mollie because Mollie's church was not RLDS. Even good-hearted Amulek wanted Mollie to share in his new-found faith.

Amulek refers to a draft about to be run in Eagleville. Nominally, the three million men between eighteen and forty-five in the North were militiamen and could be called to service at any time. Most were unorganized, however, so the draft law required deputies of the Provost Marshall General to enroll men by April 1, 1863. From these lists, names were drawn to meet local quotas. But there was no law requiring the men themselves to enroll. Resistance to enrolling was sometimes intense, as it was in Olney, Illinois, where 500 resisters threatened to burn down the town if enrollment lists were not surrendered.[19] Delays clogged the draft process in some states—California, West Virginia, and Missouri—where enrollers dragged their heels for various reasons. Since Missouri was one of those states having difficulty, this may be the reason Amulek is uncertain that a draft will actually occur.

Eagleville, however, supported the Union cause. Crowds gathered on the Fourth of July of this year to celebrate the Nation's birth and to await the news of the Battle of Vicksburg. Since the mail was delivered to Eagleville only once a week, the anxious townspeople, some of whom were relatives of soldiers, sent a messenger on horseback more than forty miles south to Gallatin to bring back news of Grant's Great Siege of Vicksburg.[20]

Amulek's joking postscript in this letter angered Mollie [See Letter #25, par. 3].

Eaglesville                    April 29, 1863

Most cherished Cousin,

[1]     I am a-going to answer your respected letter which came to hand last Friday, and I tell you, I was pleased very much to hear from you and also to get your portrait. I think it is a better looking one than the other that looked a little more funny, for I wanted [it] to look a little like my dearest cousin. I don't think it looks quite so well, but it suits very well, and I am very much obliged to you, and you shan't lose anything by it if I can help it.

[2]     Miriam, I have something new to tell you, for it is new to me. I was out to Davis [City, Iowa] last Sabbath and was at meeting at 11 o'clock. Then in the evening at three. Then after meeting I was baptized by Mr. [William] Blair. And I feel a great deal better, for I think it is the duty of everyone to begin to live in obedience to our Savior. I have joined the Church [RLDS] for that purpose, and I mean to live up to it or try to, for I have been walking in my sinful path long enough while desolation is spread abroad in our land an[d] death stands staring everyone in the face. I think it is time to turn and seek their last.

[3]    Miriam, I would have given anything if you had have been there to went with me. I would have been satisfied, but I hope you will try to live that way. Quit the follies and foolishness is the prayer of your dearest Cousin.

[4]    You say you are getting lonesome. I am sorry for you, for I know how it is by experience. I would like to be with you a while, and I think you would get over that, for if there ain't anyone down there, I shall have to come. Though, I will try it from here first by writing you a lengthy letter such as I like to have come to me. For I never get tired of reading yours.

[5]    You say you are going to Quincy. When you get there, let me know so I can direct my letters there, for I mean to write often. I have got a letter from Adam [Dennis] last Friday. He was well.

[6]    We have not had any letter from the boys since I wrote to you last, but I got a letter from Cousin Angie [Worden]. She is not well. [Words missing because of letter fold] It was so long before I answered hers. Then when I came back from down there, I wrote and did not get an answer. Then I wrote again, and she said she got both of them. I didn't know it or else I should not have written the last one.

[7]    I guess Deborah [Morey] don't like it very well because you joined the church down there. She said that she had not answered your letters that you had wrote, nor she did not talk as tho she was a-going to. If she would not answer my letters, I would let her go, for when I write to anyone and they don't answer it, I think they don't want to hear from me.

[8]    They say they are a-going to run a draft next Friday in town. Every man that goes out of the state that belongs to the State Militia with leave is liable to a fine of 30 dollars.

[9]    Miriam, the clock has just tolled the hour of two in the night and I have wrote you a tolerable long letter for the present. I must close.

[10]     I forgot to tell you that I have Grace [Robinson]'s likeness,
         but I don't think it looks near as well as yours. Miriam, write
         often. So goodnight.

         from your Nearest and Dearest,
         Cousin Amulek Boothe

[11]     Miriam, I have thought of thee often since last I seen you on
         the boat and the last kiss that I printed on thy cheek.

## ✿ Letter #21

Margaret Kennedy's second letter is from her new home in Des
Moines. She implies that, instead of cash exchanges, a tally system,
much like the one once used in Nauvoo, might have existed among
the Mormons in Pleasant Plains. In any case, her comment reveals the
scarcity of actual coins or bills with which to do business.

Not surprisingly, Margaret also has something to say about the new
draft law. Horace Greeley wrote that the draft was the foremost topic
of conversation in the nation. Some of the press were claiming that it
was unConsitutional.[21] Like Margaret, what most people discussed
was the $300 commutation clause, under which a draftee could pay
to have another serve in his place. Margaret's comment on the
provision is typical.

Nevertheless, the volunteer system of recruitment had broken
down. With the volunteer system, brokers got men who were
interested in joining together with men who wanted to stay out. The
government gave bounties to volunteers, and some men, who fully
intended to join, would wait until bounties were high before doing
so. Others, who thought they might volunteer, first sought out the
brokers of rich clients who were looking to pay the $300 for a
substitute.[22]

         Des Moines, Iowa                    May 11, '63

         Dear Friend,

[1]      I take the present opportunity to write in answer to your
         kind letter which we received on the ninth of this month,
         and was glad to hear from you, but was sorry to hear you

was sick. We are all well at present and hope this will find you in good health again.

[2]     We have left old Decatur County. I like it a great deal better here than I did there. It is a nicer place than it is there. You say you are not sorry you left that. We are not sorry yet, nor I don't think we will be. One has a chance here to get along. We can sell anything we have for cash, and that is a great advantage.

[3]     Smiths [Frank and Nancy] is well and doing well as can be expected these hard times. They have got another boy. He is five weeks old. He has got no name yet.

[4]     Well, I must tell you about our fruit. There is an orchard here on the place. We get all the apples. We have lots of tame gooseberries and tame strawberries, and we get all of them.

[5]     You wanted to know what I thought of the conscription bill. Well, I don't think much of it. It would do well enough if they could not buy their freedom, but the way it is the poor man's lives will have to go against the rich man's purse.

[6]     Well, I can't think of any more to write at present, but remains yours ever. You must excuse all mistakes for my pen is very bad.

Margaret Kennedy

Write soon if you please.

## 🌸 Letter #22

George Rockwell, still in Batavia, writes the next letter after receiving news from Iowa. As Mollie knew, the marriage of Edward Purcell meant that Martha Ann (Morey) Truman, who had been a widow since 1860, lost another chance for someone to take care of her and her three children. As it turned out, Martha did marry again, although under unusual circumstances [See Letter #82, par. 5].

The fact that George Rockwell seems interested in the marital state of his friends in Iowa may be the first indication of his own intentions [See Letter #48, par. 4].

Batavia, [Ill.]                    June 7, 1863

Dear Cousin,

[1]     I will occupy a few minutes in writing to you. I sent a letter addressed to you sometime since but received no answer as yet. Perhaps you have not received it, but I will send in care of Cousin Joseph [Bonney], and I wish you to be punctual in your answer as I am quite anxious to hear from you and also to know how you are getting along, also present and future prospects, if you please.

[2]     I am quite anxious for your welfare, one that would wish to see you do well. Is your health good as when I saw you last?

[3]     I received a letter from Cousin Grace [Robinson] last week. She says they are all well. Eddie [Purcell] is married. Well done for him. Poor Martha! [Truman] What will she do next? She must not lose many such chances. She says that Martha Cowles, Helen and Eunice Morey are still single. Where is Eunice's correspondent in the army? Is he [Henry Cowles] dead or wounded as many others are?

[4]     I should like to have the privilege of going blackberrying this fall as I did last, but circumstances are such that I cannot. Probably you will not have the opportunity, but be that as it may, I hope, ere long, we may be permitted to see each other again. If not, let us try and live so as to meet in that upper and better world where we may enjoy each other's society in peace.

[5]     I feel like thanking my heavenly Father for his kind protecting care over me. Let one and all seek an interest in that fountain that never fails health, nor a dying bed, for his hand is stretched out over all his works. Seek and ye shall find. These

are his promises to all. We may be separated here in this for a few days, but by living near to him here, we will all meet him around his throne in his kingdom.

[6] I intend to make my cousins in Mo. [Amulek Boothe and the Dennises] a visit this fall, all being well. I shall stay in this place until November. I expect then [to] return to Iowa, perhaps to spend the winter.

[7] Please write soon.

Yours, in friendship.
Give my respects to my cousins and accept the same yourself.
George Rockwell

## Letter #23

Although Grace Robinson, in this letter, does not want to put in writing how Edward Purcell died, Mollie almost certainly learned how, for his murder was spectacular. Members of Dike's Missouri Militia, with Southern allegiances, stopped Purcell on the streets of Pleasant Plains, demanding that he hurrah for Confederate President Jefferson Davis. When he refused, they shot him.[23]

Renegade raiders were difficult to tell from official ones. The most infamous renegade was William Quantrill, an ex-schoolteacher whose gang of pro-Southern thugs, including young Frank and Jesse James, terrorized northern Missouri and eastern Kansas. This year, on August 21, Quantrill's Raiders sacked and burned Lawrence, Kansas, murdering all but the women and very young children in retaliation for a Federal raid on Osceola, Missouri.[24] In October, Lincoln sent a special message to his commander in Missouri "...to compel the excited people there to leave one another alone."[25] Unfortunately for poor Edward Purcell, the "excited people" sometimes spilled over the northern border into Iowa.

John H. Clippinger, another soldier Gracie mentions, had come with the Robinsons to Iowa from Greencastle, Pennsylvania. In peacetime, he was a tinner, a maker of tin items, differentiated from a tinker, who merely mended tin pots and pans.

[Pleasant Plains, Ia.]     Sunday, October 25, 1863

Dear Cousin Mollie,

[1]     I seat myself this pleasant Sabbath morning to write a few lines to you in reply to your favor of the 17th inst. which came duly to hand last evening. We were glad to hear from you again.

[2]     I have no particular news to write. Cousin Deborah [Morey] has a young daughter [Eliza]. It is about three weeks old. They have not named it yet.

[3]     "Ma" [Angeline Robinson] has been very sick for a week, but is a great deal better now. "Pa" [Ebenezer] started away again a week ago last Friday.

[4]     I am doing the work now. Annett [Dennis] stayed with us two weeks. She is over to David [Morey]'s, and I do not know how long she will stay there.

[5]     I have not had a letter from George [Rockwell] since June, and I do not know where he is.

[6]     Robert Booth has returned from the Peak. He talks some of going back in the spring.

[7]     Rebecca Potter has another boy, and Mrs. Froudenger has got a young daughter.

[8]     Mr. Joneses have returned from N.H.

[9]     I think it is very strange that Perry [Works] does not write to me. It is now going on four months since I have had a letter from him. Tell him if he does not write pretty soon, I shall think he is too lazy to write, but I guess I can stand it as long as he can.

[10]    I cannot write any more of the particulars of the death of Edward Purcell, but if you were here, I could tell you some things that I cannot write on.

[11]    I don't see what is the reason you and Perry can't come and see us this fall, as we should be very glad to see you both. I should not be much surprised if you was to see us down as far as LaGrange this winter if nothing happens, as Pa said we could go.

[12]    I almost forgot to tell you that we had received a long letter from John H. Clippinger giving a full history of his experience in war matters. The letter was mailed at New Orleans, Louisiana.

[13]    Annett and Dianna Robertson was baptized last Thursday.

[14]    I have not had a letter from Cousin Joe and Sally [Bonney] since last spring. Please tell them that I should like to have them write to me.

[15]    Ma sends her love to you and Perry and says she would like to have you both write to her. Tell Perry to write. Give my love to him. Please write soon.

Your affectionate cousin,
Gracie

## ✿ Letter #24

The next two letters (Letters #24 and #25) were written at the same time in the Dennis home. There is a two-month period between these two letters and the previous one, Letter #23. From Angeline Dennis' first paragraph, it seems that after an initial spurt of letter writing, "the folks in Iowa" slacked off considerably. Angeline, however, accuses Mollie of being too enamored of her "new" cousins, the Bonneys. Especially, Angeline wants Mollie to remember her husband, Union Trooper Adam Dennis of Merrill's Horse Company B in Arkansas.

This year, Adam ("Addy") was stationed at Helena. (Arkansas came under the general command of the Department of Missouri, which explains the "Mo" Angeline adds to his address.) While Union forces couldn't stop the Confederate raids that started in Arkansas, neither could Confederate forces make any real gains. So far as is known, Adam never got the furlough Angeline hopes for, and the joyous time (the "shindy") did not happen. He stayed in Arkansas for the duration of the war, though he was re-assigned to Little Rock later [See Letter #58, par. 4].

Angeline's financial situation because of Adam's war service is clear from this letter. The cost of a photograph includes a trip to Leon, Iowa, some twenty-six miles north, because of the accident to James Anderson, the Eagleville ambrotypist. Many photographs at the time were ambrotypes, pictures on glass plates that required separate black backgrounds for proper viewing. A piece of black silk or paper behind the exposed plate differentiated light areas of the image, which were silver on the plate, from dark areas, which were clear and allowed the black to show through.

Angeline reports the birth of Eliza Morey and comments on the death of Effie Josephine Bonney, the second girl Sarah ("Sallie") Bonney lost. At the time of Effie's death, Sallie was in the last month of her fourth pregnancy, and she was caring for young (Jessie) Katie Belle, who was a year and nine months old. Mollie was certainly in LaGrange to help her.

The baskets Angeline mentions may have been early Christmas presents to the Dennis children that Mollie made before she left for Illinois. Angeline also mentions her daughter Annett.

Angeline includes a letter to Joe and Sallie Bonney in her lengthy one to Mollie. She even signs her letter to the Bonneys with her brother Amulek's name. It is no wonder that Amulek, writing next to her, finishes his letter first. His love for Mollie is revealed by his generous offer and an enticement for her to return.

The suitor of Mollie's named Shakespeare, whom Amulek mentions, is a mystery.

Eagleville, Mo.    Tuesday evening, Dec. 9, 1863

Dear Cousin Miriam,

[1]    It is with a joyous heart I sit down to write a few lines to let you know that I haven't forgotten you, if some of the rest have. Amulek [Boothe] got your letter this evening. I think you gave some of your relatives a pretty hard rub, but I

don't blame you much. I think some of them might write a little oftener.

[2]     You may depend we were all glad to hear from you. We have often wondered why we got no letter from you. We began to think you was so much taken up with your new relatives that you had forgotten that you had any in Mo. But since your letter came, I have altered my mind. I see you still remember some of us. Thank you. You just tell Angie [Worden] to answer your letter.

[3]     When have you ever sent me a letter without getting an answer? I have promptly answered every one that come from you. I should have written long ago, but I was waiting to get one from you. I think I wrote last.

[4]     Addie [Adam Dennis] speaks of you in almost all of his letters. I told him you was going to write to him. He says he has never got any yet. I wish, Mary, you would write to him. It would please him so well.

[5]     I got a letter from him last Friday. He was well. He talks of coming home on a furlough in a few weeks. I wish you could be here when he comes. I expect there will be some shindy cut [a festive time, as in a shindig].

[6]     Well, Miriam, I really am ashamed of myself for not sending you and Cousin Sarah [Bonney] my pretty picture. When I had a chance, the money was lacking. When I had money, there was no one to take it. There is no chance to get it done nearer than Leon. The ambrotypist in our town had the misfortune to lose his hand some time ago. I will go to Leon [Iowa] just as quick as I can and have it taken for you and Cousin Sarah.

[7]     I have got to send it to my brothers in Salt Lake. I have got Mosiah [Boothe]'s and his wife's pictures. They are pretty good looking. Hyrum [Boothe] is going to send me his and his wife's picture.

[8]     Well Miriam, times are as dull as ever here. It seems very lonesome to me since Annett [Dennis] has been gone. She has been living out to Pleasant Plains for some time. She did talk of staying out there and going to school this winter, but I guess I shall have her come home. She and George Cowin [Keown] came out last Friday and went back this morning.

[9]     Deborah [Morey] has another girl [Eliza]. Mosiah and his wife send their respects to you and want you to write to them and Cousin Joseph [Bonney] [to write], too.

[10]    You say you are going to send me a dollar for those rings. Well, I guess you won't. I know what you think; you think if you don't send money to have my picture taken, you won't get it. I guess I can raise enough to get it taken. Don't you send any here if you don't want a good scolding, for you will be sure to get it if you do.

[11]    Tell Cousin Sarah and Cousin Joseph I deeply sympathize with them in the loss of their little daughter [Effie Josephine]. Tell them not to grieve after her, for she is a great deal better off than the rest of us. Tell them I had been looking for a letter from them this long time. Ask them if they won't be kind enough to write to me once more. Tell them I am coming down to see them some of these days if nothing happens. I look at their pictures every little while and wish I could, the originals.

[12]    Give my respects to Perry [Works]. Tell him I think he might come and bring you up to see us.

[13]    Well, Cous, it is getting late. They have all gone to bed but Ammy, and he is writing to you. So you see you have got two cousins that think of you yet. I am going to write to Adam after I get yours done. Shall I tell him you're going to write?

[14]    Well Mollie, I guess Aunt [Angeline Robinson]'s folks don't get along quite as well as they did when you was there. They have rather lonesome times. Uncle [Ebenezer] is gone

a most of the time. Annett [Dennis] stayed with her a week or two this fall, but they didn't agree very well. Their tempers were too near alike.

[15]     Miriam, I expect you will have to draw on your specs to read this, it is so poorly done. But I am in a great hurry and another thing: My pen is no account.

[16]     Well Mollie, Ammy has been acting the 'possum with me. I thought he said you was going to send the money some other time. He has just handed out the dollar. I have a great mind to send it back. If I had hold of you, I would give you a gentle shaking. Never you mind. I'll remember you—see if I don't. I haven't forgot the trick you tried to play on me when you started away. How does your rings do anyway? Have you got them fixed as good as ever?

[17]     You said you was obliged to Annett for her punctuality in answering your letters. Hasn't she answered them yet? If she hasn't, she ought to be ashamed of herself, and you may scold her as much as you please. I know she is too negligent about writing.

[18]     Frankie [Francis Dennis] says he wished he could write. He would write you a long one. The children all talk about you. They all want to see you. Caroline and Susan [Dennis] says tell Cousin Miriam they have got their little baskets good as ever. They are going to keep them always to remember their Cousin Miriam by. Frankie thinks if you was here, he could beat you climbing the stairs. He often laughs about it.

[19]     Well, I will stop. Ammy has beat me. He has got his done first. Don't laugh at my writing. I can do a little better sometimes when I try hard. Please answer this.

From Your Affectionate Cousin,
Angie L. Dennis
Thursday the 11th

Cousin Joseph,

[20]     I have just sit down to write a few lines for Amulek. He intended to write himself, but he didn't have time. He started to mill this morning.

[21]     He said he thanked you for your kind invitation. He would like very much to come down to see you all this winter, but circumstances are so that he can't well leave this winter. He would like to spend Christmas with you and help eat that turkey Miriam spoke of.

[22]     Give my respects to Cousin Sarah. Tell her I often think of her, and keep a good share for yourself.

I shall remain your well-wishing
Cousin 'til death,
"Amulek Boothe" to
Joseph Bonney

[23]     Miriam, when you write to Addie, direct to (Look on the other corner of the sheet.)

Merrill's Horse Co. B
Helena, Arkansas, Mo.

That is all.

## ❧ Letter #25

Eaglesville, Mo. Dec. 9, 1863

Most Dear and Affectionate Cousin,

[1]     I have sit down to pen a few lines to you to let you know that we are well. I received your letter this evening which was dated Nov. 29th and was glad enough to hear from you, although it was a long time coming. I begun to think that you had given up writing to your best friend, although you may not think so.

[2]    Miriam, it makes me feel bad to hear you write as though you had no friends up here, for I feel as a friend toward, and I trust I always shall, you.

[3]    You must not get crusty because I wrote as I did, for it was all in a joke. I heard that there was a young man waiting on you, and they called him Shakespear. I was told by someone at Pleasant Plains, and that the reason how I heard, and if I wrote anything that did not please you, I want you to forget it and consider that it was me wrote it.

[4]    I think that Deborah [Morey] is neglectful, or she would have written to you before this. For my part, I am going to write to you as long as I can tell where to direct my letters, whether you answer them or not. When you get so you won't write, I shall think that I have one friend less.

[5]    I have not had any letters from any of our cousins for a long time. They have quit writing. George Keown came out here last Friday. He left for home this morning. Mr. [George] Morey and his wife [Sylvia] came out to see us, and his Jim horse died here. Helen [Morey] was out here this fall and stayed a week.

[6]    I will go to Iowa this winter, in time—where I was last winter a year ago. I don't know how long I will stay. I would like to be down there a while to see you and Joseph and Sarah [Bonney], but I don't know when I shall get to come.

[7]    I have sold forty acres of land this fall, the forty that I told you you might have if you and Perry [Works] would come and live on it. If you will come up here and live, you may have the rest. I will give it just as free as drink if you will live on it, for I want to leave here anyhow.

[8]    Mary, I will send you the money to pay for that likeness, and if you get it safe, I will send you some more next time. Whenever you want any money, if you will write to me and I have got a cent, you'll get it. So no more this time.

From your Cousin,
A. Boothe
Mariam, write as often as you can.
Give my love to all.

## 🌺 Letter #26

Finally, after writing to everyone else, Mollie writes to the friend she may have been closest to, Eunice Miriam Morey, and the last letter of 1863 is Eunice's reply. Eunice was the youngest of the Morey daughters and Mollie's age. The freedom with which the young women communicated explains the unabashed surliness that begins Eunice's letter, including her apparent pun on the name Pleasant Plains.

Pleasent Pains [sic]     December 27 [probably 1863]

Dard [Hard? Darn?] Friend,

[1]     I sit down this Sabbath morning to pen a few lines to see if you will do as well as I have a-done. The reason I did not write to you sooner was because you wrote to all the rest of the folks before you wrote to me. I thought that you was doing well enough hearing from the rest of your friends. You wrote in Helen [Morey]'s letter that your feelings was very hurt. I am sorry to hear it, but I think that I have got feelings as well as you. You wrote to Deborah [Morey] and did not scribble [?] a line to me. I thought that it come pretty close to home. I will not say anything more about it.

[2]     Well, Miriam, please excuse me for commencing my letter the way I did. I know that I had not ought to have a-done so.

[3]     I was down to Mr. [Adam] Dennis' last week. I went down with David [Morey] when he took Annett [Dennis] home. We made a short stay with them. We stayed all night.

[4]     I am a-going to school this winter in the old schoolhouse
        [Moffet Schoolhouse]. The name of the teacher's name is
        Wise, but he lacks of being wise. I don't like him as well as I
        did Doc Clark.

[5]     Doc is in the army. He is pretty sick. The folks say that
        Samanth Sinder [?] has gone down to see him. I don't know
        it to be so. All the folks is well.

[6]     Well, I will close by asking you to write me, if you think I am
        worthy of an answer, and I will write to you. So good-bye,
        Miriam, until the next time.

[7]     I will send you my likeness in this letter. Please to send me
        yours. This is the second time I have asked you.

[8]     Please excuse bad writing and spelling and oblige a friend.

        From your cousin until death,
        Eunice Miriam Morey


NOTES

    1. Jack Franklin Leach, *Conscription in the United States: Historical
Background* (Yokohama, Japan: Charles E. Tuttle, 1952) p. 155.

    2. *History of Harrison County, Missouri,* (St. Louis: George W. Wanamaker,
1888) p. 369.

    3. Paul E. Steiner, *Disease in the Civil War* (Springfield, Ill.: Charles C.
Thomas, 1968), p. 12.

    4. Long, *Civil War,* p. 436.

    5. Long, *Civil War,* p. 303.

    6. *Nauvoo Expositor,* 7 June 1844, p. 2; and Ebenezer Robinson, "Items of
Personal History of the Editor," *The Return,* Vol. 3, No. 2, Feb., 1891.

7. Hiram L. Andrus and Richard E. Bennett, *Mormon Mss to 1846: A Guide to Holdings of Harold B. Lee Library* (Provo: Brigham Young University Press, 1977), p. 36.

8. Early Reorganization Minutes (unpublished records) (Independence, Missouri: 1863), p. 36.

9. William W. Blair, *Memoirs,* Frederick B. Blair, ed., (Lamoni, Ia.: Herald Publishing House, 1908), p. 43-44.

10. Church policy was that those who had been baptized by high officials of apostate sects had to be re-baptized. *True Latter Day Saints Herald,* September 1862.

11. Early Reorganization Minutes (unpublished records) (Independence, Missouri: 1860), p. 64.

12. *True Latter Day Saints Herald,* 1 January 1860; and November 1860.

13. *True Latter Day Saints Herald,* 15 July 1863.

14. *True Latter Day Saints Herald,* 15 November 1863.

15. *True Latter Day Saints Herald,* June 1863.

16. *True Latter Day Saints Herald,* 15 February 1864.

17. Brigham Young, Letter of 5 June 1862 as quoted in *Letters of Brigham Young to His Sons* (Salt Lake City, Ut.: Deseret Book Company, 1974), p. 23.

18. *History of the 152nd N.Y. Volunteers,* Henry Robach, ed., (Utica, N.Y.: L.C. Childs & Son, 1882), p. 21.

19. Leach, *Conscription,* p. 257-260.

20. *History of Northwest Missouri* (St. Louis: Whitson Printing Co.), p. 520.

21. Leach, *Conscription,* pp. 282 & 287.

22. *Ibid.,* p. 155.

23. *History of Decatur County,* Vol. 2., p. 171.

24. Long, *Civil War,* p. 399.

25. *Ibid.* p. 416.

**Helen Merah (Morey) Rockwell** *(1839-1888). Both Helen and her sister Eunice Morey were faithful letter writers to Mollie. Helen's courtship and marriage to Mollie's widowed cousin, George Rockwell, in 1864 is the subject of many letters. The marriage meant George's daughter, Adrianna, would live with her father instead of with George's sister, Deborah (Rockwell) Morey, whose housekeeping he was critical of. After marrying George, Helen advised Mollie not to marry.* [Photograph courtesy of Nancy Gerlock]

*Part of Letter #36, started by Eunice Morey, and added to by her sister, Helen in 1864.*

# TOWARD MARRIAGE
## 1864

### ❋ Letter #27

Mollie knew George McNutt as early as Christmas, 1863, according to this first letter of 1864. He sent it while she was visiting the Bonneys in LaGrange, Missouri, and it was as close to a love letter as she could hope for. Though he is shy about it, George admits that the parties in Millville on the Mississippi River "bottoms" are not worth going to because she is away. He was four years younger than she and the only son of James and Sarah Bell (Case) McNutt. He had eight sisters. The closest in age to Mollie was Susan, whom he mentions.

The McNutt farm in Fall Creek township is about three quarters of a mile from Mollie's nominal home with the Stewarts. As Mollie went to and from the well-to-do Nathaniel Carrs, one of her regular employers, she would pass by the McNutt farm where George was helping his father.

In this letter, George comments on the weather, which was severe, twenty-six degrees below zero on January 4, 1864, cold enough for horsedrawn wagons to cross the frozen Mississippi River, and for 8,000 hogs on railroad cars between Quincy, Illinois, and St. Joseph, Missouri, to have frozen to death.[1] On that January day, while Mollie was in LaGrange, she saw an entire block of stores burned. Because of the cold, little could be done to save them.[2] Nevertheless, this early letter from the young farmer who courted Mollie was apparently warm enough for her to save through the years.

Payson , Adams County, Ills.     Jan. 3, 1864

Dear Friend,

[1]     I now take up my pen in hand to inform you that I am well at present, and I hope when these few lines, they will find you enjoying the same blessings.

[2]     I would like to know whether you had a very pleasant New Year or not. I don't think we had a very pleasant New Year here, for it has been snowing here pretty much all the time for four days, and last Thursday the snow drifted in some places five or six feet deep.

[3]     Sister Susan [McNutt] is not at home. She has gone on a visit.

[4]     I have not seen any of your folks [the Stewarts] for some time, but they are all well as far as I know.

[5]     We have not had but one or two parties since you left here last fall. There has been several dances down on the bottom, but I did not go to any of them, for I did not think they were worth going to.

[6]     I have not got much to write, so I will bring my letter to a close. So, goodbye. Write soon.

Yours truly,
George I. McNutt

## ❈ Letter #28

Mollie continued to receive letters from soldiers—such as the next one from Charles Worden. This, Charlie's second letter to survive, is much more relaxed than his first in 1863, and it is in a different hand. The first one might have been dictated to a volunteer who helped soldiers correspond, while this one is written much more colloquially, punctuated casually, and may have been written by Charlie, himself. Charlie was part of that army of soldiers assigned to protect the capital at all costs.

Fort Simmons , Washington, D. C.
Monday Eve, Jan. 18, 1864

Dear Cousin Miriam—

[1]     I am ashamed to write for neglecting it so long—but better late than ever—I will own up that I am negligent in answering My Letters—but shall try to be more prompt after this—

[2]     Well, Miriam, it is a good While since I wrote you last but so much the more interesting—I believe that I am indebted to you a letter—but how to express Myself in such a case, I am unable [to] say—but please excuse Me this time and I will agree to do better hereafter—

[3]     Well, what shall I write? There isn't much news of importance. We still remain where we did when I wrote you last. Everything is quite as usual. My health is tiptop and has been pretty much ever since I wrote last.

[4]     I have heard from Cousin Grace [Robinson] lately. She is well and a-going to school. I have sent her my likeness, and you must not be offended because I haven't done the same by you. I would send it in this letter but I am afraid that it might not reach you, as I know not where you may be. If this reaches you and I receive an answer, then you may look for it in the next letter, and I will agree to answer it immediately.

[5]     I hear from home often and they are all well.

[6]     Well, Miriam, I hope you have succeeded in learning your trade. I suppose I must tell you that I have been promoted to a sergeant. I first came out as a corporal and have remained so until now, and yesterday I was promoted to a sergeant. Don't you think that I have been a pretty good soldier, Miriam? Of course you do.

[7]     You must not be surprised if you should see me out there in the course of eighteen months. My time is half expired, so

the time will soon come, if providence sees fit, when I shall be free again, and in less than two months from the expiration of my term of service, you will see Charlie Worden out there.

[8]     I had the photographs of three of my sisters [Angeline, Jane, and Julia], and I have sent them to Grace—but she is to send them back to me.

[9]     Well, I must close for it is about roll call. Please answer this soon. Give my love to Cousin Amulek B[oothe]. and Cousin George Rockwell and accept a good share yourself.

This, from your affectionate cousin—
C. L. Worden

Direct the same as before:
Co. I. 9th N.Y. Heavy Artillery
Washington, D. C.

## ✿ Letter #29

Mollie's cousin George Rockwell became a member of the RLDS through the efforts of their uncle Ebenezer Robinson. Since Ebenezer's talk with him in September, 1862 [See Letter #7, par. 7] George was a changed man, and he shows how much religion affects him in this letter. "Protracted meetings" is the Methodists' name for evangelical tent meetings.

He still lives in a boardinghouse near where he had left his second daughter, Clara, with relatives, and he lists his profession as "teacher," though he had other jobs. Contrary to his plans, he visited Iowa in the spring—not fall. Later on in this year, he would return to Iowa for good. [See Letter #52, par. 26].

Aurora, [Ill.]                    Feb. 5 [probably 1864]

Dear Cousin Miriam,

[1]      I once more attempt to address you a few lines. I received your letter some time since and have neglected to answer it for the reason of my not having anything to write that would be interesting you. I have not been doing anything for several days.

[2]      The weather is very cold, but no snow. It has the appearance of some today.

[3]      I have not been to Iowa yet, and I shall not go until next fall. I have engaged work nine months and commence the first of March. I have a good place to work and good pay.

[4]      I have been attending a protracted meeting in this place of the Free Methodists, and although they do not think just as I do, yet I can enjoy myself well in meeting with them.

[5]      I do sincerely wish you could be here to go with me. I have some kind friends in Aurora, but no one can fill your place in my mind. Miriam, I do have a desire to see you prosper in all your undertakings, and I long for the time to come when I shall have the pleasure of your society, and if a kind Providence will permit, I shall visit you and the rest of the cousins in Mason [should be Payson, Adams] county. Although they are strangers to me, yet I should like to see all my cousins. You will please give them my respects and also tell them I would be pleased to hear from them. Do they look anything like Angeline [Dennis] or Amulek [Boothe] or yourself?

[6]      In my next, I will send my photograph to you. Please send yours and your brother's in one. I have not heard from Iowa for some time. They were all well then. I am expecting a letter soon. Please answer soon, and I will be more punctual in future.

George Rockwell

## ❀ Letter #30

In Gracie Robinson's first letter of 1864, Mollie learns more about Iowa friends who became soldiers. As far as is known, the Works boys mentioned by Gracie are not related to Mollie.

During the winter, Gracie and her mother, Angeline, stayed at Royal Richardson's boardinghouse in Pleasant Plains rather than at their farm on the northern outskirts of town. This made it easy for Gracie to attend school, and it made housekeeping much easier for Angeline, whose health continued to be poor.

> Nine Eagles, Decatur Co., Iowa
> Thursday, Feb. 18, 1864
>
> Dear Cousin,

[1]      I again take my pen in hand to write a few lines to you in answer to your favor of the 26th inst. which came to hand by last mail.

[2]      We are now boarding at Mr. [Royal] Richardson's. We have been here about five weeks. I have been going to school to Mr. Warnock since we came here, but the school was out last Friday.

[3]      There is a good many of the soldiers at home now who have re-enlisted, among whom are Henry Cowles, John and James Gammill, and Orville Works. They are looking for Thomas Brant every day. Leslie Works was wounded in the head at that battle of Lookout Mountain, from the effects of which he afterward Died.

[4]      I receive letters from Cousin Charles [Worden] frequently. He is still at Fort Simmons. He has sent me his likeness and is a very good looking fellow. I received a letter from him a few weeks since in which he sent Jane's, Angeline's, and Julia [Worden]'s photographs for us to look at, and I just returned them to him last week. I don't know why he don't write to you.

[5]     I haven't had a letter from Cousin George [Rockwell] for a long time. He was still at Batavia the last we heard from him.

[6]     Pa [Ebenezer] is away now, and we don't expect him home till the first of April.

[7]     I expect that we will come down to LaGrange this summer as we expect to go East on a visit. Amulek [Boothe] hasn't been out for some time. Frank [Dennis] was out not long since. They were in usual health.

[8]     Deborah [Morey] has had poor health all winter so that she has had to keep a girl. Ma [Angeline]'s health is quite poor. She sends her love to you and Perry [Works]. Give my love to Perry, and tell him to write to me soon. Please write soon.

Truly,
Your Cousin,
Grace Robinson

## ✤ Letter #31

This letter from eleven-year-old Caroline, cousin Angeline Dennis' third oldest, is typical of letters from some of the younger girls, such as Louisa Booth. Most of their letters are not as sophisticated as Grace Robinson's who was almost exactly their age.

Caroline tells about her sister Annett's working for David and Deborah Morey. It would have been appropriate for Annett, at fifteen, to begin work as a hired girl. Mollie, too, had worked for the Moreys, and in this year, Deborah Ann Morey had been ill [See Letter #30, par. 8], so Annett was needed. Caroline comments that Amulek Boothe was one of Mollie's favorite letter writers. It was to him that Mollie revealed, as she did to Margaret Kennedy, that she expected to marry soon.

Caroline's schoolgirl rhymes are not original. [See Letter #18, par. 10 for others.]

Eagles, Missouri          March 18, 1864
                          Sabbath

Dear Cousin,

[1]     It is with the greatest of pleasure that I take my pen in hand
        to let you know that we are all well, excepting Mel [Amelia
        Dennis]. She is not very well, and I hope when these few
        lines come to hand, they may find you better.

[2]     Amulek [Boothe] received your letter the other day, and he
        said that you was sick. I wish that you would come up and
        make us a visit. I would like to see you and see if you have
        grown any since you left here.

[3]     David [Morey] and Annett [Dennis] came down here last
        Thursday night and stayed till this morning.

[4]     I was out to Pleasant Plains last Christmas and the folks was
        all well. I am a-going up to Annett one day next week. They
        [the Moreys] are a-going to move in two or three weeks.
        Them and Amulek [Boothe] is a-housing together this
        winter.

[5]     Amulek said that you was a-talking about a-getting married.
        When you get married, you must fetch him up and let us
        see him.

[6]     I cannot think of any more to write this time, so I will bring
        my poor letter to a close. Give my love to all my little
        cousins down there, and you may take the largest share of it
        yourself.

[7]     You must excuse my writing and bad spelling. Write as soon
        as you get this, so goodby. This is from

        Your affectionate friend,
        Caroline Dennis

Round is the ring
It has no end
So is my love
To you, my friend.
My pen is poor
My ink is black
If you can't read this,
Just send it back.

## ❧ Letter #32

Mollie's friend Margaret Kennedy's report from her new home in Des Moines includes some disdain for the Mormons, a disdain she apparently expects Mollie to accept without being offended.

The custom of extensively exchanging presents at Christmastime, except for children, was comparatively new in America at this time, so that Margaret's not receiving any is not unusual. The figure of Santa Claus was generally unknown.[3] Some religions, notably the Calvinistic ones, reminded their members that the celebration of Christmas was not biblical and that to celebrate it in the popular way was to participate in ancient pagan rituals, an abomination.[4] Though families celebrated Christmas with visits, feasting, and gifts to children, the Fourth of July remained the nation's primary holiday.

Margaret did not know who Mollie intended to marry at this time. It may have been George McNutt, either of the two Alford brothers (Tine or Bob) of LaGrange, or even Private James McNutt Field, George McNutt's nephew [See Letter #33]. But Margaret's letter is one of many that prove Mollie intended to marry at least two years before she actually did.

Des Moines, Iowa                    March 20, 1864

Dear Friend,

[1]     It is with the greatest of pleasure that I take my seat to write
        a few lines to you in answer to your kind letter which came
        to hand about one month ago and was glad to hear that
        you was well. We are all well, excepting a bad cold.

[2]     You say that you have not heard from Iowa for some time. I
        think your friends in Decatur must be like mine. They soon
        forget you when you are out of their sight. But never mind.
        We can live as long without them as we can with them. If
        we was all Mormons, they would write and let us know how
        they was all getting along.

[3]     You wanted to know how we spent our Christmas. Well, we
        had a jollification. There was 29 at dinner at our house, and
        there was room for you if you had been here. You speak of
        Christmas presents. Well, I did not get any, so you're ahead
        of me there. So I guess we can fix that matter easy.

[4]     You said you had a very very cold winter down there. We
        had a very cold winter here. It was so cold we had to stay
        close the stove or our time would have been short for
        certain. It is pretty cold yet. The wind has blowed from the
        north for several days.

[5]     You say you are a-going to get a man this year. Well, I wish
        you good success.

[6]     Smith's folks [Frank and Nancy] is well. Hannah [Booth] was
        here today, and so was the children.

[7]     Well, I will now tell you that there has been a revival in these
        parts this winter. The Baptists have taken in forty members.
        The Methodists had a protracted meeting that lasted over
        two weeks. There was but six joined. It is but a small
        congregation they have here, but it is still increasing some,
        but slowly.

[8]     Joseph [Kennedy] sends his best wishes to you. Well, I can't
        think of anything more to write that would be interesting
        you. I remain respectfully, your friend,

        Margaret Kennedy                Write soon, if you please.

## ❧ Letter #33

James McNutt Field was the son of Joseph and Mary Jane (McNutt) Field [See McNutt Family Tree, page 288]. Mary Jane was George McNutt's oldest sister—so much older, in fact, that James, though George's nephew, was two years older than he. George and James apparently were friends as well as relatives, for they went to parties together, and when James married in 1870, his wedding was in the McNutt farmhouse. James was mentioned by Mollie to her friends. Gracie Robinson thinks James might be Mollie's intended [See Letter #42, par. 8]. His letter betrays nothing romantic, however, and in 1870 he married Amanda Bowles, daughter of a prominent Payson landowner, Holman Bowles.

Mollie's stray markings in this letter which include the name and address of Private David Tilton may be a clue to another romance, though little is known about twenty-year-old Tilton, except that he was born in Ohio, the fourth son of Austin and Julia Tilton. The fact that Jane Stewart signs her name in this letter means Jane saw the letter. Sharing personal letters with girls your own age was common practice [See Letter #67, par. 11 as well.]

James writes from Camp Butler, a training camp for Union soldiers near Springfield named for the treasurer of Illinois at the time. The Illinois soldiers who write to Mollie trained at Camp Butler. Later, the camp would also serve as a prisoner of war hospital site and become a cemetery for both Union and Confederate soldiers. During the war, Camp Butler became a boon to Springfield merchants who gouged the recruits. One soldier complained that $40 suits were only $125 in Springfield.[5] Conditions in the Camp were deplorable, too. James' first job before beginning his training was to rid his sleeping area of vermin.

After the bitter cold of January, the war was heating up. In February, Nathan Bedford Forrest, one of the ablest leaders of Confederate cavalry [See Letter #42, par. 6] commanded a furious charge at Ivey's Farm in Mississippi, his greatest victory. Now he was harassing Union outposts on the Ohio River.[6]

Closer to home, a Rebel who had gone south at the beginning of the war returned to LaGrange on March 12 and was killed by someone sneaking up behind him and cutting his throat.[7] The day after James writes, about 100 Northerners who wanted an end to the war attacked Federal soldiers on furlough at Charleston, Illinois. Five were killed and others wounded. It was one of the worst anti-war outbreaks of the time.[8] By December, Lincoln would call for 300,000 more men to replace war casualties.

> Camp Butler, Springfield, Ills.
> J. M. Field
> March 27, 1864
>
> Miss,

[1]    It is with pleasure that I take my pen in hand to let you know that I am well, and I hope that when these few lines comes to hand, they will find you enjoying the same blessing.

[2]    I am in Camp Butler now, and I thought I would write you a few lines. We will leave here tomorrow for St. Louis.

[3]    I have nothing more to write this.

[4]    Write soon and let me know when you seen George Mc[Nutt] last. You must not forget the party when you write. Direct your letter to J. M. Field, Co. G, Second Cavalry, Illinois Volunteers, Camp Butler, Springfield, Illinois.

[5]    Nothing more this time. Write to me and then I will write to you again. Write soon.

> James M. Field
>
> [Below the signature in a hand not the letter writer's]:
>
> Mifs Miriam Works' Hand
> Mollie Works

[6]    The 78 Ills Vollenters
       Mr. David A. Tilton
       The 78 Ills vols
       c/o Nashville, Tennessee
       Jane Stewart

## ❧ Letter #34

It is easy to understand what life was like in cousin Joe Bonney's home in LaGrange from this next letter by Sarah "Sallie" Abigail (Johnson) Bonney. Sallie had a two-year-old, Katie Belle, and a baby, Oliva Alberta, who at three months was still nursing. Both were ill with whooping cough, and Mollie, ill herself with an unknown ailment, was in Payson, Illinois.

As a mother, Sallie was her family's doctor, a tradition as old as the home remedies women passed on to their daughters. Many of these remedies were obtained from "Indian" or "root doctors," who were not necessarily Native Americans, but were those who practiced herbal and root medicine the way the Native Americans did.[9] Sallie knew to give Katie and Oliva a tincture of soot or castor to treat the convulsive coughs and high-pitched "whoop" that marks pertussis. Or, Sallie might let an egg sit in vinegar until its shell crumbled, before mixing the egg with the vinegar and a little honey to make a potion. Rubbing Oliva and Katie Belle's backs with ammonia or oil of amber was supposed to relieve the convulsions too.[10] The change from trusting this type of folk medicine, practiced largely by women, to trusting the more scientific medicine of the professional doctors, who were mostly men, was slow to take hold in rural or Western areas of the country.[11] In any case, the Bonney household needed help in this time of illness, and from this letter it is obvious that Sallie thought more of Mollie's help than she did of her own sister Emma's.

The card game that was most often played in the Bonney house was euchre [See Letter #59, par. 5], very popular during the Civil War. A fast-paced card game, euchre involves just five tricks before a new deal.

It is this mixture of play and pain that made Mollie's experiences in LaGrange different from those she was used to in the Mormon settlement of Pleasant Plains. The strictness of her aunt Angeline Robinson, who became a model of the good wife for the young matrons of four familes, contrasts starkly with the free-spirited Nancy Alford of LaGrange and her two mischievous sons, Sylvester Valentine ("Tine") and Bob Alford. Mollie's LaGrange friends assumed playful nicknames, like the one Sallie uses for George McNutt in this letter. Emma ("Sis") Johnson and Sallie, herself, enjoy good times and card-playing, something that was forbidden to Mollie under the strict eye of Aunt Angeline. Nevertheless, illnesses, such as whooping cough, were mixed with the joys of buying a new hat for Sallie, and parties were planned despite terrible accidents like the one to poor Mary "Molly" Coulson, a neighbor of the Bonneys.

LaGrange, Missouri  March 27 [most probably 1864]

Dear Cousin Mollie,

[1]     I seat myself this evening to answer your kind and welcome letter that I received Thursday, and I was glad to hear from you.

[2]     My children has got the whooping cough. And the baby [Oliva] is right sick. I hope she will soon be better, for you know I have a good time of it now. How I wish you was here to help me take care [of] them, for I have to nurse all the time, and then I can't keep them still, and you know Sis [Emma Johnson] is no help to take care of them.

[3]     I don't know when I can come down to see you. Not till the children gets well. I am glad to hear you and "The Farm" [George McNutt] is getting along so well. I wouldn't think you would get lonesome.

[4]     I expect you would rather see Tine [Sylvester Valentine Alford], and I don't blame you. He was here today. He is well and sends his love to you and says he won't cheat, if they do beat him. We have a game every few nights, but Tine don't seem to enjoy himself as well as he did when you was here.

[5]     Mrs. [Nancy] Alford sends her love to you and says she has a sore eye and is sick all over.

[6]     Sis says she is lonesome and would like to see you and says you must come up and see her before she goes away. They is a-going to be a dance Friday evening, and she wishes you was here to go. Tine calls on us often as usual, but he looks right lonesome.

[7]     I think you ought to come up soon. I don't think I can come
        down before May, for this disease, the children will not get
        well of it sooner, and I won't come till they get well.

[8]     Molly, I have got me a new hat. You ought to see me. How
        nice I look in it! You must get you one.

[9]     I suppose you would like to know how Cally is getting
        along? She is still down here, but she has not been to Mrs.
        Alford's since you left. She told Mrs. Alford about what she
        heard, and it made her mad, so she don't go there any
        more. Cally sends her love to you.

[10]    I must tell you what happened last Sunday to Mary and Will
        Coulson. They had been to the country and was coming
        home, and the horse run away and broke the buggy all to
        pieces and throwed them out. It hurt Mary very bad. They
        was no bones broken, but Mary was seriously injured. She
        has been in bed ever since. The doctor thinks she will get
        well now, if she is careful. Will was not hurt bad.

[11]    I must stop writing now. You must excuse my writing and all
        mistakes for I have had to stop about fifteen times. Give my
        love to your cousins. Your Aunt [Rachel] and Uncle [Samuel
        Stewart] also. Tell Perry [Works] to come see us. Sis sends
        her love to you and Perry and says you must write to her.
        Joe [Bonney] sends his love to you both and myself also.

[12]    You must tell me how you enjoyed yourself at the party. I
        could write more if I had time but I must close. Bye, telling
        you goodby. Write soon. Don't forget to come to see us.

[13]    Mollie, I have Effa [Bonney]'s picture for you when I see you.

[14]    This is Easter Monday. It has rained and snowed and blowed
        all day. I don't want [such] an Easter often.

[15]    Don't you stay down there till you wink out. When you get
        tired, you must come up. I want to see you, now. This is
        from your Cousin,

        Sara A. Bonney

## 🌸 Letter #35

In the next letter, Sallie tells what happened to her daughter Oliva because of the whooping cough. Sallie also visits her older sister, Agnes, who has a newborn.

Mollie learns that Nancy Alford is afraid her boys, Bob and Tine, may be drafted. The Alfords were Kentucky natives with Southern allegiances. As teamsters driving wagons between LaGrange, Hannibal, and Canton, Missouri, Bob and Tine were constantly on the move, and that movement made it difficult for military draft enrollers to do their job, especially in Missouri, one of a few states where the new military draft law was not well enforced.[12]

LaGrange, Mo.                    May the 1 [1864]

Dear Cousin,

[1]    I received your kind and welcome letter a few days ago and was glad to hear from you again and rejoice to hear of your good health. My health is not very good at present, but I hope it will be better soon.

[2]    I have written my troubles to you about my Dear Little Baby I lost [Oliva Bonney]. She died April the nineteenth. I suppose you have got the letter before this. Kate [Bonney] is tolerable well. The rest is well.

[3]    I haven't got much to write now.

[4]    I will come down the 21st of May. You must meet me in Quincy at Levi's store on the corner. I will come down there alone. I would like to have you come home with me and stay a while for company for me. Sis [Emma Johnson] is a-going away in two weeks, and I will be so lonesome.

[5]    Mrs. [Nancy] Alford sends her love to you and says she can't write now. She is in so much trouble about the boys [Sylvester and Robert Alford]. They are in Hannibal, and the draft troubles her. I think Tine [Sylvester] will come home to stay soon. They have been gone about three weeks. Joe [Bonney] wants Tine to work at the mill, and I think he will come back.

[6]     I must stop writing this time. I want to go to Ag[nes Johnson]'s. She has a girl a week old, so good-bye for the present. Hoping to see you soon.

[7]     Give my love to Perry [Works], and keep a good share for yourself. Answer this as soon as you get it, and let me know if you will meet me at Quincy. Mail your letter there so I will get it soon.

[8]     Remember me to your relation[s], and tell them I will be down soon. Good-bye, Mollie, till I see you.

        This is from Sallie.

## ❧ Letter #36

The character of Mollie's friend Eunice Morey is clear in this next letter. Her comments are in direct contrast to her sister Helen's. (Helen calls Mollie "Marian," another variation of "Miriam.")

Helen mentions her cousins, the Perhams. Mary Ann (Morey) Perham was Helen's aunt. Mr. and Mrs. Perham and cousin Henrietta were members of the Little River Branch of the RLDS early in 1859. The soldiers, Marion and Dunham, were not. In April, 1861, the Perhams moved to Carthage, Illinois.

Nothing is known of Mr. Hartman or Laura Young, but significantly, both Helen and Eunice mention the return of that eligible widower, Mollie's cousin, George Rockwell.

Pleasant Plains, [Ia.]              April 8th, [18]64

Dear Friend,

[1]     It is with great pleasure I improve the present opportunity to write you a few lines in answer to your kind and welcome letter which I gladly received and read with much pleasure. Your letter found me well, and I hope these few lines will find you the same.

[2]      Well, for something to write, I hardly know what to say. I was down to Mrs. [Angeline] Dennis a few days ago. We found them all well that was at home. Amulek [Boothe] was not at home. He had gone to help drive off a drove of cattle. Mr. [Adam] Dennis has not come home yet. They expected him home on a furlough the first [torn]..he has given it up..[torn]

[3]      ...[George] Rockwell has come [back?]...[torn]...come last we[ek]... very...

[4]      Well, Miriam, your aunt [Angeline Robinson] is boarding out up to town. They have been there for two or three months, although I expect you have heard of it before.

[5]      Well, Mollie, that great man, Mr. Hartma[?] has got to be papa. Don't you think it makes him feel pretty large to be the father of so nice a son? He talks of going to the gold mines this spring. I expect he will shed tears as large as buckeyes when he gives them the parting hand and the farewell kiss. Oho, don't you wish that you had have got to have been his bride. He is so kind to her when they was first wed he would get up every night and get her a cold drink out of the well. Well, enough of this.

[6]      Well, Miriam, our Jerry Blakeslee is married. I expect that when you read this news that you will cry. I felt somewhat bad when [torn] hear from Our Doc [Clark?] the [torn] [He]len wants to write [torn] to close. Please excuse not writing sooner.

Morey, Eunice

---

[7]      Laura Young was married May 21st, 1864.

Dear Friend Marian,

[8]      Eunice has give me permission to write a few lines in her letter to you. I expect she has wrote all the news.

[9]     I got a letter from Henrietta [Perham]. She said they was all
        well. She says that Marion and Dun[ham Perham] has joined
        the army. I was sorry to hear that they had gone to war.
        They was too young to undergo so many hardships as they
        will have to go through.

[10]    These few lines leaves me well, and I hope these few lines
        will find you enjoying the same blessing.

[11]    George [Rockwell]...[torn]...his best wishes...I will do...

        Helen M. Morey

## ❧ Letter #37

George Rockwell writes the next letter after his visit to Pleasant
Plains and after another stint at his job in Nashville, Tennessee.
Despite travelling through Illinois, he did not stop to see Mollie.
Travel patterns were changing because of the spread of railroads.
Whereas the Robinsons followed the river routes from Greencastle,
Pennsylvania, to Pleasant Plains just seven years earlier, George
Rockwell would take the railroad. Stopping to see Mollie was not
convenient for him.

George worked for one of the religious groups that were asked to
help with the teaching of freed slaves in Nashville, a Confederate city
that fell early to Union forces and was one of the first in line for
Lincoln's reconstruction plans. [See Letter #45.]

        Aurora, [Ill.]                     May 29 [probably 1864]

        Dear Cousin Miriam,

[1]     I will try and write to you once more. I feel almost ashamed
        to open a correspondence with you. I feel to condemn
        myself very much for not writing to you before, knowing
        that you are always so punctual in answering to your
        correspondence.

[2]     I have been in Tennessee and also in Iowa since I last wrote
        to you, which you have heard by way of Grace [Robinson], I
        suppose. I should have liked to called on you and should,
        but it being some two hundred miles out of my way and no
        direct way of conveyance, so I beg to be excused, this time,
        but I have no cousin that I would give half so much to see
        as yourself, and I hope ere long to have the pleasure of
        meeting you, but if not on this earth, let us live so that we
        may meet in heaven. When we do, parting will never come.

[3]     We are all fast hastening to the grave, but what matters
        that? Only that when we are called to chasing this mantle,
        we may put on immortality and arise to newness of life in
        God's kingdom.

[4]     Let us beware how we walk, ever trying to keep in the light
        of God. Then we have his promise that we shall not fall
        when we obey his precept. Oh, that God will protect you
        and keep you is my desire!

[5]     I had a very pleasant visit while in Iowa. They were all living
        as formerly with few exceptions.

[6]     I saw by a letter that Grace had that you intend to change
        your name before long. If so, I hope it will be a happy one,
        for in the change hangs all your happiness in this life.
        Therefore, look well to your interests.

[7]     Well, you don't want any of my advice in any such matters,
        so I will close. Please write soon. Tell me all about it, and I
        will tell you my prospects. Give my respects to your cousins.
        Tell me where they all be, etc.

        George Rockwell
        Kane Co., Ills.

## ✤ Letter #38

Though "writing a few lines" in someone else's letter is common, pretending to be another person as you write, the way cousin Joe Bonney does in this next letter, is unusual, even though the other person is his wife, Sallie. [For something similar, see Letter #24]. Luckily Sallie rescues the letter before it is sent. She had recently visited Mollie and the Stewarts.

Although the outline of the strawberry Sallie mentions is impressive, it is not the giant size of present-day varieties. To keep them longer than their season, she is canning them.

LaGrange, Mo.                    June 8th, 1864

Dear Cousin,

[1]     I take this opportunity of writing you a few lines to let you know that I got home safe Monday after I left you.

[2]     I found the folks all well. I have had a fine time picking strawberries. Since I got home, I have picked about five gallons, and I am a-picking gooseberries today. I wish that you was here to have some strawberries and cream with us.

[3]     Uncle Dave [Smith]'s folks are all well. This is all that I think of at present. Write as soon as you get this, and let us know when you are coming up to see us. Goodbye for the present,

S. A. Bonney

To Mollie Works

[4]     Mollie, you will see by this letter, Joe wrote it, and it is a short one. I intended to write Sunday, but I had company, and I have been so busy I couldn't.

[5]     I had strawberries and cream the next day after I got home, and I have them every day I want them. I wish you was here to help me eat them. I picked two gallons and a quart

Monday, and I put them up. I must go and gather some now. I will show you the size of one on this.

[6]       I want you to come up the Fourth without fail. Tell the girls [the Stewarts] to come and Perry [Works], too. Did he come up Sunday?

[7]       Mrs. [Nancy] Alford was disappointed you did not come home with me. She says you must come as soon as you can. She looks for her boys home the Fourth.

[8]       Sam [Stewart] said he would come up the Fourth. Ask Helen [Stewart] if she has got any more caterpillars on her. She had better come up and stay with me until they are gone. I haven't seen one since I came home.

[9]       I must stop writing for this time. I don't know whether you can read this. I am in a hurry. I have so much to do I hardly know what to do first. Goodbye for the present. Write soon. Give my love to all.

[An outline of a large strawberry is traced here.]

## 🌸 Letter #39

The next letter is another example of one written by two people, Eunice and Helen Morey. Helen writes a day after Eunice, correcting Mollie's impression of what Eunice wrote. Eunice seems somewhat coy about telling Mollie the news concerning George Rockwell, but Helen is frankly defensive. Eunice's prejudice against "older" widowers with children is evident here and in other letters. [See Letter #68, par. 3, too.] George was six years older than Helen with two children, Adrianna and Clara.

Neoma (or Naomi) Macy, the daughter of Dr. David and Caroline (Gibson) Macy, is just sixteen years old, and this may be why Eunice comments about her.

Mary Ann May is the daughter of one of Decatur County's early settlers, James May.

Pleasant Plains, [Ia.]          July 6, 1864

Dear Friend,

[1]     It is with pleasure I hasten to answer your kind and thrice
        welcome letter which was duly received the 3rd of July. I
        was truly glad to hear from you and that you had
        condescended to answer my letter. I sincerely thank you for
        being so kind.

[2]     Well, Miriam, I have not much news to write, but I will do as
        well as sense will allow, and that won't be much, you know.
        Well, to begin on, I will tell you about the weddings that has
        been since I wrote to you. Mr. C. Gentry, he got him a wife.
        Her name was Mary Ann May. I guess you knew her. I think
        that she was bad-off for a man to take up with him. He
        must be 35 or 40 years old. Well, he will make her a
        husband and good old Father.

[3]     That fine Neoma [Naomi?] Macy is married. She been
        married a week today. Her man's name is Whitecar
        [Whitaker?]. Perhaps you know him. He left his wife about a
        year ago. He was Mrs. Wulike's brother. He has a little girl
        about six years old. I think that Neoma could have done
        better than that if she had have tried.

[4]     I think the girls is getting scairt because the boys gone to
        war. For my part, if I could not get a young man, I would
        not prefer none at all. Don't you think so? I would live an
        old maid and die an old bachelor, as the old saying is,
        before I would do as poor as some of the girls have done
        out here.

[5]     As for Henry [Cowles] and me, we have dissolved
        partnership.

[6]     Well, Miriam, would be glad to see you. I have a good deal
        to tell you that I could not write. I heard that you talked
        some of coming a-up here this fall. I wish you would come

and spend the winter up here. Then I would be all right. I have been lonesome here without you. I have wished you back to Iowa more than once.

[7]      Well, Miriam, I guess if nothing happens I expect to have your cousin George [Rockwell] for a brother-in-law. Helen says it is not so, but never mind what she says. She is aching to write something about me, but you need not believe anything she says.

[8]      Well, Miriam, I guess I had better stow my nonsense and quit my scribbling. Please excuse bad writing and spelling and oblige a friend.

Eunice M. Morey

Write soon.

July 7, 1864

Miriam,

[9]      Eunice has give me the privilege of writing a few lines in her letter to you which I was very glad to do. I read your letter with much pleasure. I was glad to hear from you and to hear that you was well and enjoying yourself as well as you say you are.

[10]      Well, Mollie, how spent you the 4th of July? Fine, I expect. Well, I was at home all day. Martha Cowles was here and spent the 4th with me.

[11]      Amulek [Boothe] and Annett [Dennis] went past here a little while ago. They did not stop.

[12]      Miriam, you may believe as much of what she [Eunice] says as you think is so. I will tell you what she dreamt last night. She says she dreamt she was a-going to get married to an old man that is a-working on our house, and I told her that

if she wrote about George [Rockwell] and she says you need not believe what I say, you can believe as much of what I say as what she says.

[13] Well, I must stop writing, for it is supper time and I must stop writing. Write soon.

Helen Morey

## ❧ Letter #40

Another letter from George Rockwell, as an answer to the many Mollie mailed during this period, tells her about the upcoming visits of Adaline, his youngest sister, and his father, David Rockwell. Adaline had just married Philander L. Perry in April. She and her husband did move to the Pleasant Plains area in late January 1865 and lived there for a time. David Rockwell, after a brief visit, returned home to Huntsburgh, Ohio, near the first Mormon temple at Kirtland.

Again, George seems intent on seeing Mollie, but there is no record that he ever did. His cute remark about "changing your name" coming with many other references to Mollie's getting married means that she was very close to marriage at this time.

Aurora, [Ill.]                    July 10, [18]64

Dear Cousin,

[1] I will now answer your letter which I was very glad to receive, I can assure you, for there is not one of my cousins that I would so soon hear from as you. It just does me good to read your letter, but it would do me much better to see you. Then I could tell you more than I can write.

[2] I have had one letter from Cousin Grace [Robinson], and one from Deborah [Morey], one from Helen Morey, and I am expecting one from Eunice [Morey] this week. They are all well or was the last I heard from them.

[3] I have had two from Adaline [Perry]. I expect that she & her husband will come west this next winter. I am also

expecting my father [David Rockwell] home on his way to
Iowa this week.

[4]      Now I will tell you how I spent the Fourth. It was a beautiful
day with us. I remained in town until two o'clock in the P.M.
Then I went to Geneva, nine miles north, to a celebration &
a good display of fireworks in the evening. I returned at 12
o'clock at night after enjoying myself first-rate. On the whole
I am having fine times, & I am having one of God's choicest
blessing, that is, good health, & I feel to thank him for it.

[5]      Now, Miriam, I want to know if you can come to Cousin
Joseph [Bonney]'s this fall & how far it is from where you live
to Quincy or his place, for I want to see you some way this fall.

[6]      I feel very lonesome many times when I think that I have so
many relatives & know so few of them & those that I do know
are living far away from me. But I am determined to live
different after this summer.

[7]      I think perhaps I will go to Iowa & settle down for the
remainder of my days. I may go about the first of
September. I suppose you never think of returning to
Pleasant Plains again.

[8]      I will close, hoping to see you before long. Then I can tell
you more than I could write in a month.

[9]      Oh, do you think of changing your name? Please answer
this. Please accept my best wishes.

Yours truly,
George Rockwell

## ✿ Letter #41

The first letter cousin Angeline Dennis writes in 1864 reveals the
frustration she feels because she is without her husband. It is the
frustration of trying to run a farm and care for six children, aged five
to fifteen. It is the difficulty of going twenty-six miles north to Leon,

Iowa, just to get a photograph taken. (The Eagleville ambrotypist had an unfortunate accident [See Letter #24, par. 6].) Frustrating, too, is not finding time to write to friends from whom she nevertheless wants to receive letters, and finally there is the worry about her husband Adam's illness.

Disease stopped both armies, North and South. Diarrhea, entiritis, and dysentery combined with malaria to decimate regiments on both sides. Trooper Adam Dennis understood how the flux (uncontrollable dysentery) could stop the best soldier. He and his buddies called malaria "Clarendon shakes," after the town east of Little Rock, where he was stationed during most of the war. Sometimes the bugler who blew a morning "quinine and whiskey" call couldn't finish because of his own "Clarendon shakes."[13]

In this letter as in many others from her cousin Angeline, Mollie reads a familiar phrase: "when Ad gets back" or "when Ad gets home." Everything seemed to depend on the war's ending.

Eaglesville, Mo.                    Sabbath Morning
                                    July 10th, 1864

Dear Cousin,

[1]    After so long silence I again attempt to scribble a few lines. Hope you will pardon my neglect. I should have written before but have been waiting to get my picture taken. I had no opportunity to have it taken till I went to Leon. I had it taken for you, but it was not a very good picture, but it was the best I could do.

[2]    We are all well, as usual, and I sincerely hope this will find you all right.

[3]    I got a letter from Adam [Dennis] last mail. He was not well. He has the flux pretty bad. He thinks he will be home in September. I would like to have you come and make us a [?] visit when he gets home.

[4]    I was out to Pleasant Plains about a month ago. They were all well.

[5]    It seems you have forgotten us. You haven't said a word to us in a long time. Perhaps you think us rather neglectful. It is true I have been rather neglectful, but it is not because I have forgotten you. Far from it. On the contrary, I often think of you, and hope the day not far distant when we can enjoy each other's society.

[6]    Tell Joseph and Sarah [Bonney] that I have not forgotten them. I will send them my picture before long. When Ad gets home, if we can leave, I would like to come down there to see you all. Give them my best respects. Tell them to write me one more letter, and they may scold just as much as they are a mind to.

[7]    My sincere regards to yourself and Perry Works.

So good-bye,
Angie L. Dennis

## 🌺 Letter #42

Gracie Robinson's next letter in this year mentions Booth and Clark young people at a Fourth of July celebration in Leon, Iowa, north of Pleasant Plains. The Booth "young people" included the sons and daughters of Robert and Phebe (Marcelles) Booth: Horace, Robert O., Louisa, and Olive. The John Clark "young people" included Caroline (called "Call") and William, who would later marry Olive Booth. The Clark name was the most prominent one in nearby Davis City, Iowa, where the Clark Factory was busy processing the more than thirty-seven tons of wool it sold to the Union army throughout the war.[14]

The war dead now had the familiar names of Gracie's cousins, and she lists them. Her father Ebenezer's family included brothers, sisters, half-brothers, and half-sisters from her Grandfather Robinson who had married three times. George Tinker was a son of Mary, the sister Ebenezer failed to convert during his first Mormon mission in 1836. John Sterling was the son of Sarah (Robinson) Sterling, Ebenezer's oldest sister. Though Gracie may never have seen these cousins, Death's scythe, powered by war, was cutting closer to home.

Austin Cowles' son, Fourth Sergeant Henry Cowles, who lived on the west side of Little River across from Boothtown, had been wounded and captured during the Battle of Pea Ridge. He re-enlisted in this year, and Gracie relays his boast about Confederate General Nathan Bedford Forrest. Forrest, in command of all the Tennessee cavalry, was nicknamed "The Wizard of the Saddle." He had recently retaken Fort Pillow, on a Mississippi river island about forty miles north of Memphis. The complaint that Forrest's men scalped the fort's defenders was never proven, but "Fort Pillow!" became a Northern rallying cry.[15] Henry's unit was not successful, since Forrest did not surrender until after a defeat at Selma, Alabama, in 1865.

Gracie mentions a beau of Mollie's named Shakespeare, just as Amulek Boothe did last year [See Letter #25, par. 3]. Though the name is found in Illinois at the time, nothing more is known about the young man, whether his name was actually Shakespeare or he was playfully given the name for other reasons.

The "College" Gracie attends was a thirty-by-sixty-foot, two-story school building in Pleasant Plains whose grand name was meant to attract teachers as well as students. A tornado destroyed it in 1865.[16]

Nine Eagles                          Decatur Co., Iowa
                                     July 15, 1864

Dear Cousin Mollie,

[1]     I once more seat myself to address you a few lines through
        the medium of the pen. Your kind letter of June 21st has
        been received and contents read.

[2]     We are in tolerable health at present, although Ma
        [Angeline]'s health is still very poor. Pa [Ebenezer] has been
        at home since I wrote to you before. He started away the
        6th of this month.

[3]     I had a very pleasant time the Fourth. Mr. [Robert] Booth's
        and Mr. [John] Clark's young people and myself went
        together. We attended a celebration at Leon [Iowa] on that
        day. When you write, tell me if you had a good time.

[4]    I received a letter from Cousin George [Rockwell] last mail.
       He said he had received a letter from you. I also received
       one from Cousin Julie Worden a few weeks since. She said
       that they hadn't heard from Cousin Charlie [Worden] for
       some time, and she expected he was engaged in fighting.
       And perhaps the next news will be that he has been killed.

[5]    I received the news a few weeks ago of the death of two of
       my cousins that were in the army. One of them (George
       Tinker) was wounded in the battle of Ringgold and had to
       leave his limb amputated. He lived several weeks after, but a
       fever set in which terminated in his death. He was in his
       21st year. The other one (John Sterling) died of typhoid
       phenenmenid and was buried in the soldiers' cemetery near
       Culpepper.

[6]    I got a letter from Henry A. Cowles a few weeks since. He
       was then at Memphis, Tenn. He said that he expected they
       would start after General Forrest before long, and they
       intended to give him a good whipping if they had a chance.

[7]    David [Morey]'s folks are all well. Mrs. [George] Hinkle and
       Lizzie were all well the last I heard. Thomas is still <u>living</u> for
       <u>anything that I know</u>.

[8]    Well, Mollie, how is that Mr. [James McNutt] Fields getting
       along that you spoke about in your other letter? Is there any
       prospect of me having him for a cousin or not? Is he the
       one that they called <u>Shakespeare</u>? If he is, he has got a <u>fancy
       name</u>.

[9]    You said you thought I ought to come and make Cousin
       Sally [Bonney] a visit. Nothing would give me more pleasure
       in so doing if I have a chance. Perhaps it will be so we can
       come this season, at least I hope so.

[10]     I wish you and Perry [Works] would come out here this fall and make us a visit. What is the reason he don't want to come? Is it because he don't want to see his cousins? If it is, tell him to stay there, and when I come to Joseph [Bonney]'s, I won't come to see him. He hasn't written to me for about 5 months. But if he don't want to write, he can <u>let</u> it <u>alone</u>. But if I should ever see him, he will get his pay [i.e. his due].

[11]     I wrote to Cousin Joseph this spring, but haven't received any answer. What is the reason they don't write either?

[12]     The weather is quite warm and very little rain. I am afraid if there don't come rain pretty soon, our crops will be rather short.

[13]     We haven't heard from John Clipp[inger] since last August, as we neglected to answer his letter, and now we don't know where to direct. But I expect he is still living, for he was detached as nurse in the hospital, so he didn't have to do much fighting.

[14]     I suppose Perry don't talk any of enlisting in the 100 day service. There has several of the boys went from here into the 100 day call. Louis Adkins is among the number.

[15]     Mr. Jones' folks have sold their farm and calculate to move away this fall.

[16]     Well, Mollie, I have a tolerable good time this summer going to school. I study Arithmetic, Geography, and Grammar, so you see I have <u>my hands pretty near full</u>, and I have to write compositions, and that is the worst of all. I suppose you are not attending school this summer. Perhaps I shall <u>graduate</u> this term. As you know, I am attending <u>College</u>.

[17]     Well, I guess you must not complain of a long letter this time. I have small letter paper, but you wanted a long letter, so I thought I would gratify you and write on a large sheet.

[18]     Well Mollie, I guess I will have to bring this poorly written
         letter to a close, for the scholars are beginning to go to
         school, and I will have to stop and get ready. I don't know
         as you can read this. If you can't, just send for me and I will
         come and help you, as it was written in a hurry. You will
         excuse it.

[19]     Ma wishes to be remembered to you and Perry. Please give
         my love to Perry and keep a good share for yourself. Answer
         this soon, and have Perry write.

         As ever, your cousin,
         Gracie Robinson

## ❧ Letter #43

This next casual letter from Sallie Bonney reveals that Mollie most
often spent her holidays in LaGrange, something she did not do on
the Fourth of July this year.

Sallie mentions Retta [for Henrietta?] Coulson, a neighbor of the
Bonneys and one of the many Coulsons who were Mollie's friends in
LaGrange.

The hat Sallie urges Mollie to get was made with flowing chignon
ends that made it resemble a waterfall.

         LaGrange, [Mo.]     July 24 [most probably 1864]

         Dear Cousin,

[1]      I again seat myself to write you a few lines in answer to
         those I received a few weeks ago. I hope you will excuse me
         for not writing sooner, but I didn't know any news to write
         that would interest you.

[2]      We are all well and hope that you are. I would like to see
         you. I looked for you the Fourth. Why didn't you come up
         and see us?

[3]     Mrs. [Nancy] Alford sends her love to you, and says she
        wants to see you so bad, and wants you to go a-walking
        with her.

[4]     Her boys [Tine and Robert] is away. Tine was up the Fourth,
        but didn't stay long. They got a letter from him yesterday.
        He was well. I expect he will stay there till fall.

[5]     Mollie, if you get a hat, get a waterfall. They are all the fashion
        here, and I think they are pretty. They are round on the top.

[6]     Retta Coulson sends her love to you.

[7]     I can't think of anything more at present. I am going to
        church, so I must stop writing for this time. I would like to
        write more, but I haven't time. Write soon. Give my love to
        all the folks and accept same. Write soon as you get this.

        From,
        S. A. Bonney

## ❧ Letter #44

In this next letter, sixteen-year-old Phebe Louisa Booth writes to her friend, Mollie, signing her full name for the first time. [See Letter #16.] She is the youngest of the Robert Booth children. Robert and Phebe (Marcelles) Booth are not related to Amulek Boothe or his sister Angeline (Boothe) Dennis. The Booths operated a store near their farm in Boothtown, on the east side of Little River. Rebecca (Booth) Potter is Phebe's oldest sister.

            [Spring Valley, Ia.]                    August 6, 1864

            Phebe Louisa Booth
            to her friend, Mollie Works

            Dearest and Affectionate Friend,

[1]     I received your thrice and welcome letter dated July 19,
        1864. I was very glad, indeed, to hear from you and to hear
        that you was well. We are all well at the present time, and I

sincerely hope that when these few lines comes to hand, they may find you in good health.

[2]      You said that you had Leap Year [?] out there a while. I would have liked to have been there very much, for I expect that you had quite a fine time.

[3]      I want you to pick out me an old man down there, for I have got you one picked out for you.

[4]      You said that you was a-going to a show to Quincy [Illinois] the 11th[?] of last month. I like to be there to go with you, but I don't expect that I can be there. I was up to Leon [Iowa] to a show and circus last week, and we had a fine time. I wish that you had a-been there.

[5]      Olive [Booth] is not at home. She has gone down to Rebecca [Potter]. Her children has got the whooping cough.

[6]      Your aunt [Angeline Robinson] was down here last week, and she said that they talked of moving next week down to Farmington [Iowa].

[7]      We heard from Almeda [Newman] last week, and she was well, and that she liked the country there, and that she made $6 a week and Jacob [Newman] $3 a day.

[8]      Hannah Booth has a boy. It is three [days] old today. She has named it Oda Beldin Booth. You must call over some afternoon and take a look at it.

[9]      You said that you would send me your photograph, and I shall be a-looking for it until it do come. I want you to write sooner this time, for I will quit writing, for I will begin to think that you don't want to write.

[10]      Well, I will have to close for I am pretty near asleep, for I sat up all night over to Miss Graves'. Her little boy is very sick.

For that reason you must excuse bad writing and spelling, so good-bye. I shall look for that photograph until it comes.

From your friend,
Phebe Louisa Booth

[11]    Write as soon as you receive this scribbling, so good-bye. I would like very much for you to come and make us a visit this fall if you can make it convenient.

## ✿ Letter #45

This letter from George Rockwell gives a glimpse into what his life in Nashville was like working for the government in Lincoln's reconstruction program. Nashville was to serve as a model for the reconstruction of the rest of the South, but the job was left to the military, and some of the Union officers were grafters. Freed slaves were mistreated and cheated out of goods and services meant for them. At the end of 1863, a meeting was held in Nashville to organize a society for the relief of freedmen. Northern benevolent societies such as the Western Freedmen's Association and the American Missionary Association gave as much aid as they could. A camp was set up for refugee slaves, and several schools were started. By 1864, the government depended on these benevolent societies, sponsored by churches, to administer or help administer reconstruction aid fairly.[17] George had taught at the Congregational Church school in Batavia, Illinois, and went to Nashville to work for the army. For all of the unpleasantness of his situation there, significantly he does not forget his letter from Helen Morey.

Nashville, [Tenn.]                    Aug. 14, 1864

Dear Cousin,

[1]    I will write you a few [lines?], seeing that I am way down in Dixie.

[2]    I have been in this place two weeks to work for the government. I shall stay 5 more if I have my health, then to return to Ill.

[3]     I have poor board: such as sour bread and pork & beef, beans, coffee, etc. But I guess I can stand it.

[4]     I have forgotten whether I answered your last letter or not before I left. There is seven writing besides myself at this time on a long table, so you can guess how pleasant it is to think of anything as long as some are talking.

[5]     I will try and see you before long, then I can tell more than I can write.

[6]     My health is good.

[7]     I got a letter from Helen Morey last Thursday. She says they are all well as usual, so I will close. Please write as soon as you get this so I can get it before I leave.

      P.S. Direct to
      George Rockwell
      Nashville
      Box 75
      Care Department D

[8]     Miriam, give my respects to all my relations, and accept my best wishes yourself.

      George Rockwell

## 🌺 Letter #46

After nearly a month, Sallie Bonney again writes Mollie, who had been waiting for a letter from her. Mollie was with the Stewarts at the time, so Sallie tells her about the return of Olivia Donly to Canada, about Sallie's sister Agnes, and about her youngest sister, Emma, called "Sis."

Sallie, whose only living child, Katie Belle, is a two-year-old, nevertheless decides to go back to school. Interestingly she starts school in deep summer, and as a matron, she obviously does not consider herself a schoolgirl. Summer school and adult education were not unknown in Civil War times. Schools were only beginning to be regulated by school boards. Anyone possessing special knowledge, such as Sallie's teacher, could rent a schoolhouse and enroll students privately. Specialized classes, such as writing school or music school, were held at night so that they would not interfere with the regular day students' classes.[18]

LaGrange, Mo.                    August 21, [1864]

Dear Cousin Mollie,

[1]     I take pleasure in answering your kind letter that came to hand Thursday. I was glad to hear from you, but I don't like to be scolded, but I didn't blame you much. But I have been so busy I can't hardly find time to write. And Sundays, if I go to church, I have no time, so you must excuse me, and I will try and do better.

[2]     Mollie, I have been going to writing school. Don't you think I am a-getting young? I want you to come up and see us. I am tired of looking for you. Why didn't you come the Fourth? You may come as soon as you like and stay as long as you like. I am sure that is fair. I will be glad to see you all.

[3]     I can't think of much to write today. You must give our love to all our relations and please write.

[4]     Alfa [Nancy Alford] says you must come soon before all the beauty of summer is gone, for you stay housed up in the house in the winter and never look out. Her boys [Tine and Robert] won't be at home for three or four weeks.

[5]     Sis [Emma Johnson] is over at Ag[nes]'s today. Miss Donly has gone home. Will Coulson went with her. Mrs. Coulson and Mary [Coulson] spent the day here Friday. They have all left. Retta [Coulson] has poor health this summer. I haven't seen her since I got your letter.

[6]     I must stop writing. I want to go to church. Give my love to your uncle and aunt [Stewart] and all your cousins. Tell them I would like to see them all. Give my love to Perry [Works] and accept the same. Joe [Bonney] sends his love to you.

Sara A. Bonney

## ❧ Letter #47

Eunice's third letter in this year shows her religious convictions, but her high language is mixed, as always, with the homely. Here is another example of the strong belief, especially in those who called themselves Latter Day Saints, that the Civil War was the beginning of the world's latter days or end times [See Letter #13, par. 4 and especially Letter #50, par. 10 & 11 for something similar]. The Saints were reminded that Joseph Smith had prophesized not just the Civil War itself, but also where it would begin. As early as November 1860, the *True Latter Day Saints Herald* reprinted Smith's Civil War prophesy, dated Christmas day 1832 and first published in England during 1852 in *The Pearl of Great Price*, a book of his revelations and prophesies. The prophesy begins:

> Verily thus saith the Lord, concerning the wars that will shortly come to pass, beginning at the rebellion of South Carolina, which will eventually terminate in the death and misery of many souls. The days will come that war will be poured out upon all nations, beginning at that place; for behold the Southern States shall be divided against the Northern States and the Southern States will call on other nations, even the nation of Great Britain, as it is called, and they shall also call upon other nations, in order to defend themselves against other nations; and thus war shall be poured out upon all nations...[19]

It is no wonder, then, that Eunice and other Mormons believed the Civil War was the beginning of the destruction of the world. Those soldiers who would serve in it, such as Amulek, could only hasten the end. So far as is known, Eunice's announcement about Amulek's enlistment is a surprise to Mollie.

Where thirteen-year-old George Truman, eldest son of Martha Ann (Morey) Truman, goes is not known, nor is it known whether Eunice's prediction about him, her nephew, came true.

The George Moreys (Eunice's parents) were building a new home, and Mollie, on a cue from Eunice's sister Helen [See Letter #39, par. 12], teased Eunice about marrying an old workman that Eunice dreamt about. But Eunice keeps to her principles regarding age and marriage [See Letter #39, par. 4.]

Thomas Hinkle was the eldest son of George Hinkle, one of Decatur County's earliest settlers, and a long-time friend of both the Robinsons and Moreys. The Hinkles had been Mormons at Nauvoo, Rigdonites in Pennsylvania, and they had supported the Robinsons and Moffets in the Little River Branch baptism dispute.

Pleasant Plains              August 24, [probably 1864]

Dear Friend,

[1]     It is with pleasure that I sit myself down to write you a few lines informing that I am yet in the land of the living and in good health and good spirits, still looking forward with bright anticipation to the [time] when I shall see you once more in which I hope will not be long, but if we are deprived of the privilege of meeting on the earth, let us so live that we can meet in heaven. Oh, what a glorious privilege, if we keep the commandments and obey the laws of the Lord's! We can have a dominion in the kingdom of the blessed.

[2]     Well, Miriam, I hardly know what to write, but to commence, I will tell you what I have been busying myself at this summer. I have been spinning yarn. Don't you think I am getting industrious to go to spinning? I like it very well.

[3]     Well, Miriam, what are you doing down there? I think you might spend time to come up and see us. I would be glad to see you, have an hour's chat with you as we used to. I could tell you more in an hour than I could write in all day.

[4]     Well, Miriam, I expect you will be sorry to hear that Amulek [Boothe] has enlisted in the service. He enlisted about a week ago, but he has only enlisted for one year. That is better than three years. He started yesterday.

[5]    George [Henry Truman] has gone on a wild goose chase up north, or rather northwest. He said that he would not come back for twelve months. I would not be at all surprised if he comes home for Christmas, for he never was away from home over than two or three weeks.

[6]    Well, Miriam, I do not expect you have forgotten the many happy hours we have talking with Thomas Hinkle, also the talking about the time you slipped off from him the night that meeting were down to our house. I don't think that we might have the privilege of talking with him. He has passed from this world of trouble to the land of bliss. He has paid the debt we all must pay sooner or later. I hope that he is better off than he was when he was here. He is out of a world of trouble, for there is a great weeping and terrorization [?] through the land, for this is a day of much mourning and sorrow and grief, but this is only the starting point of what there will be.

[7]    Do you ever think what this war means? Does not the Bible teach us the meaning of this awful sign of black and fighting means? It is dreadful, but Miriam, if you live to more years, you will see that this is only the beginning of it.

[8]    Well, Miriam, you said that you hope that I would get that old man. Well, if you could see him, you would pity my case, for he is humped-back, and his hair is gray, and he has to wear spectacles, and besides all of that, he has not got no more than half sense. Now, think of hoping such a awful thing as that on me.

[9]    Our house is a-growing slowly. I think we will get into it in two months.

[10]    Well, I must quit my pen scratching and bring my letter to a close.

[11]    Asking you to excuse poor writing and spelling and oblige a friend. Write soon.

Eunice M. M.

I expect you will laugh when you see this poorly composed letter but you must consider who composed it.

## 🌹 Letter #48

Helen Morey tells Mollie details about Amulek, but the purpose of this letter is to announce Helen's engagement, just as Eunice had predicted.

Helen's phrase "cut a spiny" is difficult to interpret, especially because her handwriting is unclear and these may not be her exact words. The expression may refer to the extreme arching of an animal's back when it is disturbed, the spine seeming to cut through the skin. [For similar uses of the word "cut," see Letter #24, par. 5 and Letter #63, par. 6.]

[Pleasant Plains, Ia.]        August 26, 1864

My Dear Friend Miriam,

[1]     It is with pleasure that I take my pen in hand to answer your kind and welcome letter that came to hand some time ago. I was glad to hear that you was enjoying yourself so well.

[2]     Amulek [Boothe] is going to the Army. He started the 25th of this month. Annett and Amulek was out here last week. He wanted me to go out and stay a while before he went, and I went out and stayed four days. He brought me home yesterday, and he had to get back to Eaglesville by 2 o'clock. Angeline [Dennis] and Net [Annet Dennis] was to meet him there to see him start.

[3]     I was sorry to hear that he had enlisted. He is sorry, too. He hated to go when the time came to start.

[4]     Well, Mollie, I guess you think about right when you think what Eunice [Morey] said about me. I guess I will be your cousin if nothing happens. I got a letter from George [Rockwell] yesterday. He was well. David [Morey]'s folks is well.

[5]     Miriam, if George comes by to see you, come out with him
        and spend the winter out here.

[6]     Eunice has cut quite a spiny [?] about George. I think he is
        full as good as she is. I think myself just as good as this, or
        any other country, affords, and I think he is as good as I am.
        Those that don't like us can stay away. That is all. You need
        not say anything about this.

[7]     This leaves me well, and I hope they will find you the same.
        May the blessings of heaven attend you. Write soon.

        Yours truly,
        Helen M. Morey

## ❧ Letter #49

The Robinsons' move to Farmington, Iowa, is Gracie's
announcement in the next letter. Ebenezer was raising money for his
project, a railroad along the border between Iowa and Missouri to be
called the State Line Railroad [See Letter #87, par. 5]. Farmington, as
Gracie accurately describes it, would be a good base of operations.

Gracie's war news is just as detailed as ever, exactly describing
what happened to their friend, Thomas Hinkle, and mentioning, for
the first time, that group of Northerners, mostly Democrats, who
sympathized with the South and who disagreed with Lincoln's
policies. Officially, many of them belonged to the Knights of the
Golden Circle, a secret society. In 1863, a Catholic bishop of Iowa
had warned his church members to quit this secret society or face
excommunication.[20] The group was strong in Illinois, Indiana, and
especially Ohio, where their leader, Clement Vallandigham,
campaigned for office as a Peace Democrat. He was tried and
convicted by a Cincinnati military commission for treasonable
sympathies.[21] Popularly, they were not known as Knights or
Democrats, but given the same name as those venomous pit
snakes—Copperheads.

Farmington, Van Buren Co., Iowa
Sunday, August 28, 1864

Dear Cousin Mollie,

[1]     This pleasant Sabbath afternoon I thought I would write you a few lines to let you know of our whereabouts.

[2]     We arrived in this place yesterday morning about 11 o'clock. We were on the road pretty near two weeks. We had quite a pleasant journey, and I am very well pleased with "Farmington" so far. I attended church today and had quite a pleasant time. We do not know how long we will stay here, but if we can find a house that suits us, we think some of keeping house here for awhile. And if we should, we would be pleased to have you come and make us a visit.

[3]     Farmington is pleasantly situated on the east bank of the Des Moines River. The cars [railroad cars] arrive twice a day, which makes it very pleasant to live here.

[4]     Ma [Angeline]'s health continues very poor, but I think after we have been here awhile, that she will gain "or at least I hope so."

[5]     I wrote you a letter before I left Pleasant Plains which I suppose you have received ere this late hour, and perhaps answered. I expect there are several letters at the Plains for me which I think I shall get before long.

[6]     I received a letter from Cousin Charlie [Worden] a few weeks before I started away. He was well.

[7]     You wished to know in your letter about Thomas Hinkle. Mrs. [George] Hinkle received the sad news of his death a few weeks since. He was wounded in the forehead, and while they were taking him off the battlefield, another ball struck him on the head which caused his death. I do not know what battle it was in.

[8]    There are a great many of our brave soldiers that have either been killed or wounded this summer, and I don't see as the war is any nearer over now than it was two years ago. The Copperheads are getting pretty bold again and say that they won't stand the draft. But I guess the soldiers will make it all right.

[9]    I am upstairs in the room alone, and I wish you were here so that I could talk to you, and it would save me the trouble of writing. Well, I guess there is nothing more of importance to add this time, so please write soon and direct to Farmington, Van Buren Co., Iowa. Give my love to Perry [Works] and tell him I have given up looking for a letter from him.

From your affectionate cousin,
Gracie Robinson

## Letter #50

Written on the same day as Gracie Robinson's last letter, this next letter by Angeline Dennis also tells Mollie about Amulek Boothe. Angeline's is one of seven letters from August 1864 to survive, the most from any month. Beginning with Eunice Morey's letter [Letter #47] on August 24 and ending with this one from Angeline, there are four letters from people in the Pleasant Plains area within four days, a concentration that does not occur again.

Angeline grieves over her brother Amulek, since he had been helping her with the Dennis farm as well as working his own. He was a private in Company E of the 43rd Missouri Infantry.[22] Unfortunately, there is no letter from Amulek to Mollie explaining his decision, as there was when he decided to join the RLDS [See Letter #20, par. 2].

Angeline announces that Helen Morey is "our intended Aunt," a strange title, since by marrying their cousin George Rockwell, Helen would become a cousin, not an aunt. Nevertheless, the handwriting is clear here, and it may be that "aunt" like "uncle" was used casually to refer to any minor relative.

Angeline's letter from her brother Mosiah Boothe is a surprise. The deaths of their mother, Parthenia (Works) Boothe, in 1846, and their father, Lorenzo Dow Boothe, in the next year, broke up the Boothe family. Mosiah and his brothers continued west with their stepmother. While Angeline and Amulek became members of the RLDS, their brothers became members of the Utah church (LDS). Religion as well as war could divide a family.

Mosiah's mention of the peace and quiet of Utah is a hint for Angeline to come west, join the Brighamites, and avoid the turmoil of war. The two Mormon factions competed for members constantly. Some on both sides were converted to the other. Angeline's brother, Hyrum, subscribed to the *True Latter Day Saints Herald*, the official newspaper of the RLDS, even though he was a Brighamite.[23]

Angeline tries to use language impressively, and sometimes she stumbles. No doubt she means to say that Mollie is *entitled* to a large share of love from her, not *indebted* to a large share.

Eagleville, Mo.                    August 28, 1864

Dear Cousin,

[1]      After wishing you a pleasant Sabbath afternoon, I will proceed to inform you of our health which is only tolerable. I am not very well myself. Still, I am able to be about. Annett [Dennis] isn't very well, though not seriously ill.

[2]      Well, Mollie, I have rather serious news to tell you. Ammy [Boothe] has enlisted and gone to army. He started last Thursday, the day that I got your letter. I opened it and read it, then gave it to him. He didn't have time to read it. He put it in his jacket and off he went.

[3]      You don't know how it made my heart ache to give him up. Oho, he was one of the kindest of brothers! We feel truly lost without him. Everything looks lonely and sad. He has only gone in for one year. If the Lord will only spare his life! Let that be our prayer, that his life may be spared, that he may return to his home and friends in peace.

[4]      Helen Morey came out the Saturday before he went away and stayed till the day he started. Our folks were all against his going. Deborah [Morey] said she would as soon see

Dave go as to see him go. I don't know what Uncle and Aunt [Robinson] will say when they find it out. They are down to Farmington on a visit.

[5]    Ady [Dennis] has not come yet. I don't think he will get home soon, if ever. They are going to try to make him serve another year. When he does come, we will try to have our pictures taken, but there is not photographs taken near here that I know of. I want to have both our pictures taken for Joseph [Bonney]'s folks as soon as I can. I expect they think I have forgotten them, but that isn't the case. I think of them very often.

[6]    So you began to despair of getting my picture. Well, I don't blame you, for it was a long time. I had to go to Leon to get it taken, then it was so poorly done, I was ashamed to send it. But never mind. I will have a better one taken for you one of these times when a good artist comes along that can put on all the extry touches, you know.

[7]    Did you know that Helen Morey was our intended Aunt? Such is the case. I expect you will hear all about it the last of next month.

[8]    Miriam, why don't you write to Ad? He says he hasn't had a letter from you in a long time. He says he would like to hear from you again. He is still at Little Rock, Ark. I got a letter from him last Friday. He was well near right side up with care. He says the Rebs are, as they well can be, all sorts of mischief.

[9]    I got a letter from my brother Mosiah [Boothe] a few days ago. They have moved about one and fifty miles north of Salt Lake City. He says all is peace and quiet there.

[10]   Oho, that we could say that of our country, but I fear that is more than we shall be able to say soon. Turn which way we will, we only hear of wars and rumors of wars. The Indians

have broke out on the plains. They have captured a good many trains, killed women and children indiscriminately and left their bodies to bleach on the plains. There is an awful sight of their depredations in our last paper.

[11]     Well, I think the Lord has a hand in it all. He is only chastening the world for its wickedness.

[12]     Miriam, I would give a good deal to see you. I wish you was here this afternoon, then I wouldn't have to sit here in this stupid way, committing my thoughts to paper. But so it is there is a vast sight of land lies between us, but thanks to a kind Providence, we still have the privilege of hearing from each other once in awhile. And let me say to you, dear cousin, if it is ours to meet no more in this unfriendly world of tears, let us live so that we may meet beyond this vale of tears. Then we shall meet our dear parents, our brothers and sisters. There will we strike glad hands together, never more to be separated. Oho, won't that be a delightful time when we shall meet to part no more?

[13]     Oho, yes, that will be joyful, joyful when we meet to part no more!

[14]     Give my love to Cousin [Joseph Bonney]'s folks. Tell them I haven't forgotten them, and don't forget that you are indebted to a large share yourself.

         From your affectionate cousin,
         Angie

## ❀ Letter #51

The next letter marks the first that survives from Emma "Sis" Johnson, Sallie Bonney's sister, another young woman in circumstances similar to Mollie's. A year older than Mollie, Emma, like Mollie, spent a good deal of her time in the Joe Bonney household. Besides Sallie and Emma, there were six other Johnson children, and

Emma was soon "working out," that is, outside the home, as a hired girl. Her oldest brother, Jack, a livery stable keeper, and his wife Belle (Isabella) lived near the Bonneys. Emma's brother, Morten, was five years older than she and a teamster.

The Coulsons, whom Emma mentions, were friends of the Bonneys originally from Canada. Will Coulson, 25, worked in his father's sawmill. Joe Bonney was a sawyer, too, but he worked in D. K. Oyster's mill. As Emma tells Mollie, Will accompanied his Aunt Olivia on her return to Canada, while Henry, 21, may have been involved in helping freed slaves in the same way that Mollie's cousin George Rockwell was.

Emma does not want to go back to "The Hall." Unidentified in any other letter, it may have been "The Government Clothing Hall" on the southwest corner of Sixth and Maine Streets in Quincy, Illinois. There, Emma could work to make the 7,000 pants and 4,500 shirts that "The Hall" produced for the Union Army every month. She would be paid forty cents to make a pair of pants, eighteen cents for every shirt, and thirteen cents for a pair of drawers.[24] But she doesn't want to go back to "The Hall" because if she has to buy food with her wages, they will be used up. Emma apparently had a good appetite [See Letters #66, par. 2 and #76, par. 2]. She feels she could do much better at housework in a good home where her board would be part of her pay. For this she wants Mollie's help.

Quincy, Ill.                               Sept. 6, 1864

My dear Mollie,

[1]     I now take pleasure of setting down for the purpose of scratching you a few lines in answer to your kind and welcome letter which I had the pleasure of taking out of the post office last Friday, and it had been opened. You may bet I was mad. On the back it said "Opened by a mistake by Johnson."

[2]     Mollie, I am sorry to say I have been to LaGrange. I was down the second week in July, and I went home with him. I should not have went if I had have got your letter.

[3]     Will Coulson has gone to Canada with Aunt Olivia and
        Henry [Coulson] has gone down south to work for the
        government. Henry started a week yesterday. And Mort
        [Johnson] has gone to Salt Lake to drive team from St. Joe to
        Salt Lake. He is to get $50 a month.

[4]     I got a letter from Jack [Johnson] a week ago today. I also
        got one from Tine [Sylvester Alford] about two weeks ago.
        Tine was in Hannibal when he wrote.

[5]     Mollie, please find me a good home near you. I have
        thought of going to The Hall, but I don't believe I will make
        much. Board is so high, and I believe I would like housework
        the best. If it hain't too much trouble, I would be much
        obliged to you for your trouble.

[6]     I think we would have a good time if I could get to work
        close to you, Mollie.

[7]     Please excuse this, for it is getting so dark I can't see. Please
        write soon.

        From your affectionate friend,
        Emma Johnson

## 🌟 Letter #52

After all the expectations and consternation, George Rockwell's
announcement of his marriage in this next letter is casual to the point
of being offhand. The wedding was on Wednesday, November 2,
1864, in the home of George Morey, the bride's father.

No doubt the prospect of her sister marrying an older man who
was a widower with two children astonished Eunice so that her
mouth dropped open, as Helen says. Helen's comment proves that
the newlyweds were staying with the George Moreys until they could
rent the white frame house on the hill near Pleasant Plains, the old
Snook place, which they did.

Following the tradition of early weddings, friends would stay with
the couple late into the wedding night, cracking jokes and making
noise until George, the groom, would give them the "groom's treat,"

and the charivari (or shivaree) would end.[25] Later, George and Helen would visit nearby neighbors and relatives who offered the new couple a meal and lodging. This was known as a "George Washington honeymoon" because it was inexpensive and was thought to have been done first by Washington.[26] One of George and Helen's honeymoon stops is Eagleville, Missouri, to visit the Dennises [See Letter #54, par. 10].

Interestingly, Helen imagines Mollie is reading her letter as she is writing it. Therefore, because it is late and Helen is tired when she writes Mollie, it must be late when Mollie reads the letter and she, too, must be tired. The telephone was not invented soon enough for Helen.

Nine Eagles, [Ia.]                    November 14, [18]64

Dear Cousin Miriam,

[1]     After so long a silence I will try & answer your kind letter. I should have answered it long before this had it not have been that I thought I would wait until I could tell you all the [news] in this place. I came here some four weeks since & found all well as usual, Amulek [Boothe] having gone to the army, which I think very unwise in him. Everything is moving along as usual.

[2]     Oh, I was married one week last Wednesday. We have not commenced keeping house yet, but intend to the first of next week. Helen will write some in this. I have intended to come & make you & Cousin Joseph [Bonney] a visit but under present circumstances I think it will be out of the question. I should like to see you very much, I can assure you, but the cares of a large family will prevent me from doing as I intended, so you will please excuse me under these circumstances.

[3]     Deborah [Morey] says she will write as soon as she can get their likenesses taken to send to you.

Cousin Miriam,

[4]     George has gave me permission to write a few lines in his
        letter which I gladly accepted. I have been waiting with all
        the patience imaginable for an answer from the letter I
        wrote some time ago.

[5]     Eunice [Morey] sits here a-gaping. She says to tell you that
        she wants you to write to her before long, or she will cross
        you off from her book of remembrances.

[6]     George talks of renting the [Robert] Snook's place, east of
        Pleasant Plains.

[7]     Marian, I wish you was out her to spend the winter with us.

[8]     I am sleepy, as I expect you are, & I won't keep you up any
        longer, so good night. Write soon. This leaves us all well. I
        hope these few lines will find you the same.

        Helen M. Rockwell

## ❧ Letter #53

By the time Phebe Louisa Booth writes the next letter, it is winter.
Phebe's sister Rebecca has long been married, her sister Olive
recently married William Clark, and her neighbor Helen Morey is now
Helen Rockwell. Grace Robinson has moved to Farmington, Iowa,
and although there are still friends nearby, Phebe's lonesomeness
moves her to write.

Certainly Phebe's erysipelas (sometimes called St. Anthony's Fire)
would have caused her to be lonely. It is a highly contagious disease,
and standard treatment for it was to isolate the patient, destroy or
disinfect what she used, and apply cold packs to the lesions. Besides
a high fever, poor Phebe suffered with a shiny red swelling of the
infected part and a general feeling of illness. She was lucky she did
not develop blood poisoning or pneumonia from the disease.

Phebe asks Mollie to direct her letters to Nine Eagles, Iowa, since
the post office at Spring Valley, or Boothtown, near the Booth
homestead, is no longer in use.

[Spring Valley, Ia.]          Dec. 1, 1864

Absent Friend,

[1]     I once more strive to pen you a few lines in token of friendship. It has been a great while since I heard from you, so I thought I would write a few lines to see whether you are alive or not.

[2]     I received a letter from Grace [Robinson] last night. They was all well, and they were not coming back until next spring.

[3]     I wish that you were here with me today, for I am all alone, and I am lonesome.

[4]     I suppose you have heard about Olive [Booth] being married. She was married 'long in the summer. She is keeping house. She told me to tell you that she sent her respects to you, and she would like to hear from you very much.

[5]     There is quite a stir here about the rebels that the folks have caught—9 rebels—and have got them in jail in Leon [Iowa]. And they say they are a-going to hang them. And they are after six more.

[6]     We are all well at the future time. I have been sick for a great while. I had been vaccinated and then the erysipelas got in my arm, and it was very bad.

[7]     I hope when these few scribbled lines come to hand, they may find you enjoying good health.

[8]     Well, as I will have to write two more letters today, I will get tired by that time. I have not received your photograph yet. I still look for it.

[9]     Please write soon. From your devoted friend. Good-bye.

Write soon,
Miss Phebe L. Booth

Please direct your letters to Nine Eagles, Decatur Co., Iowa.

## ❧ Letter #54

Amulek and his company were defeated in the battle of Glasgow, Missouri, on October 15, 1864, as his sister Angeline tells Mollie in the next letter. He enlisted on August 18, and fifty-eight days later he saw action.

The Battle of Glasgow was one result of Confederate Major General Sterling "Pap" Price's raid into Missouri this year. Price meant to divert Union troops from the prolonged Red River Campaign that was wending its way into Louisiana. The Battle of Glasgow involved a part of Price's cavalry, called the "Iron Brigade," whose men had been taught to fight "Indian style," making good use of the terrain. It was this brigade under the command of Confederate Colonel Jeff Thompson which captured the town of Glasgow and nearby Sedalia, forcing the surrender of 400 Union soldiers.[27] One of the 400 was Private Amulek Boothe.

Amulek and the others gave their word of honor (parole) that they would not be active in the war, that is, that they would not be part of a fighting unit. They were then allowed to return home, a "French furlough." "Parole" is a French word. As was the case with Amulek, they were often re-assigned to a non-combat post, though some continued fighting as guerrillas.

Angeline is happy and then sad about Amulek, because she's lonely. Even her son Frank is away with a drove of hogs. During the summer, farmers often let hogs forage in the woods for roots, acorns, and other nuts. Then in the fall, the fattened hogs would be rounded up and taken to slaughter. The hogs that escaped these round-ups became semi-wild and developed sharp spines that gave them the name, razorbacks.[28]

Eaglesville, Harrison Co., [Mo.]
Sabbath Morning, Dec. 4th, 1864

Respected Cousin,

[1]      Though I have never received an answer to the last letter I wrote you, I am going to try it once more. Perhaps I will be more successful this time.

[2]      Brother Amulek [Boothe] just started back to his company this morning. He came home last Wednesday on a French furlough, as they call it. I suppose you have heard of the fight they were in. They were taken prisoners and paroled on the battleground. They went from there to St. Louis, then back again to St. Joseph where they now are. The most of Ammy's company came home with him but have gone back. Orders came yesterday morning to report at Headquarters tomorrow night. You may well suppose it was hard for us to give him up so soon, to part, perhaps, for the last time on earth. God only knows. His destiny is in His hands, but my only prayer is that He who watcheth the fall of a sparrow will shield him from danger.

[3]      Oh Miriam, how glad we would have been if you could have been here to enjoy the visit with us, but he has gone with the expectation of not seeing Home again till his time is expired, which is the 14th of August.

[4]      He left his photograph here for you. He intended to have written to you while at home, but his stay was so short, he didn't get time. He requested me to send it in mine.

[5]      You spoke of wanting Ady [Dennis]'s and my photograph. Ad sent home three some time ago. I would have sent one to you, but they were somewhat injured in coming. I thought I would wait till he had a better one taken. As for mine, you shall have it as soon as I can have it taken. There is not such work done here yet, but they are going to take them in that way before long.

[6]     I got my youngest brother [Hyrum Ebenezer Boothe] and his wife's picture a few days ago. They are a pretty good looking couple if they are my kinfolk.

[7]     I haven't heard from Adam for several weeks. He wasn't very well then, nor hadn't been for some time.

[8]     I am almost alone today. Frankie [Dennis] has gone off with a drove of hogs. He has been gone a little over two weeks. I look for him back next week. Annett [Dennis] has gone down to Mr. Gillen's today, so, to keep from being lonesome, I am writing.

[9]     Have you seen Cousin Joseph [Bonney] lately? They don't write anymore. Well, I don't blame them, for I haven't treated them altogether right in not sending my picture—haven't had an opportunity in having it taken or I should have sent it long ago.

[10]    I suppose you have heard Cousin George [Rockwell] is married. He and his bride [Helen] were out to see us a few weeks ago.

[11]    When you ever think of coming up into Missouri and Iowa again, you still have a few friends and two or three relatives who would like to get [a] glimpse of your face once more—not married yet, I suppose. I expect if nothing happens between this and Christmas, Annett will change her name. She is going to take a soldier [David Daily].

[12]    Well, I guess I will tell you that we are all well before I forget it. Give my love to all your relatives and to Cousin Joseph's in particular when you see them.

[13]    I must tell you that Amulek took your picture off with him this morning. Why don't you ever write to Ady any more? He often speaks about you and wonders why you don't write anymore. The last letter you sent to him he sent home

for me to take care of for him. When you write to Amulek
direct to Company E, 43rd Missouri Volunteers, St. Joseph,
Mo. Adam is still at Little Rock.

[14]    Well, I must close as I have to write a letter to Angeline
Worden, also one to A. Dennis.

[15]    Please excuse this as I am in a hurry. Write soon, and often, as
I am anxious to hear. I close by wishing you a Merry
Christmas and a Happy New Year.

From your well-wishing cousin,
Angie L. Dennis


## ❀ Letter #55

The last letter of 1864 is this happy one from Gracie Robinson, full
of underlining and casual quotation marks to indicate the adolescent
vocal stresses that alone can convey the importance of certain words.
Despite her exuberance (she writes this two-in-one letter four days
after her fifteenth birthday), her handwriting is clear and her
information accurate. The fact that she includes a letter to the
Bonneys means that she knows Mollie will be in LaGrange for the
Christmas holidays, as Mollie almost always was.

Gracie also mentions George Keown's holiday gift. A cousin of
Eunice and Helen Morey, George was the oldest child of John and
Mary Ann (Morey) Keown. He was Mollie's age, and she obviously
knew him well. Gracie suggests they "jump the broomstick," which
was a way of marrying when a minister was not available. After the
couple made their intentions known to the community, frontier
folklore demanded that they actually jump over a broomstick, a
superstition that was supposed to ward off any evil that might come
to a marriage because it began without official church sanction.

Farmington, Iowa          Dec. 26th, [18]64

Dear Cousin Mollie,

[1]    I again seat myself to answer yours of the 13th of Dec, which I received a few days since, We are in usual health at this time, and hope these few lines will find you all the same.

[2]    I haven't heard from Cousin Amulek [Boothe] for some time. "Pa" [Ebenezer] has been to visit him at St. Louis. His address is as follows:

> "4th Company, 2nd Battalion
> Paroled Men, Benton Barracks
> St. Louis, Mo."

He was well, the last we heard.

[3]    We have just heard that Cousin George Rockwell is "married." Now who do you suppose he is married to? Miss Hellen Morey is the "Victim." They are keeping house in that "white frame house" on the hill near "Pleasant Plain." Adrianna [Rockwell] is living with them.

[4]    "Pa" has gone "East." The last letter we received from him, he was in "New York."

[5]    Yesterday was "Christmas" and I stayed at home all day, but I attended Church in the Evening. I wrote a letter to Perry [Works] yesterday and have not sent it off yet.

[6]    We are having a short vacation now, but school begins again next Monday. And I think I will "graduate" this term. Won't that be "orful?"

[7]    Now I will tell you who "my fellow" ain't. It is not "Thomas Brant" nor any person that has been in the army. So you will have to guess again.

[8]    I think you and George Keown had better jump the "Broomstick" now. That ring that he sent you must have meant something.

[9]    I believe I told you about Olive Booth's being married, did I not? They are keeping house near Mr. [John] Clark's.

[10]    "Ma" [Angeline] sends her love to all. Well, I must close for this time. Please write soon and excuse this foolery.

Truly your cousin, Gracie

Farmington, Dec. 26th

Dear Cousins Joseph and Sarah,

[11]    I believe I will write you a few lines before I close. Your kind letter was received some time ago, but I have neglected to answer it, and I trust you will excuse me for not being more punctual.

[12]    I am sorry it was so that I could not come and spend the "Holydays" with you. But I intend to come and make you a visit before we return home, if nothing unusual happens to prevent [it], as I would enjoy your company very much, I am sure. And perhaps "Pa" & "Ma" will come, too. I do not know just when "Pa" will return home, but I guess it will not be a great while.

[13]    Last Thursday was my birthday. I was 15 years old. Quite an advanced age, isn't it, for these times? I will soon be as old as Mollie, if I keep on. Tell her that if she don't hurry, I will get "married" first. That is, if I can get anybody to have me. The gentlemen don't generally like "old maids."

[14]    Well, enough of this. Ma sends her kindest regards to all and wishes to see you all very much. Please answer this soon. From your

Affectionate Cousin,
Gracie Robinson

NOTES

1. Landrum, *Quincy,* p. 85.

2. *Ibid.*

3. Kay MacLean, "Publications Series III: Popular History #12: Christmas Celebrations," (Springfield, Ill.: Sangamon State University, 1979), p. 3.

4. *Ibid.,* p. 1.

5. Victor Hicken, *Illinois in the Civil War,* (Urbana: University of Illinois Press, 1966), p. 370.

6. Long, *Civil War,* p. 467, 468, & 478.

7. Landrum, *Quincy,* p. 88.

8. Long, *Civil War,* p. 479.

9. Clarence Meyer, *American Folk Medicine,* (New York: Thomas Y. Crowell, 1973), p. 12.

10. *Ibid.,* p. 18.

11. *Ibid.,* p. 15.

12. Leach, *Conscription,* p. 257.

13. Steiner, *Disease,* pp. 218-222.

14. *Biographical & Historical Record of Ringgold & Decatur County* (Chicago, Ill.: Lewis Publishing Co., 1887), p. 609.

15. Long, *Civil War,* p. 484.

16. *History of Decatur County,* Vol. 2., p. 169.

17. Peter Maslowski, *Treason Must Be Made Odious,* (Milwood: KTO Press, 1978), p. 111.

18. "A singing...or writing master would get permission to use the neighborhood schoolhouse... This was always...when the young people had leisure time, and, of course, at night time." *Historical Encyclopedia of Ill. and History of Fulton County,* (Chicago: Munsell Printing, 1908), p. 664.

19. *True Latter Day Saints Herald,* 15 November 1860.

20. Long, *Civil War,* p. 348.

21. *Ibid.,* p. 349.

22. *History of Harrison County, Missouri,* p. 334.

23. *True Latter Day Saints Herald,* September 1862.

24. Landrum, *Quincy,* p. 103.

25. Before the charivari, the women friends might toss the bride into a bed, and the men do the same for the groom. This was called "bedding" them. Missouri Genealogical Society, *Marriage Records of Harrison County Missouri: A-D* (St. Louis: 1972), p. 6.

26. *Ibid.*

27. John S. Bowman, ed., *The Civil War Almanac,* (New York City: Bison Books Corp., 1982), p. 229.

28. *Historical Encyclopedia of Ill. and History of Fulton County,* p. 660.

*First and last pages of Letter #58 from Amulek Boothe in the Post Hospital, St. Joseph, Missouri.*

**Jessie Katie Belle Bonney**
*(b: 1862). "Kate" was the
eldest of Joseph and Sarah
"Sallie" (Johnson) Bonney's
girls. (Three others: Ella May,
Effa Josephine, and Oliva
died in infancy.) Kate and
her sister, Iola Edna, kept
their father's house after
their mother died in 1871.
As noted in the letters, she
married George Larkin
"Lark" Loudermilk, and she
and her children continued
to pay visits to Mollie and
George McNutt at their
Payson, Illinois, farm.*

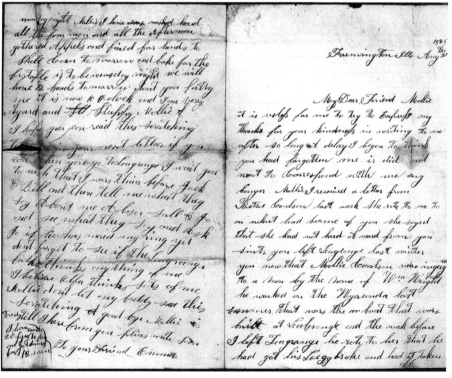

*First and last pages of Letter #67 from Emma "Sis" Johnson, sister of Sallie
(Johnson) Bonney. Mollie's age, Emma, too, worked as a hired girl, most
often for Mrs. Simpson in Farmington, Illinois.*

# THE LAGRANGE FOLKS
# 1865

## ✿ Letter #56

The first surviving letters of 1865 are from the Alfords, Nancy and one of her sons, Bob. The Alfords were a part of Mollie's LaGrange circle of friends. They lived with the David Smiths, relatives of Emma Johnson and Sallie (Johnson) Bonney. Emma calls him "Uncle Dave" [See Letter #59, par. 5]. Smith was a brickmaker from Kentucky, and this living arrangement suggests that Nancy Alford was a widow, for as early as 1850 she and her two sons, Sylvester Valentine (called "Tine") and Robert, were living with Dave and Susan Smith. Susan may have been Nancy's daughter.

Nancy is forty-two at this time, fifteen years older than Sallie Bonney. But in this first letter of 1865, it is the younger Sallie who is reluctant to continue the merrymaking—not Nancy.

Mollie's LaGrange friends chose aliases for themselves, and some of these playful nicknames are known, such as the one Robert Alford assumes in the fragment of his letter which remains. Emma Johnson was appropriately called "Bridget," a common house servant's name [See Letter #66, par. 1]. The LaGrange "folks," as they were known, dubbed George McNutt "The Farm," [See Letter #34, par. 3] because, unlike them, he was a farmer, and Nancy Alford was called "Alfa" probably because of its similarity in sound to her surname and also to suggest she was the oldest of the crowd, alpha being the first letter of the Greek alphabet. [See Letters #46, par. 4; #59, par. 5; #62, par. 4, and #67, par. 15.]

Robert Alford's mischievousness is obvious. His comment on Mollie's Iowa friends proves that Mollie discussed her Mormon relatives with the folks in LaGrange. Bob's older brother Tine Alford was just as much of a tease as Bob was. [See Letters #34, par. 4 and #72, par. 4]. However, none of Tine's letters remain. Bob was nineteen at the time he wrote this, while Tine was Mollie's age, born in 1844. During the war, the Alford boys drove team between Canton, Hannibal, and LaGrange, Missouri. After the war, they became tobacconists in LaGrange.

LaGrange, Missouri        February 6, 1865

Dear Friend,

[1]    We are all well here and at Sallie's and hope this finds you the same. Emma [Johnson] is still here but things looks very dull on the God-forsaken hills of LaGrange. I want you to be sure to keep your promise and come over in May and we will go visiting every day.

[2]    Tine [Sylvester Alford] heard in Millville the other day that Perry [Works] was going in the army. If it is so, when you [w]rite let us know.

[3]    Tine and Emma is still after Sallie [Bonney] to let them have a party, and she says it is too late in the season. It is time to go to work.

[4]    You will here find the bow Tine stole from you and forgot to give you.

[5]    There is no news—nobody dead or married.

[6]    Give my best respects to Perry. Bob [Alford] and Tine also sends their respects to your brother.

[7]    So, no more at present.

Affectionately yours,
N. Alford

## ❧ Letter #57

[undated fragment]

[1]     ...too much fatigued. The people in Iowa have got horns on
        them like an oxen, but don't plough well.

[2]     I shall now bring this to a close, Mollie. Be a good girl and
        don't eat any dirt.

        Yours respectfully,
        Robert Alford

        Alias Nicodemus Efenhamer

[3]     P. S. Mollie, you need not answer this till you hear from me
        again, and I don't know when that will be, maybe never.
        Just as the notion takes me.

        Robert Alford

## ❧ Letter #58

A precious letter from Amulek Boothe while he is stationed at the
St. Joseph, Missouri, post hospital after his "French furlough" tells
something of his life there. Though he is no longer a part of it, there
is still fighting near his old battlefield. On the day he writes, there is
fighting at Sturgeon, Missouri, about twenty-five miles east of
Glasgow, and skirmishing continued throughout February at Macon
and at Switzler's Mill on the Chariton River. But Amulek seems more
interested in something other than war, even though Mollie's
suggestion does not suit him.

Amulek tries sarcasm as he tells Mollie about his niece Annett
Dennis' wedding. His dislike for her husband becomes a continuing
theme in his letters. Annett's husband was one of Amulek's officers in
his regiment. That may explain all. [See Letters #94, par. 5; #96, par. 7,
and #101, par. 10].

Western Branches of the U.S. Christian Commission
Post Hospital, St. Joe, Mo.
Feb 7th, 1865

Dear Beloved Cousin,

[1] I have set down this evening to pen a few lines to you to keep up an acquaintance, for you are a-getting to be quite a stranger for the last year, and I don't like it a bit. But being as it is you, I will look over it and blame myself, not you. I know you would wrote if you had have heard from me.

[2] I got the letter that Joseph [Bonney] and you sent and was glad to hear from you. It found me well, as this leaves me. I was sorry to hear that Cousin Joseph's family had been sick, for I have seen so much sickness since I have been in the hospital that I am afraid I will hear of some one of my dear cousins being dead, which I feel for so much.

[3] I got a letter from home last week, and they was all well, except Angeline [Dennis]. Her health has been poor for several days.

[4] Adam [Dennis]'s health has been very poor for some time. I got a letter from him since I came here, the first that he has wrote to me for a year, and I have answered it. He is at Little Rock, Arkansas. If they keep him three years, his time will be out about the time that mine is—next September.

[5] Annett [Dennis] is married since I left home. I have been at home once. I left on Sunday, and she was married the next Saturday. I think she had better get married while I was there. She got a good clever young man, but I don't know what kind of a man he will make. He was our first lieutenant, then he went home and got married. He is teaching school now. His name is David Daily.

[6]    I am still at the hospital. I am cook here now and it keeps
       me busy, for there is so many to cook for. I have been cook
       very near all the time since I have been out till I came here.
       Then I sawed wood for some time, but they have put me in
       the kitchen to cooking.

[7]    Mary, we have the nicest weather here that I seen. There
       has been no snow this winter here. It has been an
       exception. I have a nice time here these nice evenings. I
       have got acquainted some with the young ladies. I have
       been waiting on one real good looking, but she is too much
       of a lady for me. It is just to pass away time while I am here.

[8]    You think I can take Eunice Morey, do you? Well, I hardly
       know whether she will suit or not, but I will see about that
       when I get home. It will be fixed up right.

[9]    Angeline will send my photograph to you. She spoke of it in
       her last letter.

[10]   Mary, I would like to come down and make a visit the best
       kind, but I can't till my time is out. Then I will.

[11]   I have wrote about all the news for this time, so I will close
       for the present. Hoping to hear from you soon. Give my
       compliments to Perry [Works].

       Your cousin,
       A. Boothe

       direct to St. Joseph, Mo. Post Hospital

## ⁕ Letter #59

   Emma Johnson's second letter to Mollie recounts events that only
Mollie would know. The Alford boys are familiar, as are some of the
Coulsons, though Ada Coulson and how she died is a mystery. Emma
also mentions Molly Coulson still slowly recovering [See Letter #34,

par. 10]. Mrs. Silawa is unknown, but Mrs. Catharine (Drawbaugh) Oyster was the wife of Joe Bonney's employer, David K. Oyster, a prominent family in LaGrange. She was the sister of Daniel Drawbaugh, the Pennsylvania mechanic who claimed to have had a workable telephone as early as 1866 but who later lost the patent fight to Alexander Graham Bell by a single vote in the United States Supreme Court.[1]

Emma does get that job with the Simpsons [See Letter #63].

LaGrange, Mo.           February 27, 1865

Dear Mollie,

[1]      I will now attempt to scratch a few lines in answer to your most welcome letter which we had the pleasure of receiving a few days ago. I will not treat you the way you treated me. You was gone almost two months before you wrote to any of us.

[2]      Mollie, I suppose you want to hear about Bob and Tine [Alford]. Bob is in Hannibal. He went about a week ago. Tine is here yet, but I expect he will go this week to Hannibal. Bob did not get any Valentines. Tine got two very nice ones. One was from Canton, and one Kate Crandelle sent. I have some of her writing and compare[d] it together [with] the other one come from Hannibal. Tine says, "Hooray for the Canton and Hannibal girls."

[3]      Henry Coulson has come home, and also Charlie Coulson got here Friday evening. Henry has been home about three weeks. Callie just went home about a week ago.

[4]      I have not went to a party this winter in LaGrange. There has been a great many, too. Will Coulson and Callie went almost every night. Ada [Coulson] had not been dead a week till Will went to dances—and danced, too. There has been a great many talking about the way Will done, Mollie.

[5]     I go up to Alfa [Nancy Alford]'s and play euchre once in a while and to church sometimes. Two weeks ago last night there was three couples went from Joe's, and I went with Tine. We went to the Baptist Church. I had a beau from the country, but I played off on him and went with Tine. Tine was here a few minutes ago but has gone downtown now. Alfa has had the chills but is better now. Uncle Dave and Sue [Smith] is well.

[6]     Sallie [Bonney] has the toothache and has had it ever since last night.

[7]     Will Smith has come home from the army from the 4th Missouri. I must tell you about the young soldiers.

[8]     Mrs. Silawa[?] has a young son, also Mrs. [Catharine] Oyster has a young son.

[9]     Mollie, I am going to Farmington [Ill.] in about two weeks. I expect to go to Quincy the last of this week. Mollie, you must come to Quincy to see me before I go away. Old Mother [Margaret] Simpson has wrote to me to come and live with her, and I am a-going to go. I have give out going to St. Charles. You had better go to Farmington with me.

[10]     Molly Coulson is mending slowly. Mollie, that nigger has gone under that was so sick the time Ada died. She was buried yesterday.

[11]     I will have to bring my letter to a close. I can't think of anything of importance to write. Please write soon. If you write, direct to Quincy to your friend,

Emma L. Johnson

## ❧ Letter #60

The next letter, the first from the newly married Helen (Morey) Rockwell, is full of news about Mollie's Iowa friends, including the tragedy to the Robert Booths [See the next letter, too]. Helen also gives another example of the custom of distributing children to relatives when their mothers die. Not only her cousins, the Perhams, were affected, but as she knows, her own husband, George, followed custom with his two girls [See Letter #2, par. 5]. The belief that children must be raised in a family environment that included a wife and mother was strong. After George married Helen, his daughter Adrianna joined his new household, making Helen an instant mother. Adrianna is the "Ady" mentioned here.

Helen's advice to Mollie concerning marriage is honest and sad. Her suggestion about finding "a good library" in the Rockwell home is simply another way of saying, "If you want to learn about marriage, come live with us." Though she writes nothing of it to Mollie in this letter, Helen is four months pregnant.

Pleasant Plains, [Ia.]        March 27, 1865

Dear Cousin,

[1]     It is with pleasure that I sit down to while away a few leisure moments in scribbling to you. We received your welcome letter two weeks ago. I had been waiting for George [Rockwell] to write, but I will write now, and he may write some other time.

[2]     He has gone down to Mr. [Robert] Booth's today. Mr. Booth has met with a great loss. He has had his store broken into and his money all taken. About $2,000.00. He feels bad enough about it.

[3]     I got a letter from Henrietta Perham the other day. Her mother [Mary Ann] is dead, and she says the children are scattered. The boys [Marion and Dunham] is in the army, and the rest of them is in Ohio, all at different places. It looks hard to see children scattered, but as soon as a mother is gone then children's homes are gone.

[4]     We are all well. I hope these few lines will find you the same.

[5]     David and Deborah [Morey] is well. Their little girl [Eliza] is a-trying to talk. You have two more cousins out here now. Deborah's youngest sister Adaline [Perry] and husband [Philander] is out here. They have been here some two months. He has rented a place of Mr. Booth. They will move down there this week.

[6]     I was glad to hear from Amulek [Boothe]. He don't think enough of his folks in Decatur to write to them.

[7]     George is a-going to start to Illinois the last of this week and will be gone about three weeks.

[8]     Miriam, you stay single until you are twenty-one or thirty. Then you are young enough, then. Now you can go and come when you please, but when you get married, you'll find that you can't go as you could before. A man has as good a chance as ever. There is someone at home if he is gone.

[9]     You said you hoped that George and I never would fight. I don't hardly think we will, for I think he could whip, and I would hate that.

[10]    Miriam, if you want a good library you had ought to live with us this winter, but never mind.

[11]    If things will grow, we will have something to eat next fall. I wish you would come out next fall. I will send you a piece of my wedding dress, and you must not make of it. Olive Booth's was off from the same piece, so you will have a piece of hers too.

[12]    I can't think of anything more at present so good-bye. Write soon.

        Helen M. Rockwell

[13]    It don't seem to me as that was my name, but so it is. Ady
        [Rockwell] says to tell you that she has that basket yet that
        you sent her.

[14]    [Lightly inked on the letter above Helen's name are the
        words "Booth Carr." Below the postscript, possibly in
        Mollie's hand, are the words "i say can you see by...Miss
        Mollie Works" "Miss Lizzie Flyer[?]" and "Miriam Works."]

## ✿ Letter #61

Despite being written just four days after Lee surrendered to Grant
at Appomattox Court House, this next letter of Gracie's does not
mention the end of the Civil War. Instead, Gracie is intent on telling
Mollie about the Robinsons' return to Pleasant Plains from their sojourn
in Farmington, Iowa. Though he would travel constantly, Gracie's
father, Ebenezer Robinson, conducted his business from his farm near
Pleasant Plains for many years after this return.

Gracie notes the visit of Adaline, the youngest sister of Deborah
Morey and George Rockwell. Adaline and her husband, Philander
Perry, did not stay in Iowa, settling instead in Connecticut, the place
where the Rockwells began. George's trip to Aurora may have been
to settle the fate of his other daughter, Clara, who was living with
relatives in Illinois.

Gracie's beau is not known, but her interest in marrying, at the age
of sixteen, is as keen as Mollie's, who was nearly twenty-one.

        Pleasant Plains, Iowa          April 13, 1865

        Dear Mollie,

[1]     After a lapse of some weeks, I again resume my pen for the
        purpose of answering your letter which I received before
        leaving Farmington, and I thought I would not write until
        we got home. We arrived a week ago last Monday after a
        pleasant journey of about eight days.

[2]    I have not seen Deborah [Morey] yet, but I saw Adaline
       [Perry] and her husband [Philander] the first evening we got
       home. We met George [Rockwell], when we were coming,
       on his way to Aurora. Helen [Rockwell] is keeping house in
       Pleasant Plains. George is going to work at his trade this
       summer with Mr. [Royal] Richardson.

[3]    We are now on the farm, have not got things fixed up much
       yet, but expect to have our house finished this summer. Pa
       [Ebenezer] and Mr. [Robert] Booth think of starting next
       Monday for Farmington.

[4]    Mr. Booth has been robbed of about $1500 this spring.
       Robert [Booth, jr.] lost $400 and Horace [Booth] $33. They
       talk of selling their farm and moving away, but I do not
       know whether they will or not.

[5]    I believe you knew Joseph Denton, did you not? He died last
       fall in the army. Oh! Mollie, you don't know the changes
       that have taken place since you were here. Many of the best
       young men have died or got killed. There are a few good
       ones left, but not many.

[6]    Is your "beau" in the army or not? If he is, I am afraid you
       will not see him very soon. You must tell me all about him
       when you write, as I would you, if I had any. But as I had
       not, you cannot expect me to tell anything about him. I
       have a photograph here, though, that I will show you if you
       will come up here. It is a real pretty one, I think. But it is a
       person you never saw.

[7]    Why don't Perry [Works] write to me? I have not received a
       letter from him for three (3) months.

[8]    It is about time to retire, and I am very tired, so I will close
       this poor letter. There has been somebody here every day
       since we came home, so you may know that I have not had
       anything to do.

[9]     Ma [Angeline]'s health still continues poor. She and Pa join
        in love to you and cousin Perry. Please write soon. Direct to
        Nine Eagles.

        From your Affectionate Cousin,
        Gracie

## 🌸 Letter #62

Sallie Bonney's first letter to Mollie in this year is written two
weeks after Lincoln's assassination although she does not comment
on it. Missourians had conflicting feelings about the Civil War. In
Canton, eight miles north of LaGrange, a newsboy hawked the news
of Lincoln's death by shouting: "Here's your latest news, Old Abe's
dead, pity he hadn't died years ago." A crowd restrained a soldier
who was ready to kill the boy, and the boy was later fined $16.00
and sent down the Mississippi River on a steamboat.[2]

Mollie had returned to the Stewart farm near Payson, and Sallie
teases her about George McNutt ("that 'Farm'"). Sallie herself seems
somewhat out of sorts; she is near the end of the pregnancy that will
result in her last child, Iola Edna.

Sallie notes coyly that her sister Emma, who is working in Illinois,
has not written yet. This marks the beginning of a tiff between the
two sisters. [See the next few letters.]

        [LaGrange, Mo.]          April the last [probably 1865]

        Dear Cousin Mollie,

[1]     I take pleasure in writing you a few lines to let you know
        how we are. We are all well and hope that this may find you
        the same. I expect you are out of patience awaiting for a
        letter, and I don't blame you much.

[2]     I would have wrote some when Nance [Alford] wrote to
        you, but I didn't know she was a-writing to you till it was
        sealed up, and I kept a-putting it off. As you know, I don't
        like to write. I hope you will excuse me, and I will do better
        next time.

[3]     Why don't you tell me how the folks is down there? You
        never said a word about them and how Perry [Works] is,
        and tell him to write to us. The gals is all alike. They have so
        much about the boys to say that they can't think of
        anything else. That "Farm" [George McNutt] takes your
        attention, I guess.

[4]     Alfa [Nancy Alford]'s boys has been away from home all spring
        in Hannibal, and now Bob [Alford] has gone to Idaho. He
        started last Tuesday. Tine [Sylvester Alford] is in Hannibal yet,
        and Bob said he would give you from now till he gets back to
        tell him how many white beans it takes to make three black
        ones.

[5]     The folks is all well here. Mary Coulson has got able to go
        around some. She is in Canton now. She is not very well yet.
        We have not heard from any of our kinfolks [Emma Johnson,
        especially] since you was here. We don't know whether they
        are in Farmington [Illinois] or not. If you have heard from
        them, write and tell us and about all the rest.

[6]     I have wrote all I can think of at present. I hope you will
        answer this soon, and come and see us when you can, and
        tell Perry, too. Goodbye, Mollie. Our love to you both.

        From Sally

## 🌸 Letter #63

Emma's letter is from Farmington, Illinois, about twenty miles west
of Peoria. The day she writes, Lincoln's funeral train, on its way to his
burial in Springfield, has stopped in Chicago where thousands paid
their respects.

From Emma's letter it is obvious that the tiff between Sallie and her
is growing, though Emma seems more concerned with helping out
her other sister, Lucy, by telling Mollie about Lucy's plan.

Emma's employer, Mrs. Margaret (Cordner) Simpson, was a widow
who managed a one hundred sixty acre fruit farm in Fulton County,

Illinois, with the help of her twenty-six-year old son, John. How Emma came to find a job so far from LaGrange is not known, but there were Simpsons living near the Johnson farm in Missouri who may have been related to these in Farmington, and Emma's sister Lucy was also living nearby. In any case, many of Emma's letters come from the Simpson farm.

Could it be that Emma is fond of Tine Alford? [See Letter #76, par. 3, too.] Was she Mollie's rival? If so, it was a friendly rivalry, for she proposes that they both "cut a splurge" in LaGrange with new finery. Like "cut a spiny" [See Letter #48, par. 6] and "cut a shindy" [Letter #24, par. 5], Emma uses "cut" colloquially to mean perform a conspicuous action. Together with the Scottish or Old English meaning of "splairge" or "splurge" (to spatter or splash) the phrase "cut a splurge" can only mean "create a splash or show, a great display." It does not have the more modern meaning of "lavish spending."

Farmington, Illinois          May 1, 1865

Dear Mollie,

[1]     I received your most welcome letter a few minutes ago and was truly glad to hear from you once more. I am sorry that we are so far apart, but I can't help it.

[2]     Mollie, there is a good place here close to me that I can get for you if you will come. It is only a half a mile from Mrs. [Margaret] Simpson's, and it is a good place. There is a young girl about my age and another about twelve years old. The youngest goes to school. They are very pleasant folks. The grown girl is not very stout. Mrs. Bond says that she will give a girl a dollar and a half all the time. Mollie, it is not a hard place. I know you would like it.

[3]     Lucy [Johnson] says if you come out and don't like to stay at Mrs. Bond's, you are welcome to stay at her house as long as you please. Girls is very scarce here. Some get two dollars and a half a week. Mollie, if you will come, I will send you money to come on.

[4]     I have not had a letter from Joe [Bonney]'s since I left, but
        Lucy has heard from them. They was all well. I am not going
        to LaGrange till I can beat Sallie [Bonney] dressing. I am
        going to have a silk dress before I go. If Sallie don't like me,
        she needn't to. She has found out about us reading the love
        letters.

[5]     Mollie, I had rather stay in Quincy or in Missouri rather than
        here, but I know that Sallie don't like me, and I don't want
        to bother her. I would have went to St. Charles if it hadn't
        been for her.

[6]     If you don't come to Farmington, try and get you a black
        silk dress by this fall year, so we can cut a splurge in
        LaGrange when I come. I have a-got me two new calico
        dresses. I will send you a piece of them. I went to Lucy's
        Saturday afternoon, and came back Sunday evening. It
        rained all night Saturday night and my riding dress was all
        mud when I came home. I went to town last week and
        bought 20 yards of muslin.

[7]     Mollie, I had my photograph taken last week. I will send you
        one, and you must not forget to send me one, and one for
        Louisa Riddle, and if Perry [Works] has any taken, hook one
        for me.

[8]     I will not write to Sallie and Joe till they write to me, if that is
        never. I was so sorry that I did not get to see you before I
        left Quincy. It always is a great pleasure to hear from you.

[9]     Oh, yes, I got a letter from Tine [Sylvester Alford] about two
        weeks ago. He told me to tell you that he was well and sassy
        as ever. He is going to send me his picture. I must stop.
        Please write soon to,

        Emma Johnson

## ❧ Letter #64

Mollie wrote Emma near the end of May, but Emma does not answer until this letter in mid-June. Here, Emma confesses the details concerning Lucy, and she reveals that she has been at the Simpson's since March. Emma's brother Mort is a teamster like Tine and Bob Alford. Emma takes pride in telling Mollie about another young man who has sent his photograph. There may be something in that!

The hat Emma mentions is in the shape of a gypsy hat, a style that was popular thirty years before she wrote this.

Farmington, Illinois      June 17, 1865

Absent but not forgotten Friend,

[1]     Please pardon me for not answering your most welcome letter sooner. I received your letter about three weeks ago and have been very busy ever since. We have had the carpenters here shingling the house and doing some other work and finishing cleaning house and a great deal of company, so I have not had time to write any sooner. I hope you will forgive me, and I will do better next time.

[2]     Mollie, I wrote a short note to you for Lucy [Johnson]. It was because I could not help it. She wanted me to write, and I could not get out of it. I would be real glad if you would come, but I don't want you to go to Lucy's if you do come.

[3]     Mollie, we are going to have a great time in Farmington the Fourth. How I wish you was here to go with me! Is there anything going on in Quincy the Fourth?

[4]     I got a letter from Joe [Bonney] the last of the week for the first since I have been in Farmington, and that is over three months. I do not intend to write to them for three months.

[5]     Mollie, if I had hold of that girl that has been taking my letters out of the office, I would give her fits.

[6]     Mollie, brother Mort [Johnson] has got back from Salt Lake. Charlie Coulson got his thumb and four fingers of the right hand sawed off in the sawmill two weeks ago yesterday. Oh yes, I guess Henry [Coulson] sent me his photograph about two weeks ago.

[7]     Mollie, I have got my white hat done over and got a bunch of fruit on it. There is a peach, plum, pear, apple, acorn, strawberry, gooseberry, and two grapes. I will send you a piece of the ribbon to you. I just cut it off of the string behind. The shape of my hat is what they call the lavinia regina.

[8]     I got me a new white waist yesterday and black buttons to go on it, and also I got a pair of garters that cost $3.50.

[9]     I received a letter from Tine [Sylvester Alford] soon after I received yours. He was well and said for me to give you his best respects as he says he was afraid to write to you.

[10]    I will have to close. It is late. Please write soon to your friend, Emma, and excuse bad writing and correct all mistakes.

        From your friend,
        E[mma] Johnson

## ❦ Letter #65

Despite Lee's surrender, the war is still going on for Milton Frame, a Payson soldier who writes Mollie while he is at Decherd, Tennessee, on the railroad line south of Murfreesboro. Milton's troop, the Illinois 148th Infantry, did not see exceptional duty. Organized on February 21 of this year at Camp Butler, the men left for Nashville the next day, and by the first of March they were on their way to Tullahoma, Tennessee. There, they had guard duty until they left for Decherd on June 18.

Milton's homesickness for his buddies, the Lamberts and George Morris is real. At sixteen, Jesse Lambert enlisted as a musician (either a drummer or a bugler) in Company K of the 78th Illinois Infantry, and his troop saw some fierce battles. He was mustered out on June 7, 1865, so Milton's information about Jesse is right. Milton, too, will soon be back in Illinois to be discharged and get his final pay on September 9.

After Mollie married, all of her children were delivered by the midwife, Widow Frame, who always kept a remembrance of her husband in her apron pocket—a plug of chewing tobacco. The relationship of this midwife to Milton is suspected, but not clear.

Decherd, Tennessee          June 26, 1865

Dear Friend,

[1]     I seat myself down to answer your kind letter I received last night. It found me well at present. We have moved from Tulahoma, a Sunday week. We marched fifteen miles. We landed in Decherd, a Sunday night.

[2]     Well, Mollie, I ain't got much to say this time. I ain't seen John Lambert since I left. He was well when I left. I don't think we will be home till my time is out. All I wish is I keep my health. I like to be a soldier so fur. All the boys is well [at] present.

[3]     Well Mollie, you told me that Joe Lambert is home. I like to see Joe and Jess [Lambert]. I heard that Jess was in Springfield when Joe came home. They was glad to see them.

[4]     I keep well. I think I be home the first of April, nothing happening.

[5]     I heard that George Morris and Mary Beebe is married. All I wish is to be at the shivaree. I like to know what Samuel Stewart is a-doing.

[6]     Will have to close my letter. No more at present. Write soon.
        So goodby for this time. You are my friend till death. Direct
        your letter to

        Decherd, Tennessee
        148th Regiment
        Care of Capt. Root

        from Milton Frame

## ❧ Letter #66

Peevishly, Emma, whose alias was "Bridget," scolds Mollie in this
next letter. She also reveals how important the Fourth of July was as a
national holiday. Special events, visits, and entertainments were
planned with much the same intensity as the Christmas holiday
season is today. Although Valentine's Day and Christmas were
celebrated privately, The Fourth was a community celebration where
regular work routines were interrupted. Decoration Day (Memorial
Day) would not be established until after the War, and Labor Day did
not exist. The Fourth was the only summer holiday generally
recognized, and in the North, its celebration became a show of
loyalty to the Union. This year, three days after the Fourth, four of the
seven who were convicted of conspiring to kill Lincoln were
hanged.[3]

The custom of "mittening" that Emma mentions is an ancient one.
After rural church services, the young men of a congregation would
line up outside the church door, each offering his hand to a young
woman of his choice in order to escort her home. If she accepted, her
hand would stay in his; if not, she would yank it back, leaving
him—figuratively—with her mitten only. To "mitten" a young man
was to reject him.[4]

The custom recalled the legend of the tenth century saint, Wilfreda,
who spurned the persistent love of King Edgar of England. Once, as he
pursued her, he caught her hand and knelt, just as she was running
away into a church. Despite his pleas, she continued up the steps and
into the sanctuary, leaving her hand, miraculously, still in his.[5]

Emma also uses that time-worn epithet for the Devil, "Old Scratch."

Farmington, Illinois          July 23, 1865

Dear Friend Mollie,

[1]     I hope you will answer this scratching, as this is the third
        letter I have wrote to you, and have not received a word in
        answer. I have begun to think you have forsaken Bridget, as
        she is so far away.

[2]     Mollie, what kind of a time did you have the Fourth? I hope
        better than I had. There was a celebration in Farmington
        and a free dinner. There was not half enough of dinner for
        the folks. Don't you think I got a biscuit smothered with
        molasses and two bits of currant pie, and neither was fit to
        eat, and to mend the matter, I had to be stuck along with a
        brother of John Bowley's.

[3]     I would not have been with him but his niece come over the
        night before and went with me, so if I had have mittened
        him, I would have made the girl mad. I hate him worse than
        the Old Scratch. Don't you pity me? I will be smart enough
        for him next time.

[4]     Have you heard from Bob or Tine [Alford] lately, or from
        LaGrange? I received a letter from Joe about six weeks ago,
        and I do not intend to answer him for 3 months. He waited
        3 months, and I intend to [too.] If they don't want to hear
        from me, I don't want to hear from them. Sallie [Bonney]
        would rather give anything or do anything for Molly
        Coulson than for you or me. Anytime I am willing, I can live
        without her half.

[5]     I believe I wrote to you that Mort [Johnson] had got home.

[6]     I will have to bring my poorly composed letter to a close.
        Please write soon. I would be glad to hear from you every
        two weeks.

[7]     Mollie, if you see any advertised letters for me at Quincy, won't you please send them to me? Please excuse bad writing and correct all mistakes. Mollie, tell me what you have got new this summer. Goodbye, Mollie.

Write soon to your friend,
Emma L. Johnson

## ✽ Letter #67

The next long letter from Emma is very chatty as it ranges over a number of subjects just as if Emma were speaking directly to Mollie. Included in the letter she had received from Mollie was a remnant of cloth, another example of exchanging specimens and photographs in letters.

Emma's questions to Mollie about dress are full of the frustration of being a poor hired girl and yearning to be fashionable. Styles of clothes did not change as rapidly then as now. In an earlier letter, for instance, Emma mentions getting a lavinia regina hat, one that was popular thirty years earlier. [See Letter #64, par. 7]. Though black silk dresses and balmoral skirts were prized, hired girls in rural western communities probably dressed for everyday work much as they did in the 1830s. Emma and Mollie would have worn a "frock slip," a loose-fitting wool, cotton, or flaxen gown with sleeves that was "rainy-day" length (not so long that it trailed in the mud.) The gown was held in place by a drawstring around the waist. A collar of similar material had a drawstring around the neck, and perhaps a few buttons.[6]

Of course, Emma and Mollie would have better dresses, often made of silk. The alpaca collar Emma mentions was a thin cloth made from a mixture of alpaca wool and either silk or cotton. Often it did not actually contain wool from the South American alpaca. Most alpaca cloth sold during this period was really mohair.[7]

How lonely Emma must have been, and how tired, as she spends the last few moments of the day dreaming of new clothes in her cramped room, writing by candlelight!

Farmington, Illinois          August 27th, 1865

My Dear Friend Mollie,

[1]     It is right for me to try to express my thanks for your kindness in writing to me. After so long a delay I began to think you had forgotten me or did not want to correspond with me any longer.

[2]     Mollie, I received a letter from Rettie Coulson last week. She wrote to me to know what had become of you. She said that she had not heard a word from you since you left LaGrange last winter.

[3]     You knew that Molly Coulson was engaged to a man by the name of William Wright. He worked on the *Wyaconda* last summer. That was the [steam]boat that was built at LaGrange, and the week before I left LaGrange, he wrote to her that he had got his leg broke and had it taken off. Rettie wrote to me that it was a lie, his leg had not been hurt. So him and Molly has played it quits. So Rettie wrote to me.

[4]     Sallie [Bonney] told Tine [Alford] and me that she had an invitiation to a wedding, and we would not have a bid. They were to be married this fall. It was last spring that she were a-bragging, but I guess she were slipped up on that time.

[5]     Mollie, when you go to LaGrange, don't let on that you know a word about it, or maybe Rettie won't like it, if she hears that I told you. Sallie thinks a great deal more of Molly Coulson than you or I, but I don't care, do you? We can live without her love.

[6]     Mollie, what are you going to get this fall that is nice? I mean far as a dress. Mrs. [Margaret] Simpson wants me to get a plain collar, alpaca. I don't know that I will. If I do, then I can't get a black silk. Do you intend to get a silk this

winter? I want to, before we go to LaGrange again, to dress as fine as Molly Coulson. You know she has a checked silk and talked of getting a black silk. I don't think Henry [Coulson] will get her the black silk.

[7] Mollie have you got a dress of this piece you sent me? I think it is so pretty! I have got 22 yards of muslin this summer, 9 yards is bleached, and the rest is unbleached. I have not yet got a new dress since the spring. I sent you a piece of them.

[8] I received a letter from Tine about 4 weeks ago and answered it last Sunday.

[9] Oh yes, I have got a balmoral skirt and a new pair of shoes. They are as good as hers.

[10] Mollie, if you won't come up here to stay, get me a place down there next spring. I want to be close to you, for I think more of you than my sister I have got. Mrs. Simpson don't keep help in the winter. I don't know what I will do this winter. I think some of going to school this winter.

[11] I would like to see your love letters.

[12] The folks all went to church today, but me, I did not go. I can [do] so, Monday night.

[13] Mollie, I have washed hard all the forenoon, and all the afternoon gathered apples, and fixed for hands to shell corn tomorrow, and bake. Festival is to be Wednesday night. We will have 12 hands tomorrow. Don't you pity me? It is now 10 o'clock, and I am very tired and sloppy.

[14] Mollie, I hope you can read this scratching. Tell me in your next letter if you can.

[15] When you go to LaGrange, I want you to wish that I was there before Jack and Belle [Johnson] and them. Tell me

what they say about me, also Sal and Joe [Bonney], and see what they say, and ask Joe if he has made my ring yet. Don't forget to see if the LaGrange folk think anything of me. I believe Alfa [Nancy Alford] thinks lots of me.

[16]     Mollie, don't let anybody see this scratching. Goodby, Mollie, till I hear from you. Please write soon to your friend,

Emma

Tuesday. I have made 20 pies today and got dinner for 12 men.

## 🌠 Letter #68

Lincoln is buried, the war is over, and slavery has been abolished by the ratification of the Thirteenth Amendment. Now is the time for living the peace, and with young women like Mollie and Eunice, both of whom are now well into their twenty-second year, when and who they will marry is most important. With each of Eunice's reports, there is a lingering wonder about another chance missed. Her caustic remark about housing is especially telling.

Again, unexpectedly Mollie learns about Amulek from Eunice, not from him. Mollie writes him immediately, for he gets her letter the day after Christmas [See Letter #69, par. 1].

Schoolteacher Doc Clark apparently said or did something for which Eunice never forgave him [See Letter #79, par. 2], but her tone as she writes about him and the famous blackberrying party [See Letter #22, par. 4] is nostalgic. Despite the longing for past times, she finds room to lecture Mollie about her membership in the Christian Church. Though her friends in Iowa always assumed she would become Mormon, Mollie was never baptized a Mormon. Compare Eunice's reaction to Mollie's religion with Eunice's sister-in-law Deborah Morey's [See Letter #20, par. 7].

[Pleasant Plains, Ia.]          December 11, 1865

My Dear Friend,

[1]     I hope that you will excuse me for not writing you long
        before this. I have been very busy doing our fall work up
        that I could not start to write to you, and I have not got
        through yet. I am trying to get ready to go to school next
        week in Eldorado to Mr. Grumball. I wish that you was here
        to go with me, and it would seem like old times again.

[2]     Well, Miriam, Doc Clark has got back to this county again,
        and he is keeping school in the Alden District, and Jane
        Moffet is going to him. I wonder if he ever thinks of the
        time that he helped us in school. I often do, and have often
        thought of the pleasure that we have taken to gather those
        there many blackberries grown down there. Do you think of
        the time that we went down into Missouri? George
        [Rockwell] often talks of it.

[3]     Well, Mollie, the girls are as fond of the old widowers as they
        was when I wrote you last. There was a girl 22 years old that
        married an old man with 5 young ones. Don't you think that
        she was hard-pushed? And they tell me that I will marry
        some old man, but I will stay single first. What do you think
        about it? I know that you will believe as I do.

[4]     Call Clark is married two weeks ago to a man from Ohio. He
        took her back with him. Well, Lois and Emma Good was
        married the same week that Call was. I heard that there was
        26 married that has no homes. I think that they had better
        stay single. Amulek [Boothe] was married two or three
        months ago to Maryann Gillen [Gilliland].

[5]     Well, for something else. I heard that you got converted to
        sectarianism. Is that so? I hope that it is not the case. I want
        you to write and tell me what your belief is in regard to the
        Christians. You have heard the true gospel in its easy and

simple [?] [?], and I hope you have not forgotten it. If you read the Bible you will see a great deal of difference in the teaching of the Mormons and the teachings of the different denominations.

[6]　　You must not get offended at me for asking you. I always hoped that you and me would belong to the same church, but if that is the case we will never to believe alike, but that need not make us enemies to each other because that we can't see alike. I am not of that disposition, and I don't think that you are.

[7]　　Well, Miriam, I will bring my scribbling to a close for it is dinner time. I wish that you was here to help me to it. Goodby till the next time.

Eunice Morey

to Miriam Works.

NOTES

1. Alvin F. Harlow, "Old Wires and New Waves," *Dictionary of American History,* (New York: Charles Scribner's Sons, 1976), p. 21.

2. Landrum, *Quincy,* p. 109.

3. Long, *Civil War,* p. 694.

4. "It was fun to see those long lines of boys reaching from either side of the church door... and the girls...run the 'gauntlet.'...it would only be known whether the young man 'got the mitten' or not when the journey home was started..." *History of Fulton County,* p. 665.

5. Michael Ohlmert, "Points of Origin," *Smithsonian,* May 1984, p. 50.

6. *Historical Encyclopedia of Illinois and History of Fulton County,* p. 658.

7. *Webster's New International Dictionary of the English Language* (Springfield, Mass.: G & C Merriam Co., 1930), p. 63.

**George Irvin McNutt** *(1848-1932).*
*Marrying Mollie in 1866, he took her
to the 1849 farmhouse in Fall Creek,
Illinois, that he had inherited—as the
only surviving son—from his parents,
James Alexander and Sarah Bell
(Case) McNutt. He raised wheat, oats,
and ran some stock, often comparing
yields with Mollie's Missouri cousin
Amulek Boothe. He was a partner
with cousin Joe Bonney in a lumber
business, and even loaned money to Mollie's brother, Perry. The
farmhouse was often full—with George's sisters and husbands, with
children and grandchildren, or with the Bonneys.*

*First page of Letter #71 from Grace Robinson in 1866.*

# ALL THINGS COME TO THOSE WHO WAIT
## 1866

Of the eight letters which survive in 1866, two are from Amulek Boothe. His January letter is written after nearly half a year of not writing and much has happened to him. He misspells his bride's surname, however.

Because he has not written in a long while, he asks questions based on what he knew about Mollie in years past, giving a clear picture of her life then—even of her weight.

> Eaglesville, [Mo.]          January 7, 1866
>
> Dear Respected Cousin,

[1]     It is with respect and love that I seat myself again for the purpose of answering your long written letter which I received the next day after Christmas. It was sent in care of George [Rockwell], and I have not been there since he got it. They ought to have sent it to me, but did not till Annett went out, and she got it.

[2]     I expect you thought strange of me for not answering it before; however, your letter found us all well except Ad[am Dennis]. He was very sick at that time, from which he has recovered. The rest is all well. I have had a very bad cold this winter which settled in my lungs, which come very near

setting me into the consumption, but I am over it and feel
quite saucy.

[3]     You wanted me to come and make you a visit before I was
        married, but it is too late. I would like to have come and
        seen you on my return home from St. Louis, but I was not
        very well, and I wrote Cousin Joseph [Bonney] a letter
        before I left there and told him the reason why I did not
        come that way. But it seems as though he never got the
        letter. I think I have wrote one letter to you since the one
        you answered.

[4]     You wanted to know if I was a-going to get married. I was
        married the seventh day of September. Her name was
        Maryann Gillen [Gilliland]. You have seen her. If you
        remember, she was here when you was out to Ad's at that
        party. She is about the size of you. She weighs 120 pounds.

[5]     Tell Cousin Joseph that I would like to come out and see him
        and Sarah if I had time, but can't this winter. I think you had
        better come out here and see the folks. I wish you would.

[6]     Do you live with your uncle [Samuel Stewart] or do you
        work out? Tell me how you get along. How is Perry [Works]?
        You never say anything about him. I would like to know it
        all. You may think I am very inquisitive, but that is my
        failing.

[7]     What kind of a time did you have on Christmas and New
        Year's? I tell you it was dry times for me both days. Annett
        [Daily] and her man [David] went to Pleasant Plains to see
        the folks. I wish I had been there, too. I would have passed
        the day very well and better if you had been there.

[8]     That present will come in the next letter. I have not got it
        yet. I am going to the [Mississippi] river in a few days and I
        will get it then. I will know whether you are at Joseph's or
        Payson.

[9]     It is getting late and I must close. So farewell, dearest cousin.
        May blessings attend you where'er you go is the desire of
        your cousin. Please excuse this for it is I. Give my love to
        Perry and your cousins.

        Yours truly,
        Amulek Boothe

        Maryann says you must come and see us. She sends a piece
        of her dress and sock that she has.

## 🌸 Letter #70

Grace Robinson's next letter is one of the few not written to
Mollie, but to Mollie's brother, Perry Works. After long pleading for
him to write, Grace got a letter from Perry late in 1865, and now it is
she who has waited a long time to answer. In his letter to Gracie,
Perry must have asked her some questions about the Mormon
religion [See par. 4.] How Mollie got this letter is explained in the
letter Grace writes the next day, Letter #71.

Adaline (Rockwell) Perry, George and Deborah's sister, is still
living in Pleasant Plains with David and Deborah Morey while her
husband, Philander, is in Wisconsin.

        Nine Eagles, Iowa            April 17th, 1866

        Dear Cousin,

[1]     I now seat myself for the purpose of answering your letter of
        December 8th which I received "long ago." I have put off
        writing so long that I declare I am almost ashamed of
        myself. I expect you will never forgive me for neglecting you
        so long, but I have had considerable to occupy my attention
        the past winter & did not write many letters. Perhaps if I
        had tried very hard, I might have had time to answer yours.

[2]      There has been considerable sickness around here this spring. One of our nearest neighbors have lost four children— disease, spotted fever.

[3]      Where is Miriam? I have not had a line from her for nearly nine months. I should like very much to hear from her. If I have time, perhaps I will write her a few lines in this letter. If I do, I want you to be sure and give it to her, will you?

[4]      I think you and Mollie ought to come and make us a visit this summer, and then I will talk to you about religion and everything else until you will get tired hearing me.

[5]      I do not think you had better get married this year. I am not going to, but there is a very good reason: because there won't any person have me.

[6]      Well, I must hurry with this scribbling, as I want to take this over to David [Morey]'s tonight & have Cousin Ad[a]line [Perry] put it in the post office at Leon tomorrow, as she expects to go.

[7]      I presume it will be difficult for you to read this miserably written letter, but you will please excuse haste & please write soon. Don't wait as long as I have.

Affectionately, your cousin,
Gracie

[Writing to:] Mr. Perry Work

## 🍀 Letter #71

From what she tells Mollie, it is likely that Gracie has not written in a long time, perhaps since April of 1865. The tragedy of the Moffet children is especially sad. Alfred and Lydia Moffet often informally "adopted" orphans and other needy children like Adoniram Wright [See Letters #12, par. 5; and #14, par. 2].

John Crawford, arrested in the Dr. Mullinix affair that Gracie mentions, was one of Mollie's many schoolteachers. Dr. Parmentus E. Mullinix came from a family of physicians. His brothers and his father were physicians. Some say Mullinix was returning from a dance in Mercer County, Missouri, on the night of April 6. Others say that he was seeing a patient. Whether theft or revenge for a lost love was the motive for the crime, Crawford was acquitted. "The evidence was not strong enough to convict him," one chronicler reported.[1]

The unnamed baby born to David and Deborah Morey on February 25, 1866, that Gracie mentions is eventually called Elsie Louella.

Gracie brings Mollie up to date with news about Pleasant Plains friends and about their cousins, the Wordens of New York. Like many soldiers, Charlie Worden returned from the war and quickly married. He continued to live in and around Auburn, New York, as did his sister, Angeline.

As Gracie reports, the Booth family is still gambling on striking it rich in Colorado where gold, and by now, silver, too, continued to magnetize the imagination of so many. [See Letters #15, par. 13; #16, par. 4; #18, par. 6; #23, par. 6].

　　　[Nine Eagles, Ia.]　　　　　　April 18, 1866

　　　Dear Mollie,

[1]　　I did not go over to David [Morey]'s last night with Perry [Works]'s letter, so I thought I would write you a few lines and put in an answer I sent to him.

[2]　　Are you offended, or what is the reason you have not answered my last letter? I looked for a missive from you so long that I have got clear out of patience, and concluded that you never intended to write me again, but you will have to hear from me whether you wish to or not.

[3]　　I have some bad news to communicate. Mr. [Alfred] Moffet's have buried four children this spring, namely: Jane, Sophronia, James, and Julia. No tongue can tell what they

suffered during their sickness. Jane was crazy all the time she was ill. I tell you it seems lonely to go there now. We miss the children so much.

[4]     Dr. [Parmentus] Mullinix was murdered a week ago last Friday night (the 6th) about six miles below town (in Mo.) John Crawford is suspected as being one of the murderers. They have got him arrested, and the trial is now going on. I wish you knew all the particulars as they are too dreadful to write.

[5]     Frank Smith came home from the army this spring and only lived eight days after. They suppose that he was poisoned. Nancy [Smith] takes it very hard. She is now at her father's [Mr. Dale].

[6]     Cousin Adaline [Perry]'s buried their little boy last winter. She is at David [Morey]'s. Her husband [Philander] has gone back to Wisconsin.

[7]     Deborah [Morey] has got another daughter. They have not named it yet.

[8]     I suppose you have not heard that Cousins Angie and Charlie [Worden] are married. Angie was married last November to Mr. Linus D. Worden, so you see she has not changed her name.

[9]     Mr. [Robert] Booth, Robert, and Horace [Booth] are going to the Peak this spring. Robert was married in February to a Miss Ophelia Delap, a young lady from Wisconsin. She will be sixteen in May—quite an "old maid," won't she?

[10]    Caroline [Call] Clark was married last fall to Mr. William Biggs from Ohio. They are now at her father's.

[11]    Henry Cowles was baptized last Sunday into the Methodist Church. He is a very good young man. I presume Lizzie Gammill thinks so at least.

[12]    The most of the young folks is having grand times out here since the soldiers returned home. I wish you would come out here this summer. There are some splendid young gents here, I tell you. I think you would enjoy yourself very much if you would see proper to visit us.

[13]    I suppose you are not married yet, are you? The relatives are all well as far as I know. I have never seen Amulek's wife [Maryann Boothe] yet. We have not heard from there since Christmas.

[14]    By the way, Mollie, we had our house finished last fall. I wish you would come and see us if you can. Ma [Angeline] sends her love to you and Perry [Works] and wishes very much to see you both.

[15]    I believe I have written all the news this time. If found worthy, an answer will be very gladly received.

        Yours affectionately,
        Gracie

[16]    P.S. Write and tell me how you are getting along. I am prospering splendidly, I tell you, and I only weigh 103 pounds—ain't I fleshy. I wish you would send me your photograph. I got quite a number of photos, and would like to have yours to put with them.

## ✿ Letter #72

This short letter from Sallie Bonney reveals that as late as June of the year that Mollie married some people thought she was romantically involved with Tine Alford.

The visits between LaGrange and Payson were frequent and seem to be easier now that the war is over. Even strawberries can be sent from one place to the other.

Sallie's baby is Iola Edna (called "Ola"), whose first birthday was the day before this letter was written. Sallie's oldest, Jessie Katie Belle (called "Kate") is four.

June 10, [1866]                    LaGrange, Mo.

Dear Cousin,

[1]     I received your letter in due time and was glad to hear from you. I got my berries a Monday. They was all right. I am very much obliged for them. I would like to see you. Tell your cousins to come and see us. I would like to see them. I will look for you, too.

[2]     My baby [Iola] is a-walking now. Katie [Bonney] is well and says she wants to see Mollie.

[3]     Joe [Bonney] ain't very well. Joe says you must [come] and see us when you can.

[4]     Mrs. [Nancy] Alford and I is talking of coming down, but not soon. This fall, maybe. She sends her love to you and says she will come if she can. Tine [Alford] wants her and I to come and see you very bad, for some reason, I guess. Maybe you know. I don't. I haven't told him what you said in your letter. His ma read the letter. She laughed and said she would tell him.

[5]     Katie says she would like to know why Mollie don't hurry and come now.

[6]     Give my love to Perry [Works] and all the folks and accept the same yourself. No more at present. Write soon as you get this.

From your cousin, Sallie

## ✺ Letter #73

Another letter after a long period of not writing comes from Amulek Boothe just before Fourth of July celebrations. He refreshes Mollie on the Iowa news and reveals how she might travel to Iowa for a visit, a different way of travelling than he and Mollie used in 1862. By "cars" he means railway cars, and the "hack" was the mail wagon.

Interestingly, Amulek's bride is Maryann, and Mollie's given name, "Miriam," was sometimes interchanged with "Marian" or "Maryann" by Amulek and others. What he suggests that Mollie do with the locket seems oddly appropriate because of his affection for both "Maryanns."

Eaglesville, [Mo.]          July 1, 1866

Ever-esteemed Cousin Mollie,

[1]    With love and respect towards you I once more take my seat at the table to address you with a few lines to let you know that we are all well and hope this may find you the same. I received your letter long since, but I neglected answering it which I am ashamed of, but I have been busy this spring, and I have not wrote a letter since the last I wrote to you.

[2]    Adam [Dennis]'s folks is well, except Angeline. She is complaining some. Annett [Daily] was well last Friday. They live in Eaglesville. He [David Daily] is teaching school there.

[3]    I have not been to Pleasant Plains since last fall. I don't know how they are getting along. I thought some of going out there on the Fourth, but I was so busy that I hardly think I shall.

[4]    I have rented the farm and have got 35 acres of corn in, and it keeps me busy with no help. I have got in 10 acres of oats besides.

[5]    Adam has traded his farm off for another, four miles north of where he did live.

[6]    Mr. [Robert] Booth has gone across the plains, and Robert and Horace [Booth], and Charley Potter. Robert is married.

[7]    There is going to be a celebration in Eaglesville on the Fourth. They are fixing for [it] now.

[8]    Mary [Boothe] and I wish you would come up and stay with us. You would do as well here as there, and then we could all see you. If you will come, I will do all I can for you, and then you need not to have to work out for a living. I will get you what you need just for your company, for I feel for you as a sister and want to see you do well.

[9]    If you are not married yet, come up and stay this winter anyhow. If not all winter, long enough to make a visit. You could come to Chillocothe on the [railroad] cars, then from there on the hack, or I would come to Chillocothe after you, if you would come.

[10]   I will send you a locket with Maryann's miniature in it. You can have yours taken on the other side. I would have mine taken, but you have got it.

[11]   Tell Perry [Works] he must come up here and see us. How is he getting along? I would like to see him and Joseph [Bonney]'s folks. Give them all my respects, and you take some, too.

[12]   Maryann, let me know when you get married, and maybe I will come to the wedding. So, no more from your dear cousin,

       A. Boothe

[13]   Fare thee well until I hear from thee again. Mary sends her love to you.

## ❧ Letter #74

Emma Johnson writes Mollie immediately after arriving in Quincy from working at Mrs. Simpson's in Farmington, Illinois, and she wants to see Mollie again to tell her the news.

The practical joke Emma and Mollie played seems to have involved baking a boot jack in a gooseberry pie.

J. W. "Jack" Johnson, Emma's married brother, is most probably returning from Wisconsin where he worked now and again. Emma's bachelor brother, Mort, whom she likens to Mollie's brother Perry because both sent money to their sisters, proposes a common arrangement for unmarried people. If Mort's plan would have worked, he and Emma would appear to be an ordinary family, and Emma would seem suddenly "old" to herself—no longer a girl.

Emma has heard some sad news regarding Mollie and George McNutt ("The Farm").

Quincy, Ill.                    July 10, 1866

My dear Mollie,

[1]     I take pleasure this morning of penning you a few lines in answer to your kind and welcome letter which I received about two weeks ago. I was truly glad to hear from you once more. I did not think you would write to me as you waited so long.

[2]     I suppose you will be surprised to hear that I am in Quincy. I left Farmington the last day of June. I expected to see you the Fourth in Quincy and hunted all day for you but did not hear from you. Were you in Quincy the Fourth or not? When are you going to LaGrange? Are you going soon? If you do, let me know, and I will go, too.

[3]     How have you enjoyed your life this summer? Have you enjoyed yourself as well as you did last winter? I have not seen a bit of pleasure since I left LaGrange. Only the Fourth. I had a very pleasant time the Fourth.

[4]     I suppose you had a nice time when Sallie [Bonney] was down. What did Sallie say about the Gooseberry Pie? Rettie Coulson wrote to me that Tom [Coulson] told Sallie about the pie, and she said that we was both bad girls, but I'll bet that was not all she said about it. I have often thought about the gooseberry pie, and the pie crust, and the boot jack.

[5]     Oh Mollie, I have a letter from Jack [Johnson] the other day. He will be home this fall if he has good luck. We will have to give LaGrange a call when he comes.

[6]     Mort [Johnson] is at Taylor's a-harvesting this week and last, but he will be back soon. Mort sent me money to come on and has give me a great many presents. I believe my brother is as good as yours. Mort is talking of going to housekeeping this fall. If we do, you must come and stay a long time with me. We will have a good time. You know Mort, I believe. I hope he will go to housekeeping. I will look old—won't I?—at the head of a household.

[7]     You told me that you and "The Farm" [George McNutt] had fell out. Do not give him his picture till I see it.

[8]     I think you might come and see me. I should have liked to have come down to have seen you very much, but I left before Sallie went down, and you did not ask me to come. I thought you did not think about asking me. I did not get offended at it. I thought you did not mean it an insult.

[9]     I must bring my letter to a close, as I can't think of anything of importance to write. Please write soon, a long letter to your friend and well-wisher,

Emma Johnson

direct to Quincy

## ✿ Letter #75

Apparently, the word that Mollie was contemplating marriage had reached the folks in Pleasant Plains, Eagleville, and LaGrange. But who was courting Mollie at this time is somewhat of a mystery. In LaGrange, Emma Johnson thinks Mollie's intended is Bob Alford, perhaps because Emma is sweet on Bob's brother, Tine. [See next letter.]

In Pleasant Plains, however, Gracie Robinson is anxious to know the facts, as this letter confirms. Her mother, Angeline, wants to buy Mollie her wedding dress, a generous gift. Together with her news about murder and adventures, Gracie cannot resist telling Mollie about her own beau, even though she coyly uses a dash for the word. For what happens to Gracie and her beau, see Letter #82.

Pleasant Plain, Iowa
Monday Aug. 6th 1866

Dear Mollie,

[1]     I am again seated for the purpose of acknowledging the receipt of your welcome letter of the 18th ult. [ultimo, in the last month] which came to hand last Friday—Now Mollie! I think you deserve a real good scolding for not writing to me long ago. I had almost given up hearing from you again, but it seems you have not quite forgotten me.

[2]     You wished to know where I spent the fourth. Well, I will tell you: There were two couple[s] of us went to Decatur City, but when we got there, we did not find "things" as we had expected, and we went to Leon and staid [sic] until evening, and then came home. I enjoyed myself very well indeed. Miss Louisa Booth and myself were the Ladies. I will leave you to guess who the gentlemen were that were with us. Suffice it to say they were Soldiers, and own brothers.

[3]     Now I want to know if you are really in earnest about getting married. If you are, Ma says she will get your wedding dress. Please write and tell me if you wish it this fall. If you don't get married in the fall, we would like to have you come and spend the winter with us if you can. The stage runs from Leon to town every other day now, so we get our mail three times a week. Mr. and Mrs. [Royal] Richardson were here yesterday—they would be pleased to see you.

[4]     You say your admirer is "good looking." I would like very much to have his photo, but I don't believe he is better looking than my—[beau]. I tell you I have got the photograph of the best looking young man in Decatur County. I would like to send it to you and see if you would recognize it, but I am afraid you'd want to keep it, and I could not consent to that until I get another.

[5]     There are a great many weddings taking place around here now. Ann Adkins and Doc Clark have been married about 3 months. They are living in town. Sarah Hedrick was married 3 weeks ago yesterday to Ed. Seymore.

[6]     Mr. James W. Alfrey was murdered some time since, by Jacob Williams in Mo—He was buried with Masonic honors—Williams has run away and I guess crossed the plains.

[7]     Robert Booth has returned home; he did not go all the way to Pike's Peak. I guess he could not stay away from his wife long enough. The rest have got through safe and will probably come back this fall.

[8]     The relatives are all in usual health as far as I know. Deborah calls her babe Elsie Louella. Cousin Adaline Perry has gone back to Wisconsin to her husband; she was baptized before she went away. Mr. Alden's folks are all well she has got her loom up in the cabin and is weaving this summer.

[9]     I will send you a few pieces of my dresses. I have been peacing [sic] me a quilt which makes me rather short of calico pieces.

[10]    Some people think I am going to marry before long—but "I can't see it."

[11]    Well, it is getting to be pretty near night & I will have to close. Ma sends her regards & Perry. Why don't he answer my letter? Tell him I think he is a bad boy—

[12]    Please write soon to your loving cousin,

        Gracie

[13]    My compliments to my future cousin. Please tell me what his name is—

## ❧ Letter #76

More than two months after her last letter, Emma is working at Mrs. Simpson's in Farmington, Illinois, again. It is late when she writes her friend Mollie, and she is suffering. (Notice her plaintive addition to the letter's dateline.) It is hard to remember that she is only twenty-three years old.

        Farmington, [Ill.]         Sept. 16, 1866
        At Mrs. Simpson's all alone, Sunday

        To Miriam Works

        My dear friend Mollie,

[1]     Please excuse me for writing two letters to your one. This is a very lonesome rainy day. I suppose you will be surprised to hear I am alone on such a day. Today is communion day, and there is to be an extra sermon, too. I would liked to have gone, too, but I could not go.

[2]      Mollie, I have had the toothache for about two weeks. I went to the dentist on Thursday to have my teeth taken out, but he would not pull it, as they was my upper front teeth. He put something in to kill the nerve, and it made my mouth so sore that I can't eat anything but bread soaked in tea or coffee. Don't you pity me? You know how well I like to eat. I hope it will be better soon.

[3]      Mollie, I heard a few weeks ago that Mrs. [Nancy] Alford said she wished that Bob [Alford] would come home and marry Mollie Works, and last week Belle [Johnson] wrote to me that Bob had got home, so you had better be a-getting ready. I also heard that Tine [Alford] is very attentive to Molly Coulson. If they marry, I say joy be with them. I hope you will do better than to get either of them.

[4]      Belle wrote to me that you was a-going to LaGrange the last of this month or the first of October, and she wanted me to come over there this winter and stay with her. Jack [Johnson] wants to work away from home. I hope you will put off going till winter, if I go. I don't know yet whether I can go or not.

[5]      Mollie, send me a little piece of all your new dresses, and tell me of all the fine new things you have gotten.

[6]      My wrist is far from well yet. This rainy weather is so bad on it. It pains me all the time in the rainy weather.

[7]      Please tell me when you have heard from LaGrange. I will have to bring my scratching to a close. When you get this, please write the same day. I want to hear from you so bad.

[8]      We have a great many apples this year. I have commenced making cider.

[10]    It has been raining here for two weeks past.

[11]    Is they any cholera in Quincy as you know of?

[12]    Please excuse bad writing and correct all mistakes and
        please write soon to your true friend,

        Emma Johnson
        Farmington, Illinois

## ✿ Letter #77

The final letter of 1866 is one *from* Mollie, rather than to her.
Saved by her husband, it is written two weeks before their wedding
and represents how unwilling Mollie was to be married in the Stewart
home, where she was uncomfortable. She chose a household she
loved, the Bonneys', even though it meant special arrangements in
another state, Missouri, and a special trip to Monticello, the seat of
Lewis County, to obtain a license.

Her friend Tine Alford married Kate Crandelle of Hannibal the day
before this letter was written.

        LaGrange, [Mo.]             Nov. 8, 1866

        My Dear George,

[1]     With pleasure I again seat myself to answer your kind letter
        which I received today. I was glad to hear from you, dear.
        The time seemed long since I got your last letter, although it
        was only a week this morning.

[2]     I wrote to you last Friday. I suppose you have received my
        letter by this time. Well, Perry [Works] did give you my letter
        at last, did he? I suppose he thought it would be very
        consoling to you after he had carried it around four or five
        weeks. I guess he thought, Better late than never. He is a
        great boy.

[3]     I suppose Tine Alford is a married man by this time. He
        started for Hannibal last Monday morning. He was to be
        married the 7th and is coming home the 13th.

[4]     I tell you we are having some gay times here now, especially
        our Dutch friends. They have a dance every few nights.
        There is one tonight, only a few steps from here. I can hear
        the fiddle plain and hear them call off. I think they might
        have invited their Dutch sister, don't you?

[5]     I will change the subject. You still think you will have to go
        to Monticello, do you? I am sorry that I didn't conclude to
        go to Quincy with you. I didn't think it would be so much
        trouble, but we will have to do the best we can now.

[6]     I wasn't particular about staying here, but my cousins
        wanted me to, so I thought it would do just as well. I don't
        think you will have to get licensed, but perhaps you will.

[7]     I will be ready the 21st of this month, and, beloved one, I
        hope you will. I wish you would tell me how many you think
        will come and who. I hope Ella [McNutt] will come. We
        want all to come that can. We want to know how many can
        come so we can arrange things according. We will try to
        provide plenty for all that come.

[8]     I will write a few lines to Perry and also to Uncle [Samuel
        Stewart]'s folks and send in this letter. You will please see
        that it is handed to them soon. I wrote to Mary Jane [Field]
        last week and told her that you would let them know when
        to come, for I could not tell her till I heard from you.

[9]     Well, my dear, I shall have to close, as it is getting late.
        Please answer this letter as soon as you get it, and let me
        know the arrangements. Send your letter to Quincy, if
        possible, for I will get it so much sooner. If there is any
        letters come to Payson for me, you will please take them out
        of the office and keep them for me.

[10]    Well, dear, it is time to close. May the blessings of the Most High be with you and protect you is my prayer. Remember me kindly to all inquiring friends.

From one that loves you sincerely,
Mollie
To her ever dear George. Write immediately.

NOTES

1. *Record of Ringgold & Decatur County*, p. 639; the particulars are also recorded in *History of Decatur County, Vol. 2.*, p. 171.

*Royal and Martha Richardson's hotel in Pleasant Plains (now Pleasanton), Iowa. It was one of the first hotels in Pleasant Plains and housed wounded Civil War soldiers (as young Gracie Robinson reports) as well as the Robinsons themselves while their home was being built. In later years, both Mollie and Gracie stayed with the Richardsons when they would visit the area.*

**James Alexander McNutt** *(1801-1869) and* **Sarah Bell (Case) McNutt** *(1808-1887). Parents of 13 children, ten of whom reached maturity, they established the McNutt farm in the township of Fall Creek, Illinois, buying bounty land from a War of 1812 veteran. Their only son, George Irvin, inherited the farm, as James had stipulated in his will.*

*Children of Mollie's friends and relatives playing in the log house (since demolished) on the McNutt family farm in Fall Creek, Illinois. This was Mollie and George I. McNutt's first home, since his father and mother, James Alexander and Sarah Bell Case McNutt, were in the main 1849 farmhouse. Mollie's second son, James Ernest, was born in this log house.*

# KEEPING HOUSE

# 1867

## ✿ Letter #78

From now on, the letter writers are careful to address Mollie as Mollie McNutt and often to include messages to her husband, George, as Sallie Bonney does here early in 1867.

Sallie accuses Grace Robinson of being "a great girl," a mildly derisive term emphasizing Gracie's immaturity and therefore her irresponsibility in writing regularly. In the same way, Mollie derided her brother Perry as "a great boy" for casually forgetting a letter she sent to George [See Letter #77, par. 2].

Though who Sallie means by "Grissom" is not known, she does mention another of George's sisters, Harriet Ellen ("Ella") McNutt who is seventeen at the time.

LaGrange, Mo.                    January 6, 1867

Cousin Mollie,

[1]    I will write you a few lines to let you know that we have all been sick since we got your letter and are not very well yet. We were all down at once. We should have wrote long before this if we had been well, and I don't write much now. Write soon as you get this and let us hear from you.

[2]    Mrs. [Nancy] Alford is sick now. The rest of the folks are all well, I believe. They all send their love to you and your husband [George McNutt]. I have had two letters from Jane

[Stewart] since you was here. We accept your kind invitation to visit you and think we should do so next summer.

[3]     We want you and George to come up this winter and see us. You can come if you think so, I know. The folks thinks your husband is good-looking.

[4]     Mollie, I haven't heard from Grace [Robinson] yet. She is a great girl, I think.

[5]     Write and tell me about them wildness [?] and who Grissom married. Give my love to Perry [Works] and tell him to write to us.

[6]     George, we want you and Mollie to come and see us as soon as you can. You know we can't come this winter, and you musn't wait for us. We would like to see you very much.

[7]     Give my love to Ella [McNutt], and tell her I would like to see her.

[8]     George, I look at them pictures nearly every day and wish I could see you and Mollie, so you must not forget to come and see us.

[9]     I must bring my letter to a close. I have the neuralgia in my head. I can't hardly do anything for it. You must excuse this short letter. I don't feel like writing. You must write as soon as you get this. Give my love to your father and mother [James and Sara Bell McNutt] and keep a good share for yourselves.

Goodbye for the present,
from Sallie and Joe

## ❧ Letter #79

As for the frequency of Mollie's letter writing, especially to her friends in Iowa, Eunice Morey's letter in the spring of 1867 tells much. It also reveals how Eunice feels about marriage and pregnancy, though her warning to Mollie is too late because Mollie is already five months pregnant.

George McNutt towered over his bride, who was so short that one of their playful stunts was for her to skip and dance under his outstretched arm. George's height was one of the details in Mollie's letter to Eunice, and predictably Eunice has a comment on tall husbands, including Mollie's and Martha Cowles'.

Two years younger than Mollie, Martha Cowles is the daughter of Austin Cowles and his second wife, Irena. Martha, Eunice, and Mollie were schoolmates. For what happens to Martha and the "tall Delap," see Letter #87, par. 7. "The prettiest man" that Eunice brags about is revealed in Grace Robinson's letter of this year [See Letter #82, par. 5].

Eunice's mentioning of her cousin Martha Keown and their friend Grace Robinson's "largeness" remains a mystery, but her quick request to Mollie that George McNutt not read this letter indicates that Eunice may not be referring to the weight of the girls but to significant parts of their mature female bodies.

[Pleasant Plains, Ia.]        April 6, 1867

Dear Friend,

[1]    Your letter dated March 26th came to hand yesterday and I make a hasty reply. I was surprised when Father [George Morey] gave me the letter and found it was from you, but I was truly glad to learn that you had not forgotten me. I had made up my mind that you had entirely forgotten me, for it has been over a year since I have had a letter from you.

[2]    Well, Miriam, you wanted to know if [I] see Doc Clark. Oh yes, I often see him. He's just the same old Doc Clark. He asked me one day if I was mad at him yet. I told him, no, but that I wanted to keep my word seeing that he did. I guess that Ann [Clark] has got enough of him, for he is not one of the best of men in the world, for he is so quick-tempered. I

guess that she has got her hands full with him and the baby. Ann looks nice, you may bet, with a baby. She says, first a man, then a baby.

[3]     Well, Miriam, I will just warn you now: Be careful how you do. Don't do that bad, Miriam, for nothing in the world.

[4]     Miriam, there's plenty babies up here this spring. It has been a good year for babies, and all that could afford one have got one or have signed for one.

[5]     Martha Cowles is married at last. She got a man so tall that he can pick off plums without climbing the tree. I see that there is an advantage in getting a tall man, so when I choose a man, I will pick me one [the] height of yours. When I get married, I will write the height of my man.

[6]     Well, Mollie, you wanted to know how I enjoyed myself this winter. Well, I have enjoyed myself very well, but I would have enjoyed myself better if you had been up here with me, for I don't think that I have my match up here unless you is here.

[7]     Well, Mollie, you spoke of sliding downhill when we were children. Oh, how often I think of it and wish that we were children again, so that we could be together! To look back to that time, it don't seem long, but how soon the years pass away and separate friends and, perhaps, forever. Oh, how I wish that I could see you, but we are denied of that privilege now, for many a long mile separates us, but I still live in hope of seeing you some day.

[8]     Have you forgotten the promise that we made that the first one that got married should come and see the other? And it will fall on you to come and see me.

[9]     Well, Mollie, you say that you have the best and prettiest man in the world. Well, I hope that he is, but when you see mine, then you will not think so, for I think that I have got the prettiest man picked out. Oh, I wish that you could see him. You must have your man come up here and live by me and then I will be all right again.

[10]     I have been lost ever since you have went away. Now, do come up here and live, for it will not do for two old friends like you and me to be separated always.

[11]     Deborah and David [Morey] are well and their family. Helen and George [Rockwell] are living in the Plains yet, and George talks some of going to the Peak with Mr. [Robert] Booth this spring.

[12]     George Keown has bought him a piece of land joining ours. He is going to build as soon as he can raise the means. Martha [Keown] is at home yet. She is as large as I am.

[13]     We had a meeting here yesterday, and Florind Miller was here. She is as large as Grace [Robinson].

[14]     Well, Miriam, I can't think of anything more to write. I wish you much joy and a long and happy life and plenty as long as you live. Mollie, don't let your man read this letter for nothing in the world. He would think that I was an awful girl. Don't let him see it.

[15]     I remain, as ever, your friend. Write and tell me what trade your man follows and how you like keeping house. Oh, how I wish I could step in and see you keeping house! I know that I should laugh and expect that you would laugh at me if I was married and keeping house.

[16]     Mollie, I bought me a saddle last summer. I wish you was here, and we could take a horseback ride.

         E. M. Morey  I will send you some pieces of my new dresses.

## ❧ Letter #80

After she returns from visiting Mollie, Sallie Bonney is sick, so her husband Joe must write this letter. In Joe's colorful language, a person who has died has "gone up" (to heaven).

LaGrange, Mo.            June 23, 1867

Dear Cousin Mollie,

[1]      Sallie [Bonney] says that she will whip me like the devil if I don't write you a few lines to let you know that she is not gone up yet. So I reckon I shall have to do it. She was not well for some time after she got home, but she is all right now, I think, for she can scold a blue streak. She has got Fanny staying with her.

[2]      Jack and Belle [Johnson] are staying here at present. They are a-going to Wisconsin before long.

[3]      I can't think of much to write at present. But I think I will come down to help you harvest. Don't you think that I would make a good hand in the harvest field?

[4]      Uncle Dave [Smith] has been sick but is better at present. The balance of the folks are all well. It is pretty hot weather here. I have not heard from any of the relatives for some time, but I thought that I would write to Grace [Robinson] soon. The children are all well at present.

[5]      Write soon as you get this and let us know how you are all a-getting along. This is all that I think of at present. Write as you get this and let us hear from you. Tell George [McNutt] to come up and see us.

From your cousins,
J. E. and S. A. Bonney

## ❦ Letter #81

The next plaintive letter from Emma Johnson is the last one that survives from her for twenty-five years [See Letter #108]. She is working in West Quincy, Missouri, where the land is not as protected by bluffs as it is just across the Mississippi River in Quincy, Illinois, so high water is a problem.

Worse than living in the water is being an old maid. However, four months after this letter is written and less than a year after Mollie's marriage, Emma is wed, on November 5, to John Coulten in LaGrange, Missouri. They move to Shenandoah, Iowa, and by the fall of 1868 she is a mother [See #84, par. 3].

West Quincy, [Mo.]               July 7, 1867

Dear Mollie,

[1]      I, at last, find time to write to you. I received your letter just as I was leaving Farmington [Ill.] I have thought very much since I have been here that I would see you, but have not had a chance to see you, so I will give up and write to you.

[2]      Mollie, I will give up. All the girls is married but me. I will be the old maid of the Johnson family.

[3]      I have not been to LaGrange since May. I am at T. J. Loftiss [Loftus?] at West Quincy.

[4]      The river is very high now. I am tired of living in the water, and if I can't get another place, I will start to old Farmington in September, but if you can get me a good place to work out where you are, I will not go to Farmington this winter.

[5]      You know I have worked a great deal from home and can do almost any kind of work. My wrist has troubled me a great deal but is better now.

[6]      I suppose you have heard that Lizzy Bozarth is dead. She died four weeks ago of consumption.

[7]      Mollie, when I wrote to you last, I wrote to Mollie Works. Now it is Mollie McNutt. I wish you much happiness and pleasure.

[8] I will look for an answer to this. Till I hear from you, I think this summer will be very sickly, or rather this fall. Write soon. I will have to close.

Remember me as a friend,
Emma Johnson

## Letter #82

The unusual relationship that developed between Eunice Morey and her sister, Martha Ann (Morey) Truman, is explained clearly in Gracie Robinson's only letter of this year. Since 1861 when her husband William Henry Truman died, Martha Ann had been a widow with three children, living with her parents George and Sylvia Morey. There were attempts to find Martha Ann a husband [See Letter #22, par. 3], but not until Hyrum G. Hall arrived was she successful.

Hyrum Hall and his family had been followers of James Jesse Strang. Strang brought his followers to Beaver Island, Michigan, where he crowned himself king. Claiming to have a letter from the prophet, Joseph Smith, Jr., that made him the true successor of the Mormon Church, Strang, like members of the Reorganized Church of Jesus Christ of Latter Day Saints, opposed polygamy. Later, however, he began practicing it. Because of this radical change, many of his followers denounced him.

Ironically, Strang failed to name his own successor. After he was mortally wounded by a U. S. Coast Guardsman in a policing action, the Strangite sect dissolved.[1] Ex-Strangite Hyrum Hall, who had lost his wife in 1865, moved to Pleasant Plains, Iowa, with his three children. There he met the widow Martha Ann (Morey) Truman. Poor Martha Ann would die eight months to the day after her marriage, though it is not known whether she died of complications in childbirth.

Havens, Hyrum's son, was Eunice's young man. He was eighteen in 1867, five years younger than she. Mollie's George was only four years younger than Mollie. Eunice had held to her principles! [See Letters #39, par. 4 and #68, par. 3.] Lamentably, Eunice died a year and three months after she married.

Gracie's marriage prospects, too, are revealed in this letter. Family tradition has it that the young man was a doctor, but nothing else is known, possibly because Mollie did what Gracie asked her to do.

Gracie's way for Mollie to get to the Pleasant Plains area does not exactly match Amulek Boothe's: Gracie's is north and Amulek's south [See Letter #73, par. 9], but either would work. Like Amulek, she means railway "cars," not automobiles.

Pleasant Plains, Iowa          Sunday, August 25, 1867

Dear Mollie,

[1]     Feeling rather lonesome this evening, I concluded that the best thing I could do would be to answer your last kind missive which I duly received some time since, and I trust you will pardon my seeming negligence.

[2]     I know you would forgive me if you only knew the circumstances that have surrounded me since I last wrote you. I have written to only one person (excepting Pa [Ebenezer]) during that time.

[3]     David and Deborah [Morey] were here today—went home a short time ago. They are all well. Adam and Angeline [Dennis] were here in July with their little boy. They named him David Morey. I have not seen Amulek [Boothe] yet. He is talking of bringing his wife [Maryann] and son, Hiram, out this fall, but I think it rather doubtful about their coming.

[4]     Pa has been away nearly all summer, but came home yesterday morning. You may guess we were delighted to see him.

[5]     Eunice Morey was married last May to a boy by the name of Havens Hall, 18 years of age. His father [Hyrum] was a widower with three children, and so Martha Truman thought she would be Eunice's mother-in-law, and last Sunday she married Mr. Hall. So you see they are rather "mixed up." Eunice is living at home yet.

[6]     I attended a party last Saturday night. Did not get home till nearly 3 o'clock. Had a tolerable good time.

[7]     What has become of Perry [Works]? I have not heard from
        him since last winter. Tell him I will not like him if he don't
        come out here. It would only take him about two days to
        come here from LaGrange if he came by the way of Keokuk.
        The cars run to Chariton [Iowa], and the mail comes in
        every day out of Leon [Iowa], so he could come right
        through. I wish you would persuade Perry to come here,
        and you come with him. Tell Cousin George [McNutt] to
        come along, and if he cannot come, to let you come
        anyhow. And I will promise to send you back in a month or
        two, for fear if you did not go back, he might run away or
        do some other dreadful thing.

[8]     I promised to tell you my intended's name in this letter.
        Well, I would if I had any. When I last wrote you, I was
        engaged to be married to a young man whom I believed to
        be every way worthy of my affections, and I loved him
        devotedly, but I have since found that he was not as noble
        as I thought him to be. Oh, it was hard to believe and cost
        me more sorrow than I ever want to see again, but I am
        now free. He still suffers, and, I fear, will never be happy
        again while he lives, but as he said to me in his last letter,
        "He has no one to blame but himself." I have not replied to
        his last missive and, perhaps, never shall.

[9]     Now, Mollie, please never tell this to any one. There is
        hardly any person here that knows anything about it. I
        sometimes think I will never marry, as it seems as though I
        could not love another as I have loved him. But time alone
        will tell.

[10]    I mean to visit you as soon as I can. I want you to tell me if
        you are keeping house by yourself, or are you living with
        your husband's parents [James and Sara McNutt]?

[11]    Joseph [Bonney] has not written to me for a long time. I
        want you to give him a good scolding for me. You promised
        me your photograph after you were married, but I have not
        seen it yet. I will send you mine as soon as I can.

[12]    If you you come out here, I will play some for you. I took
        music lessons a while last winter. We have a melodian. I will
        not tell you how well I can perform, but leave you to judge
        for yourself when you hear me.

[13]    We have quite a number of apples and peaches now. The
        peaches are not quite ripe, but the apples are splendid.
        Come out and I will give you some.

[14]    Ma and Pa join me in best wishes to yourself and husband.
        Give Perry a good whipping when you see him. I would
        help you if I were there.

[15]    Now Mollie, please answer this soon, for I want to hear from
        you so much. I will endeavor to be more prompt in future.

        Affectionately your cousin,
        Gracie

[16]    I have a ring I want to send to [Bonney]. I would send it to
        you and then you could send it to her, but I am in hopes to
        hear from Joe soon. I got the ring for her some time ago but
        forgot to send it when I last wrote. Tell Cousin George to
        write to his "Western Cousin" if he pleases. Yours,

        Gracie

## ✤ Letter #83

The last letter to survive from 1867 is one from Joe Bonney filled
with news about births and near births. Mollie's firstborn had arrived
twelve days before, and it is this that prompts him to write,
commenting on how she "got along" with the delivery. She named
her boy, Irvin Perry, "Irvin" a McNutt family name and "Perry" for her
brother, who had sent her the money to come to Illinois.

Sallie's illness continues, and it is unclear whether she went with
Joe to the Fleck wedding or he is using the editorial "we" in his letter.
His use of the phrase "laid in" to mean "give birth" is unusual, too.

LaGrange, Mo.                    Sept. 8, 1867

Dear Cousins George and Mollie,

[1]     We take this opportunity of writing you a few lines. It is an answer to your letter. We had been very happy to hear from you for some time. We were glad to hear that Mollie got along so well.

[2]     Sallie [Bonney] would come down to see Mollie if she was able. She has not been able to go downtown for the past six weeks. We want Mollie to come down to see us as soon as she can.

[3]     We were at a wedding last night. Molly Coulson was married to Mr. Samuel Fleck, our city barber. Some of the family was opposed to it. They had the driest wedding that I ever saw.

[4]     Tine's wife [Kate Alford] hain't laid in yet, but will soon. Tom Coulson's folks are all well. Alfa [Nancy Alford]'s folks are all well. Mrs. [Catharine] Oyster has gone to see her folks in Illinois. Jack and Belle [Johnson] have gone to Wisconsin, but I don't think they like it very much there. Sis [Emma Coulten] is still staying with us. Ret[tie Coulson]'s folks are getting along as well as could be expected.

[5]     This is all that I think of at present. I got a letter from Uncle [Ebenezer Robinson] not long ago. He was in Ohio then.

[6]     Tell Perry [Works] to come up and see the folks. George, we want you to come up soon. Come with Mollie. This is all this time. Write soon as you get this.

From your cousins,
J. E. and S. A. Bonney

NOTES

1. D. Michael Quinn, *The King Strang Story,* (New York City: MacMillan Co., 1978), pp. 122 & 125.

**Myrtle Dell McNutt** *(1882-1970), at five years of age. As Mollie hoped for a girl, after giving birth to four boys, so her cousin, Grace (Robinson) Gurley, hoped to give birth to a boy after four girls. Both were rewarded—first Grace, with Zenas Robinson Gurley in 1881, and then Mollie with Myrtle Dell nearly a year later.*

*Three Morey girls whose births are mentioned in the letters Mollie receives. From left,* **Elsie Louella, Evangeline Estelle** *(the youngest) and* **Eliza Miriam.** *All daughters of Mollie's cousin Deborah Ann (Rockwell) and David Butterfield Morey, they were invaluable help to their mother after she became paralyzed.*

Photo courtesy of Nancy Gerlock

# CHILDREN AND INHERITANCE
# 1868 & 1869

### ❦ Letter #84

The only letter which survives from 1868 is one from the Bonneys that reports events concerning Tine and Kate (Crandelle) Alford and the visit of Emma (Johnson) Coulten to LaGrange.

Mollie and George lived for a time in LaGrange, but it is obvious from this letter that they do not know what has been happening in the Bonneys' hometown since late summer.

The prominent Oyster family owned much LaGrange property, including its first sawmill. For a time, D. K. Oyster was Joe Bonney's employer. As Joe explains, the Oysters did much for LaGrange, even though the heyday of the Mississippi steamboat town was passing. Railroads carried more and more of the goods formerly hauled on the river.

The first mention of Perry Works in New Carrollton, Missouri, is in this letter. For what happens to him there, see Letter #87.

The body of this letter is in Joe Bonney's hand, but the postscript is in Sallie's, the last writing of hers that survives.

LaGrange, Mo.                    Oct 10th, 1868

Dear Cousins,

[1]     We take the present opportunity of writing you in answer to your letter of Oct. 8th. We were glad to hear from you but that it was a long time a-coming. Guess you forgot that we lived over this way.

[2]       We are all well at present & hope these few lines will find you the same.

[3]       We have got lots of kinfolks. Sis [Emma Coulten] has got a baby. They call it Ora Edward. Belle [Johnson] has got a gal. They call it Iola Belle. Mort [Johnson] has got married [and] is a-living in West Quincy. Molly Coulson has got a babe. They call it Luellor [?] Clyde. This is all of the babies at present. We'll have some more after a while.

[4]       We are a-going to have a fair here this week. It commences Oct. 13th. Come up and go to the fair. It is a little below [David K.] Oyster's house. They are a-going to have a fine time.

[5]       Tine Alford's wife [is] dead. She [Kate] died about the 14th of Sept. with the inflammation on the bowels. The rest of the folks are all well. I have not heard from Uncle [Ebenezer Robinson]'s folks for a long time.

[6]       We are a-building a railroad from Quincy through LaGrange. They are at work on it now. D. K. Oyster has the contract of grading the road sixty miles.

[7]       Mollie, we are a-coming down to see you this winter, to see you this winter and stay six months. We have got an old blind horse that goes on three legs. We will get some poles and make us a sleigh, then look out the first snow. We are a-coming.

[8]       We got a letter from Perry [Works] some time since. He [is in] Carroll County, New Carrollton.

[9]       Don't think of anything else if you don't write & tell us all about it. Tell George [McNutt] to have a-plenty of straw for my old hoss when he comes.

[10]       This is all at present. Guess you don't want any more this time. Write soon as you get this & let us know how you is.

From your Most Affectionate,
Sallie Bonney & Jo Bonney

[11]    Mrs. [Nancy] Alford has Tine's baby [Robert]. They all take
        Kate's death very hard. She died sudden. She sat up
        Saturday and died Monday night. Write soon.

## ✠ Letter #85

Another letter from Phebe Louisa Booth survives from 1869. By
now she is twenty-one, and unlike her sister Olive, she is unmarried.
Grace Robertson, another of Mollie's friends from Iowa, did not write
in Phebe's letter as Phebe thought she would.

[Pleasant Plains, Ia.]              March 20, A.D. 1869

Dearest Friend,

[1]     I once more strive to answer your thrice and welcome letter
        that came to hand a few days ago. I was very much pleased
        to hear from you once more and to hear that you was well. I
        would like to see you, but you are so far off that we will
        [not] get to see each other very soon, for we are so far
        apart.

[2]     We used to have a great deal of fun together, but we don't
        see much fun together now. It has been a great while since
        we saw each other. I have almost forgotten how you used to
        look.

[3]     I have been a-going to school this winter, but our school
        was out today. I wish that you had been here to went with
        us. We had a great deal of sport.

[4]     Grace Robertson is here tonight. She came here last Friday
        and she is a-going to stay here till Sunday. Olive [Clark] and
        Robert [Booth] has gone to meeting tonight over to Mr.
        [John] Clark's schoolhouse tonight to meeting.

[5]     Mollie, I would like to have your picture very much. I would
        like to see how you look nowadays. It has been a great while
        since I saw you, and if you will send me your likeness, I will
        send you mine in return. I would like to have your picture
        very much.

[6]     I don't expect you would know me if you would see me, for
        I have growed homely since you went away from here, and
        I am a great deal larger, too. I am half as taller than Olive is.

[7]     Well, Mollie, as I have nothing of importance to write, guess
        that I had better bring my letter to a close. I will try and
        write more next time, for Grace [Robertson] is a-going to
        put a little in, and so I can't write any more. So goodbye.
        Write soon.

        From Phebe L. Booth

## 🌺 Letter #86

Though Joe Bonney signs this 1869 letter with both his and Sallie's
name, he alone wrote it. Sallie's illness is not known, but for her
sister Emma to visit her from Shenandoah, Iowa, it must have been
serious. Two years later, on July 23, 1871, Sallie died.

Mollie and George are now living in the loghouse on the McNutt
farm, and George is helping his sixty-seven-year-old father, James,
run the farm.

LaGrange, Mo.                          June 27, 1869
Sunday afternoon

Dear Cousins,

[1]     We take the opportunity of writing you a few lines to let you
        know how we are getting along. Sallie [Bonney] is sick, has
        been sick for about four months, is not able to set up an
        hour at a time. She thinks it is hard to have to lie in bed so
        long.

[2]     Sis [Emma Coulten] is here to see Sallie. We would like to
        have you come and see us while Sis is here. We see hard
        times this year.

[3]     I have not much time to write and can't think of what to
        write, but if you will come over here, I will tell you what I
        don't write.

[4]     Sis says be sure and come while she is here. She says that
        she ain't a-going to stay but two weeks.

[5]     The acquaintances here are all well. Henry Coulson is
        married and lives in Tom Coulson's house. Mrs. [Nancy]
        Alford's folks are all well.

[6]     This is all at present. If you can't come, write soon. This
        from your most affectionate cousins,

        J. E. and S. A. Bonney

        to George and Mollie McNutt

[7]     P.S. Sis says she can beat you showing boys. She wants to
        see your boy [Irvin McNutt]. Sis sends her love to you both.
        All at present.

## ✿ Letter #87

From what Gracie writes at the beginning of the next letter in this
year, Mollie has not written often to her since marrying George, and
Mollie's brother, Perry, has not written at all. Who Perry married is
not known, though it was a woman from Bogard, Missouri, near
where he had moved [See Letter #84, par. 8]. The marriage did not
last. The couple mutually agreed to part without formally divorcing.
As Gracie reports, something similar has happened to one of Mollie's
schoolmates.

Ebenezer Robinson's attempt to establish the State Line Railroad
failed, and he did sell out as Gracie hopes he will, returning as much

of the money to investors as he could.

It is generally believed that Gracie's "my ——" (meaning her beau) is Zenas Hovey Gurley, Jr. [See Letter #96, par. 6].

Pleasant Plains, Iowa             August 1, 1869

Dear Mollie,

[1]     It is with pleasure that I seat myself this afternoon to answer your kind missive which I received some weeks since. You certainly do deserve a scolding for being so negligent, but I suppose when people get married they almost forget everyone but their "darling," so I will try to excuse you on the plea of family cares and having your mind and attention taken up with husband and child [Irvin Perry]. Glad that you did not forget us entirely.

[2]     It has been very rainy this season until a few weeks past. I expect the corn will not be as good as usual. The wheat is about half a crop.

[3]     I was rather surprised to hear that Perry [Works] was married, but I suppose it is no more than we should have expected. He has not written to me for a long time and I suppose never will now. Tell him I am going to be married some of these times and shan't ask him to my wedding.

[4]     The letter you wrote to George Rockwell was received. He got your letter at the office and opened it and took out the picture and put [it] in his pocket, and the letter he lost on his way home. If you want me to, I will get your picture and send to you the next time I write, as George and Helen [Rockwell] are so negligent that I am afraid they won't write. George said he expected I had better get the picture, but I am going to try and have them write if I can get them at it.

[5]     Pa [Ebenezer] has not been at home since about the first of May. We are looking for him all the time now. I hope he will sell out the R. R. and come home and stay as he is calculating to do.

[6]     Ma [Angeline]'s health is quite poor this summer, but I am
        in hopes it will be better when the weather gets cooler. I will
        send you Ma's picture and mine in this letter. Write and tell
        me what you think of them. I do not think mine is a very
        good one, but you know it is not often we can get good
        ones here. We had ours taken Friday. I wish you would send
        me yours and the baby's the next time you write.

[7]     Martha Delap's (Cowles) husband has left her. They had sold
        their farm & she came home in a visit, and while she was
        here, her husband left & took the money they had received
        for the farm. She did not know he was going, as he had no
        cause to leave her, and I suppose they never quarrelled in
        the world! She has heard that he is in Wisconsin where he
        came from.

[8]     By the way, Cousin Angie Dennis has another daughter
        named Elizabeth Ida.

[9]     I must write another letter tonight to my _____ [beau]; your
        future cousin, you know. So goodbye, and believe me as
        ever.

        Your Cousin,
        Gracie

Some events in 1869 affected Mollie deeply. After the last letter in
this year, on August 29, Eunice (Morey) Hall died of consumption,
and on September 12, 1869, James Alexander McNutt died, leaving
the McNutt farm to his only surviving son, Mollie's husband George.
Mollie and George moved out of the loghouse and into the main
farmhouse, their home for the rest of their lives.

**Zenas Hovey Gurley, Jr.** *(1842-1912) and* **Grace (Robinson) Gurley**
*(1849-1932) taken most likely when they were married, 2 April 1872.*
*Mollie's cousin Grace was the Robinsons' only daughter, while Zenas was*
*the son of the man who ordained Joseph Smith III president of the RLDS.*
*The Gurleys bought the Ebenezer Robinson farm in Pleasant Plains after*
*Grace's father moved to Davis City, Iowa, and remarried; however, they*
*spent most of their early married life in Lamoni raising 10 children, one*
*of whom—Julia—married Mollie's son, James Ernest McNutt. Besides trips*
*to Utah to convert Brighamites (LDS) into Josephites (RLDS), Zenas lobbied*
*the 47th Congress for passage of the Edmunds Act that outlawed polygamy.*
*Though he, Gracie, and other relatives eventually broke with RLDS, he*
*continued to preach independently while working as a deputy prison*
*warden and an Iowa state legislator.*

# OLD FRIENDS, SETTLED LIVES

# 1870s

## ✿ Letter #88

The year 1870 was significant for Mollie and George, though only one letter survives from it, a chatty one from Adam and Angeline Dennis' oldest son, Frank. When he was twelve, he raced Mollie up the stairs and wished he could write [See Letter #24, par. 18]. Now he is twenty years old, quoting corn prices, building fence around his own acreage, and going to church meetings for other than religious reasons.

As Mollie became more settled as a housewife and mother on the McNutt farm (her second child, James Ernest, was born on October 24, 1870), she obviously continued to keep in touch with many of her friends and relatives in Iowa.

    Eagleville, Mo.               April the 16, 1870

    Well Cousin,

[1]    I received your letter a few minutes ago and was glad to hear from you. We are all well at present. I hain't saw Amulek [Boothe] for a good while. They was all well the last time I heard from them. I hain't saw Aunt [Angeline Robinson] for a week. They was well.

[2]    Well, Mollie, it has snowed today and covered the ground. We have got us white, and it's saved.

[3]     Pa [Adam Dennis] has gone with my brother-in-law [David Daily] to Nebraska to sell a span of mules. I am going to start to go to Poweshiek Co. [Ia.] in a few days to take my cousin home.

[4]     You said there was lots of pretty girls out there. If you want to see girls, just come out to meeting tomorrow, as it is Sunday. There is more than you could shake a stick at in a week. I have lots of fun out here, you bet. There's Sunday school going on now.

[5]     Well, Mollie, tomorrow is Easter. I wish I was down there to help you eat eggs. I'll bet I could eat one if I would try right hard.

[6]     How does corn and wheat sell out there? Corn sells from 75 to 100 1/2 cts.

[7]     Well, Mollie, I have been building fence today, and my fingers is so stiff that I can't hardly write.

[8]     Well, Mollie, you said you only weighed 75 pounds. I can beat that a little. I weighed 100 and 35 the last time I was weighed.

[9]     It's getting late. They have all gone to bed but me. So, good evening for this time. Call again. Excuse poor spelling and bad writing.

[10]    Well, Mollie, this is Sabbath evening. I have just came from meeting. We had lots of fun, you bet. I saw lots of pretty girls.

[11]    You said you had an album. I have a new one to fill. You won't forget to send me yours.

[12]    I hain't seen Grace [Robinson] for a long time.

[13]    Well, Mollie, Pa gave me 30 acres of land. He said I might
        have all that [I] could raise for 5 years for fencing and
        breaking it. I guess that I will build me a little house and
        keep "bach," and then you must come and see me.

[14]    You said you wanted my photograph. I will send you one. It
        ain't [a] very good one, but it is [the] best one I have.

[15]    Excuse poor spelling and bad writing.Please write soon as
        [you] get this. This is [your cousin,]

        [Frank] Dennis to M[ollie McNutt] Howdy

## ✿ Letter #89

George Rockwell's version of what happened to Mollie's lost letter
is somewhat different in this 1871 letter than Gracie's version two
years earlier [See Letter #87, par. 4]. Because he has not written Mollie
in such a long time, George is careful about identifying exactly what
has happened. This makes it easier to understand the events in the
lives of people mentioned in earlier letters.

Eunice Rockwell is one of George and Helen's children. Mollie had
returned her photograph with the "lost" letter just as George Rockwell
was returning Mollie's photograph in this letter.

        Nine Eagles, [Iowa]              August 14, 1871

        Cousin Miriam,

[1]     I have once more attempted to write to you. It is so long
        since I have written a letter that I have almost forgotten
        how to commence one.

[2]     I received a letter from you near one year ago. I was at the
        Plains & took it from the office & opened it & took Eunice
        [Rockwell]'s likeness from it & read enough to find out who
        it was from & then placed it in the envelope & started for
        home, but went into the woods to get some lime & sand in
        which I lost your letter. I went & looked for it, but could not
        find it. So you see that I never knew the contents of your

letter, & I believe this is the second letter I have written since that time.

[3]      We are all well as usual. The health of our community is very good this season.

[4]      Deborah & David [Morey] & the children are well. Father [George] Morey & the old lady [Sylvia Morey] are well. They have Martha [Truman Hall]'s three children living with them & Havens Hall. Lisabeth Crandel is working for them.

[5]      Geo. Keown is living on the road running north from the corners, west of Father [Morey]'s house. They have got a girl two weeks old yesterday. Sam Keown is at work up north. David is at home.

[6]      Uncle [Ebenezer Robinson] is at home now, but talks of going to Burlington soon. Grace [Robinson] is not married yet—no prospect of being [so]. She is a good girl & is liked by all. Laskey Alden is still single & living at home.

[7]      [Alfred] Moffet's people are all well. Irene is not married yet, nor no hopes.

[8]      Martha Cowles [Delap] is at work in Clark's factory. She and her husband will never live together again.

[9]      I think Louisa Booth is living at home this summer, still single. Horace Booth is west, to work on the railroad. Robert [Booth] lives near his father-in-law's, four miles northwest of Leon. John [Booth] is living with his folks.

[10]      I suppose Grace has kept you posted on most of the changes in our town. I live on the old [George] Hinkle place. Our crops are very good. My family consists of five: Adra [Adrianna]; [Eunice] Alderilla, she was five years [old] the sixth of this month; & George Watson, who will be two years old next October.

[11]    I heard from Ad [Dennis]'s last week.They are well, with the exception of little Grace, who has had her leg taken off below the knee. It was first caused by a sprain in getting the cows.

[12]    Doc Clark has just come from Eagleville where he has been living the past year. He is as poor in purse as a man can well be.

[13]    Miriam, you will please pardon me for my neglect in the past, & I will endeavor to be more punctual hereafter. I will send your likeness in this, but I wish you would send your family likeness in some form, as I want all my relatives' pictures to frame. I will send ours to you as soon as I can.

Write soon,

George Rockwell

## ❧ Letter #90

From 1872 to 1912 are ten letters from Amulek Boothe that poignantly reveal a passage of time in both his and Mollie's life. Through his aging eyes come reports about Pleasant Plains and Eagleville, and these reports are mirrors of events affecting her own life in Payson, Illinois. The three letters in 1872 are all from Amulek, and they are written after Mollie and George visited Pleasant Plains and Eagleville sometime in late spring of that year. It is apparent from this letter and others that Amulek and George had much in common, except George is readier to try new endeavors. That is what is behind Amulek's reference to the oxen, animals commonly used in an earlier day to move a family west after pulling up stakes.

Mollie visited Carrollton, Missouri, whether because her brother Perry was nearby or for some other reason is not known.

Eaglesville, [Mo.]                    June 21st, 1872

Respected Cousin,

[1]     I received your letter some time ago, and it found us all
        well. Hoping this may find you and family well.

[2]     We are all well except myself. Last Monday I mashed my
        foot very bad, and I can scarcely hobble around.

[3]     I have got in a tolerable fair crop, and it looks very well. I
        have got some plowed over twice. My first planting is
        almost knee high. My wheat looks very well. It has been
        very wet here since you left till about 2 weeks back. It has
        been very dry, and I expect it will continue so.

[4]     I have built me a crib 24 feet long, since you was here, that
        will hold about nine hundred bushels of corn, and I am
        going to husk mine all out. I have got some two hundred
        bushels husked now.

[5]     Well, George, you ask us to come down this fall to see you.
        If I can, I would like to. I don't know yet. You are closer than
        I expected, and I hope you will visit us again.

[6]     I wish you were here to spend the Fourth with us. They are
        going to have a big time this year. We can raise more
        people here on the 4th of July than they can anywhere.

[7]     I have not been up to Ad [Dennis]'s since I saw you last. I
        guess they are well. Ad had a very serious time with his
        hand that was sore when you was here. I heard he was
        about to sell out. I don't know whether he will or not.

[8]     If you leave there anyways soon, write and let me know, for
        fear that I might happen to come down. You need not look
        for us, for fear we don't come. You come, and fetch them
        oxen this fall, and let's go!

[9]     I can't think of anything else to interest you, so I will close. Give my love to Mary and the children. So, good night.

from Amulek Boothe
to George I. McNutt

## ✿ Letter #91

Amulek's second letter in this year explains his financial situation and the difference in prices between Illinois and north central Missouri.

Adam Dennis has long returned from the war, and many of his children are grown and married, as Amulek notes. Adam, himself, has gotten a job with a relative in Powschiek County, Iowa, where he is receiving remarkable pay.

One of Charles Worden's sisters, Ursula (Worden) Wolford was the fifth child of Mollie's aunt Jerusha (Works) Worden of Throopsville, New York. Ursula and her husband had moved to Cameron, Illinois [See Letter #93, par. 11] southwest of Galesburg, and not far off the east-west route from Pleasant Plains that passed through Keokuk, Iowa. As Amulek reports, visiting their niece would not be difficult for the Robinsons, who planned an extensive trip east to visit Angeline's sister, Jerusha.

The Robinsons' only daughter, Grace, was married in April of this year to Zenas Hovey Gurley, Jr., whose father was one of those who had ordained Joseph Smith III as leader of the Reorganized Church. The Gurleys had moved to Sandwich, Illinois, from Blanchardville, Wisconsin. They, like the Halls, rejected the Strangite version of Mormonism when "King" James Jesse Strang started practicing polygamy. Young Zenas often passed through the Pleasant Plains area on Mormon missions, and Gracie Robinson sometimes paid special attention to these young missionaries [See Letter #15, par. 4]. After their wedding, Zenas and Grace lived near "The Colony," a settlement that eventually became Lamoni, Iowa, west of Pleasant Plains.

Eaglesville, Mo.                    October the 5, 1872

Dear Cousin or Cousins,

[1]     With respect I sit down to answer your letter which came to me this week. It found us well, hoping the same with you. I

should have written before, but I have neglected it, [not] being through with my work. Today is raining and I get to stay indoors. I have been plowing, cutting corn, and working in cane for some time and am not done yet.

[2]      You say you had over 8 hundred dollars worth of wheat while I had 15 dollars worth. Wheat was not good this year. Oats and corn is good—only worth 15 cts. I will raise as much as I did last year.

[3]      We thought of visiting you this fall, but as you have gone back to Ill. we will have to give it up this fall. We are not prepared to go so far.

[4]      You spoke of me coming down there and buying a place. I could not sell my place for enough to pay over one third of what I would have to pay for that, and I could not make the rest for a long time. It would cause me to live very hard and work very hard and close to make the pay, even if I were to get it on time, although I would like to live close to you, if it were so that I could. We will come and see you as soon as we can.

[5]      Well, Frank Dennis told me that Uncle Eb and Aunt Angeline [Robinson] was going to visit Cousin Ursula [Wolford], then back to New York to see Aunt Jerusha Worden. Likely they will come that way and call to see you.

[6]      Ad [Dennis]'s folks is well, what is at home. He himself has been gone ever since about the Fourth of July to work. He is about a 150 miles from here in Iowa. He is getting a 150 cts per day now, and, through harvest, he got 200 per day.

[7]      Tell Mary that I have not wrote an answer to her letter yet while [she was] in Carrollton, but this will do for both till you will want to hear from me again. The next will be hers. She may think I am partial in answering your letter first, as she wrote long ago, but no partial thought have I towards either.

[8]     Well, I don't think of anything more that will interest you, so I will close by wishing you luck and success. Write when you can, and I will do the same. No more. Farewell from,

A[mulek] Boothe

to George McNutt and wife

## 🌺 Letter #92

Maryann (Gilliland) Boothe, Amulek's wife, writes a short note in his last letter of 1872, acknowledging Mollie's compliment on the Boothe hospitality while the McNutts visited the area. George and Mollie stayed both in Eagleville and Pleasant Plains on their 1872 visit. If Maryann appears rushed, she is to be excused; she was the mother of four at the time, aged five, four, three, and one.

What Amulek means by a Tom and Jerry cough is revealed in the next letter, #93.

Eaglesville, [Missouri]          Dec. 22, 1872

Dear Cousin,

[1]     I received your letter the day before yesterday and was glad to hear from you...[unreadable portion]... will fare well, except this Tom and Jerry cough that is raging that George was speaking of in his letter. It is well scattered here. My horses is just taking it. I have not heard of only one dying from it, yet.

[2]     Dave Daily was here today, and he read your letter. They are well, and so is Ad [Dennis]'s folks. We are all trying to do the best we can.

[3]     Christmas is drawing nigh, and I wish you and George and Joseph [Bonney] was here. I would get a great big turkey and have a jolly old turkey roast.

[4]     I don't hear from Aunt [Angeline Robinson]'s folks as often as you do. Uncle [Ebenezer] has been here once by himself and stayed about 15 minutes.

[5]     Since you were here, Maryann and I was to Dave Morey's
        this fall. George Rockwell had not got home then. I stopped
        at Olive Clark's last spring, as I came home from Dave
        Morey's, and she was surprised to think you had gone so
        clost by and she did not get to see you. She wanted to see
        you the worst kind.

[6]     Mary is going to write, so I will close by wishing you a
        Merry Christmas and a Happy New Year.

_____

[7]     [Unreadable]...I would have written before, but I am such a
        poor writer I was ashamed to write. However, I will do the
        best I can.

[8]     I would like to see you all the best kind, if I could. I was glad
        to hear you say you felt welcome while you was at our
        house, for I know you was, and I would [have] like[d] to
        have [had] you stay longer with us.

[9]     You said you would send your photographs to us if we
        wanted them. We would like to have them so well, and we
        will send you ours, soon as we get them taken.

[10]    Well, Mary, my washwater is hot, and I will have to quit
        writing for this time. I guess you will say, "I don't want Mary
        to write any more, if this is the best she can do." So
        goodbye for this time. Write soon.

        from Mary Booth[e]

_____

[11]    You wanted to know if there was any express here. There is
        no express office nearer than Princeton. There is a hack
        comes from the south. The rest of the mail comes on
        horseback.

[12]    You will see this was not mailed as soon as it was wrote on
        account of neglect sending it to the office.

[13]     Tell George to hurry on with his oxen. I am waiting.

from your sincere cousin,
Amulek Boothe

Write when you will. Give my respects to Joseph.

## ✤ Letter #93

Amulek's letter in 1873 is written a month before Mollie gave birth to her third son, Zenas Virgil Sylvester (called "Dick"). The McNutts are now firmly established in the McNutt farmhouse. George's mother, Sarah Bell (Case) McNutt, lives with them, but all George's sisters are married.

Amulek reveals some of the snobbery that the Robinsons were accused of. Authenticity and authority were important to Ebenezer Robinson, as they were to many who had come out of the chaos that flooded Nauvoo after the death of Joseph Smith. Whether Ebenezer claimed to be of the "Upper 10," as Amulek accuses him, is not known, but obviously Amulek feels slighted and so humorously places himself higher in the hierarchy.

Relations between Amulek and his youngest brother Hyrum who lived in Grantsville, Utah, were easing after many, many years. Amulek's ploy regarding Hyrum eventually works [See Letter #110, par. 7].

Eaglesville, Mo.                    March the 25th, 1873

Dear Cousin,

[1]     As it is too blustery to work, I will write you a few lines. We are well at the present, hoping the same with you. We have had some fine weather this spring, and the most of [the] farmers have got their wheat sown, and today is as blustery a day as we have had this winter. The snow is flying so at times that you could not see a neighbor's house. We are trying to get along the best we can, but that is hard enough.

[2]    You say you have got back home where you expect to
       remain. If so, I fear you will not come to see us anymore. I
       am glad you are at your old farm, unless you were closer to
       us. That I would like better.

[3]    Mary and George, I would like to live neighbor to you if it
       were so I could, but as I can't, I will try and arrange matters
       so we can come this fall and make you a long visit—stay all
       night, anyhow.

[4]    I received a letter from Hyrum Boothe. He is getting along
       real well, far better than I am.

[5]    Ad [Dennis]'s family was well the last I heard. I have not
       seen Ad to speak to him but once since July. He has rented
       out his farm, and is teaming—and Frank, too. Bub is
       working out. Dave Daily is taking photographs in Eagleville.

[6]    Uncle [Ebenezer Robinson]'s folks I have not heard from
       since I last wrote to you. They don't come near me, for
       why? I can't tell—unless it [is] because I am Number 1
       instead of Upper 10.

[7]    Tell George we expect to have a railroad through Eagleville
       this summer. Then times will be livelier than now.

[8]    Hogs is worth 325, and corn the same old price, 20 cts.
       Wheat is worth 140 cts pr bushel. Eggs is 8 cts, butter is
       worth 12 ½ cts.

[9]    Tell George that our horses have all had that 'tarnel
       whooping cough in this country that he spoke of in his
       letter, and some cattle has had it, and some persons in town
       had it, so I heard. I don't think I had it. If I did, I did not
       know it. I have only heard of one horse dying from it.

[10]   Where is Perry [Works]? Is he married yet? I don't hear
       anything about him. He ought to come out here and see his
       cousins, aunts, and uncles.

[11]     I guess Ursula [Wolford] still lives at Cameron yet.

[12]     Hyrum says if I don't come out to see him before long, that
         he will come out here. So I reckon I had better not go, or he
         will never come.

[13]     Well, Mary, I have wrote all that I know and more, too, so I
         had better quit. It is so seldom that I write that I can hardly
         compose a letter anymore. I have wrote more to you and
         George since you were here than anyone else.

[14]     Give my respects to Perry, George, and the children. So, no
         more this time, and a little more next time.

         From your Cousin,
         Amulek Boothe          Write again, and tell George to write.

## ✿ Letter #94

Amulek never visited the McNutts, though he is careful to explain
why, as he does in the last letter of 1873. As for his news: Gracie and
Zenas Gurley's first child, Angie Marguerite, is nine months old;
Adrianna Rockwell, George's child that he and Helen raised, married
Bennett Scott during this summer when Adria was nineteen; and for
further adventures of Annett (Dennis) Daily, Amulek's niece, in
Kansas, see Letter #96, par. 7.

         Eagleville, [Mo.]              Sabbath, Sept. 14, 1873

         Dear Cousin,

[1]      I take my seat to write you a few lines. We are all well at this
         time, hoping this will find you and family well.

[2]      We expected to come to visit you this fall, but I am behind
         so with my work that I can't get off before cold weather. So,
         I guess we will have to give up coming. Deborah [Morey]
         intended to come with us. My potatoes is to do, and cane
         to work up, and plowing to do—with much other work, so
         you will please excuse me. I would gladly come if it were so
         I could without losing at home.

[3]       Crops is only tolerable, it being so dry. I had so little wheat that I will say nothing about it. There is enough raised to supply the country. Corn is light and chaffy. Corn is 25 cts.

[4]       I will have 20 head of hogs to fatten, and water scarce. I have dug two wells and lost them both. So, I guess I will haul water for them. I have 52 head of hogs now.

[5]       Ad [Dennis]'s folks lost one child last week. It was 3 or 4 weeks old. The rest was well. Grace [Gurley]'s folks are well and so are Dave Morey's. Adria Rockwell is married one of Al Scott's boys. Dave Daily and Annett started last Tuesday to Kansas. They have sold out and moved.

[6]       I know of nothing more to write that will interest you, so I will close. Write when you will, and give my love to Perry [Works] and all.

Your Cousin,
Amulek Boothe

## ✿ Letter #95

As he becomes more and more taken up with family and farm, Amulek travels less. Even so short a distance to Pleasant Plains is a bother, yet he is surprised that his aunt, Angeline Robinson, who was often ill, has not seen his children. He has one boy, Hiram Ebenezer, and three girls: Olive Jane, Louisa, Viola Elizabeth, and Nora ("Norey") Angeline, named for his aunt and sister.

Eaglesville, Mo.            May 9th, 1874

Dear Cousin,

[1]       As I have not had any letter from you for a long time, I thought I would write and see if I could get one. This is 2nd time I have wrote since hearing from you. I expect you are like me—since you have got married, you don't think so much of writing.

[2]　　To conclude my letter, this leaves us all well, except myself. I have had the toothache for several days very bad. I hardly slept any last night.

[3]　　Ad [Dennis]'s folks are usually well, and so is Net [Daily]'s family. I have not had any letters for almost 12 months from no one, so you can guess that I write.

[4]　　I have never been out to Pleasant Plains yet to see the folks, but I am going as soon as I get my corn in. I am going to stay a week. I have got 5 acres to plant yet. I have got 11 acres planted. It has been raining here for 2 days, and it is so cold that I am afraid the corn will rot that is planted. The season has been very cold. The late frosts has killed all the early apples.

[5]　　There has been considerable improvements made since you were here. I don't think you would know the place. There has been several frame houses and large barns built, and as nice a schoolhouse as there is anywhere around. The schoolhouse is close enough to us to hear them sing and preach when it is still. It stands in sight of our door. There is meeting today there, and Maryann [Boothe] has gone while I write. There is Sabbath school there this spring and summer, and we had singing and writing school last winter.

[6]　　We will soon have 2 children large enough to go to school. We have 3 children: Olive, Louisa, and Hyram. We sent the two oldest children's picture to Aunt Angeline [Robinson], as she has never seen the children yet.

[7]　　When you write, tell me what has become of Perry [Works].

[8]　　I must write to Joseph [Bonney] soon, for he wrote the last letter. I would like to see him and you all. I think you might come up here to see the folks and eat peaches, and I can talk at you, for I have to work so hard that I can't hardly write. You can tell that by the straight marks I make.

[9]     Well, Mary, do you grow old as fast as I do since you were
        married? As time passes swiftly along, we must conclude
        that we are getting old, although it seems but a few days
        since we were young together, but now we will soon be old
        folks. I feel as young as ever, but don't look so.

[10]    Well, I will close for this time. So remember as your Cousin,

        A[mulek] Boothe

        To Miriam McNutt

## 🌸 Letter #96

Despite its salutation, Amulek's 1875 letter is directed to George
McNutt more than to Mollie, while Maryann Boothe writes Mollie the
postscript. What Amulek means by his cows "playing off" on him is
not clear, though it apparently is a rejection phrase taken from
courting and may mean his cows refused to give milk.

As Amulek reports, Grace's husband, Zenas Gurley, is away on a
mission for the RLDS, preaching against polygamy (or "spiritual
wifery") to the Brighamites in Utah territory. His arguments must have
hit a nerve because one night while he was away from his Utah
boardinghouse, according to his landlady, two men leading a
riderless horse asked about him. The riderless horse was meant for
his dead body.

        Eagleville, [Mo.]                    Apr. 1st, [18]75

        Dear Cousins,

[1]     I got your letter dated the 22. We was very glad to hear
        from [you], as it had been so long since we heard. Our
        family is tolerable well at this date, except colds.

[2]     The weather has been fine for some time, until yesterday. It
        rained, and last night it snowed. It is very muddy. No
        farming done yet, except a very few that has sown wheat.
        There was no snow here the day you wrote.

[3]     You have got wheat enough sown to bread your little family,
        I should think. I have some fall wheat sown and some rye.
        Rye was worth more than wheat in the winter. Corn is worth
        65, wheat 75, oats 40, while beans 350 cts pr bushel.
        Potatoes—don't know. Butter—don't know, for we hain't
        had any for two months.

[4]     Our cows played off on us this winter. We will milk 10 this
        summer. I have 19 head of cows and heifers. We ought to
        have butter now, had we not? I have one span of two-year-
        old mules and three work horses.

[5]     I have built me a barn this winter. It is 28 by 24. That is all I
        have done this winter—only chores and get wood. It takes
        me all the time to do nothing. If I was there, I could help
        you do the same. I might chop a little, though.

[6]     You spoke of the relatives. Ad [Dennis]'s folks is well and live
        where they did. Grace [Gurley] lives with her father and
        mother [Angeline and Ebenezer Robinson]. Her man [Zenas
        Gurley] has gone off preaching. He went last fall, and she is
        staying there. I don't know how long he will be gone. I
        hain't been to Uncle [Ebenezer]'s since you were here.

[7]     Annett and Dave [Daily] still lives in Kansas—the southwest
        part. Their address is Peace[?] P.O., Rice Co., Kans. He has
        got him a farm. He broke out 30 acres and planted it in corn
        last year, and the grasshoppers gathered it for him—only
        left one sackfull. Big rent, weren't it?

[8]     You spoke of us coming down. I don't know when we will
        get there. I would like to come and see you dreadful well,
        but we just don't get started. That is the reason, but we will
        come if we keep well, and you do, too. I would like to go
        and see my brothers soon. One has been ailing for some
        time.

[9]     Has Mary had good health since you went back on your
        farm? I was afraid she would not get stout any more. Tell
        her to slip in a word in your next letter. I got your letter the
        next Monday after you wrote it.

[10]     Well, I have wrote enough for this time, I guess. So, I will close by wishing you all good luck and good health. Write again. Give my respects to Perry, Mollie, and the children.

Yours truly,
from Amulek Boothe

[11]     Well, Mary, as Amulek has quit writing and did not fill his paper, I will try to write a few lines to you.

[12]     I would like to see you all, the best kind, if I could. I don't know whether we will get down there this summer or not. I would like to, real well, if it is so we can. I thought when you left here that we would have got down to see you before this, but we failed to do so. We would like, very much, to have you all come and see us again.

[13]     Well, I guess I will have to quit scribbling for this time. So, good-bye. Write soon.

From Mary A. Boothe

Excuse bad spelling and writing, if you please.

By the end of the 1870s, four of Mollie's six children were born, all boys. She and George had visited Decatur County at least once, and the folks in LaGrange were still an important part of their lives. Joe Bonney and George McNutt became partners in a lumber and sawmill operation that was based in LaGrange but did business in Canton, Missouri, as well. Joe, who did most of the actual work of the business, tried making extra money by installing kitchen cabinets, and all the while, he sent somewhat formal "business" letters to George telling about lumber being delivered or going to be delivered. Katie [Jessie Katie Belle] Bonney, his oldest daughter, begins writing Mollie the other news, because Sarah "Sallie" (Johnson) Bonney, Kate's mother, is dead, and Emma "Sis" (Johnson) Coulten is living in Shenandoah, Iowa.

The changes in Decatur County are profound, too. Six of Amulek and Maryann Boothe's seven children are born by then, and all but the first are girls. Adam Dennis had sold his farm near Eagleville, Missouri, and he had taken his wife Angeline and their family to

Kansas. They would return by spring of 1880, though, and operate a hotel in Lamoni, Iowa. One of Helen and George Rockwell's children would be born in the fall of 1875 and die in the spring of 1876. A year later, George Rockwell, himself died, and Helen moved in with her mother, Sylvia (Butterfield) Morey. Finally in the late 1870s, Deborah Morey would develop those pains in her knees that would eventually result in her paralysis [See Letter #99, par. 2].

These developments had much more to do with Mollie's life than the other event of this decade, the death of her uncle Brigham Young in 1877. Though Young's death would bring on a controversy over the value of his estate which would lead to the excommunication of his first children, Vilate and Elizabeth, Mollie's life was unaffected by the turmoil in the lives of these two cousins whom she had never seen. Rather, she was most affected by the cousins, aunts, uncles, and other relatives who did not go to the Valley of the Great Salt Lake, both the ones who were members of the Reorganized Church and the ones who were not.

**Mary Elizabeth Robinson** *(b: 25 June 1886). The daughter of Ebenezer Robinson and his second wife, Martha Ann "Mattie" Cunnington, Mary was born 22 days after Ebenezer's seventh grandchild, Gladstone, was born. Ebenezer was 69 when he married Miss Cunnington. (The honorific "Miss" was used to emphasize that she had not been married before.) Their second child, Ethel, lived a month and three days in 1890. After Ebenezer's death in 1891, Mary's mother Mattie married Charles Wickes, printer of* THE RETURN, *the newspaper serializing Ebenezer's autobiography and promoting the Whitmer version of Mormonism—the Church of Christ.*

*Middle pages of Letter #103 from Zenas H. Gurley, Jr., when he was lobbying for the Edmunds Bill passsage in Washington, D.C.*

**James Marks Works** (1821-1889). *The youngest of the Works, he was the only one to follow Brigham Young west and become a Brighamite. He is said to have worked for a time in "The Lion House," Brigham Young's home, helping with chores. Despite the intense competition between the Josephites (RLDS) and Brighamites (LDS), each trying to win converts from the other, Mollie's letter writers do not hear from their Uncle James.*

Photograph courtesy of Mary Hemphill.

# Passing of the Older Generation
# 1880s

## ❧ Letter #97

By this time, Pleasant Plains has changed its name to Pleasanton because of a conflict with another Iowa town with the same name. After many years, Gracie Robinson (now, Grace Gurley) and Mollie start writing to each other regularly. Although the first letter in 1880 is the only one of Grace's to survive after eleven years, she has already written Mollie about Deborah (Rockwell) Morey's illness [See Letter #99, par. 2], an illness that began in 1877 or 1878. Nevertheless, Grace does not know about Mollie's six-year-old son whose name has special significance for the Gurleys. By this time, Grace is the mother of four girls: Angie, 7; Evelyn, 6; Julia, nearly 3; and Ida, the baby. Mollie, meantime, has borne four boys: Irvin Perry, 12; James, 9; Zenas, nearly 7; and Albert, 3.

The influence of Angeline (Works) Robinson on many of the girls who grew to womanhood in the Pleasant Plains area can hardly be exaggerated. Because she was often ill, Angeline needed a hired girl much of the time. Two of her first helpers were sisters, Adliza and Deborah Rockwell, her nieces. Adliza, who went with the Robinsons when they moved from Nauvoo to Greencastle, Pennsylvania, married at fifteen. Angeline then recruited Adliza's sister Deborah in Ohio before the Robinsons moved to Iowa. Deborah, too, married young. (Her husband, David Morey, always claimed he proposed marriage because Angeline Robinson overworked Deborah.) Angeline then took in her orphaned niece, Mollie Works, as a hired girl, and Mollie admitted she learned much from her aunt. Even after Mollie left for Illinois and Grace Robinson was old enough to help her mother, Angeline hired fourteen-year-old Annett Dennis [See Letters #23, par. 4 and #24, par. 14]. Annett's failure as a hired girl is a strong clue as to how strict Angeline Robinson was with the girls.

Angeline's Mormon faith was remarkable to Ebenezer even before he married her, and it did not falter through the difficult years migrating from Kirtland, Ohio, to Far West, Missouri, to Nauvoo, to Pennsylvania, and finally, Iowa. Once, when Mollie and Gracie excitedly anticipated Fourth of July celebrations in Pleasant Plains, Angeline's strict faith showed itself. She demanded that the girls stay home and forgo celebrations, out of respect for a neighbor who had recently died. In another instance, Mollie remembered that Aunt Angeline would not even allow the girls to use the porch swing on the sabbath.

Angeline's faith and values, hard as they were, touched many households through the girls who worked for her and who later became wives and mothers themselves. Her passing was noted beyond her small community. Ebenezer had her coffin faced with glass and topped with a silver plate. Old friends, many of them officials in the RLDS, were her pallbearers. They buried her on the Robinson farm among the apple trees she loved.

Pleasanton, Iowa                    April 15th, 1880

Dear Mollie,

[1]     Your kind letter was duly rec'd, but at the time it came, my darling baby Ida was very sick, and on Thursday evening the 11th of March her gentle spirit was called home to God. She was sick for three weeks with brain fever, a part of the time suffering greatly; and yet my cup of sorrow was not full, for just four weeks after my baby died, my dear mother [Angeline Robinson] passed calmly and peacefully to the bright world beyond.

[2]     She came with my father to our baby's funeral and seemed as well as usual, and I, feeling sad and lonely after losing my baby, came with my children and stayed two weeks with her. (My husband [Zenas] came with me & stayed a few days, then went home to attend to his business.) I went back home the first of April, little dreaming that in less than a week I should be summoned to the bedside of my dying mother, but such was the case. She died Thursday evening, the 8th instant, and last Sabbath she was buried, here in the orchard, according to her request.

[3]    Three weeks ago, Pa [Ebenezer Robinson] & Ma went to
       Leon and had some pictures taken, and Ma gave me some
       to send to you. She said she would like to see you. I have a
       scarf of hers that I wish you to have. How shall I send it? I
       remember Ma spoke some time ago about sending it to
       you.

[4]    We will stay with Pa this summer. He is not feeling at all well
       and does not wish to leave home.

[5]    Deborah [Morey] is just about as she was when I last wrote.
       Her disease seems to be an affliction of the spine.

[6]    I have not seen Amulek [Boothe] since last fall, but I heard
       they were well a few weeks ago.

[7]    I would be very glad indeed to get your pictures. As you
       know, I have none that are good.

[8]    I am glad your brother Perry [Works] is doing well. How far
       does he live from you? Is your Aunt [Rachel] and Uncle
       [Samuel Stewart] still living?

[9]    So you have a namesake for my husband! He thought the
       name a pretty one. Yes, you spell it correctly, Zenas.

[10]   If you can visit us this summer, do so, as we would be glad
       to see you.

[11]   I had intended to send one of Zenie's pictures in this letter,
       but find they have all been given away. Will send one when
       he gets more taken.

[12]   Rebecca Potter's oldest son is married and lives on the old
       place in Eldorado, where Father [Robert] Booth used to live.
       Old Mr. Booth & wife [Phebe] live near Davis City.

[13]   Wm. Clark lives in Davis City, is a merchant there, and lives
       in fine style. You know his wife was Olive Booth. She is the
       same jolly soul as ever. If you would come out here, we
       would visit her. She has three children, the eldest a girl of 14
       [Minnie], and two sons.

[14]     Hoping this may find you all well, I will close. My father &
         husband both join me in kind regards to you all.

         Affectionately,
         Gracie

[15]     I have just learned that Angie Dennis has returned from
         Kansas, came this week and is going to live in Davis City so
         her four youngest children can go to school. The rest are all
         married, except Frank. I hope to see Angie soon. Adam is
         still in Kansas.


## ✿ Letter #98

Mollie learns what has happened to the Dennises in Amulek's
letter of 1880. He also prepares Mollie for Deborah Morey's news
concerning Sylvia (Butterfield) Morey [See Letter #99, par. 17].

Amulek is answering Mollie's question about an organ, probably a
melodian, that Grace Gurley, when she was Grace Robinson, bragged
about [See Letter #82, par. 11]. Significantly, Mollie and Maryann
Boothe got more practical gifts.

         Eagleville, [Mo.]              September 19, 1880

         Dear Cousin Miriam,

[1]      I take my seat to write to you. We are well at this date,
         hoping the same with you.

[2]      I was out to Uncle [Ebenezer Robinson]'s last Wednesday,
         found them well, and I read a letter from you to Grace
         [Gurley]. You was wondering if I got your children's pictures.
         I did and much obliged. I wrote to you, but it seems as
         though you didn't get it, so I will try again. I supposed you
         had got it and neglected writing, like me.

[3]      Times is tolerable here. Has been dry through the summer,
         but is raining plenty [now]. Wheat was light, and so is corn.

[4]     Deborah [Morey] is no better. Old Mother [Sylvia] Morey is
        dreadful low. She can't live long. She was glad to see me
        when I called to see her. Helen [Rockwell] looks bad. There is
        a cousin out there on a visit. It is Deborah's sister's child
        [Herbert Palmer] from Pennsylvania. A pert looking chap he
        is.

[5]     Sister Angeline [Dennis] lives in Davis City. She moved up
        last spring. Ad [Dennis] will come up this fall. Frank [Dennis]
        fetched the family up and married while here and went back
        to tend Ad's farm in Kansas. Bub [Dennis] is married and
        Doll and Phebe [Dennis]. Annett [Daily] lives in
        Independence, Jackson Co., and Dave [Daily] lives in
        Colorado. Has been there a year last spring. He has a mine.

[6]     I still live in Mo. where I did, and I hain't come out to Ills.
        yet to see you and George. I suppose Perry [Works] is
        married from Grace's letter you sent.

[7]     Caroline Dennis lives at Lamoni, keeping hotel. Lamoni is a
        town on the railroad between here and Davis City, 11 miles
        from here. There is another road built from there to our
        county seat. It runs three miles east of Eagleville.

[8]     Mary[ann Boothe]'s father [Hugh Gilliland] and brother is
        living with us yet. They have been here for two years, so you
        see I have got a great big family—nine in all. Our house is
        small, you know, so when night comes, you see, we have to
        just hang around on pins and be as comfortable as possible.

[9]     Tell George the cholera has been working on my hogs. I had
        43 head and sold 13 and there is 3 or 4 alive yet. Twenty-six
        of them was fat, just ready to sell, when they took to
        dropping off—after eating some four hundred bushels of
        corn, raising them, and fattening.

[10]    Corn is 20 cts, oats 20, wheat 6, flour 300 to 350, dry cows
        choice 225, hogs 410.

[11]    Mary has got her a sewing machine, but no organ yet.

[12]     George raised a right smart sprinkle of wheat, didn't he? 800 bushels. He certainly won't have to buy much flour. I shan't tell you how much I raised. Still, I eat flour when I buy it, and that is ⅔ of the time. I had 18 acres sown. If you want to know how much I had thrashed, guess at it. I'll not tell.

[13]     Tell George I would like to pitch horseshoes with him. I could knock the socks right off of him.

[14]     Mary has gone visiting, and I am writing. I am in the best business—ain't I?—for Sunday. I could write more, but I reckon I'd better quit. I hate to hop on to another sheet of paper. Maybe there won't be any left for the next time.

[15]     So, good-bye for this [time]. Give my love to the children and respects to George and Perry and wife, if he has any, and the same to yourself.

From your Cousin, Amulek Boothe

## 🌸 Letter #99

For the first time in seventeen years, Deborah (Rockwell) Morey writes to Mollie, but not before Mollie has written her to find out about her paralysis. As difficult as it was for Deborah, she managed to run her home with help from both her oldest girl, Eliza, and Elsie, her fourteen-year-old. She even bore her last child, Blanche, while paralyzed.

As Deborah explains what has happened to herself and her family, Mollie learns that Adliza, the first of the nieces to have helped Aunt Angeline Robinson, is still living where she was married, in Greencastle, Pennsylvania (not Greensville, as Deborah has it).

It was near Greencastle that the Rigdonite branch of the Mormon faith, which included the Ebenezer Robinsons, started a colony. There Ebenezer published *The Conococheague Herald*, the area's first newspaper. It was devoted to persuading Mormon sects that only Sidney Rigdon was the true successor to Joseph Smith, Jr. Adliza Rockwell lived and worked for the Robinsons during this period, which was also when Grace Robinson was born. However, Adliza met and married Solomon Palmer, and the Robinsons went on to settle in Iowa after the Greencastle colony failed. Now, thirty-two years later, Adliza's twenty-two-year-old son, Herbert, and her twenty-six-year-old son, Sylvester, have moved to Iowa (near Webster City). It is young Herbert's visit to his aunt Deborah Morey that Deborah describes in this letter.

The news about Adaline, another of Deborah's sisters, and especially what's happened to George Rockwell's children, Clara and Adrianna, would interest Mollie. George Rockwell had died three years before, and that is why his widow, Helen, is living with her mother, Sylvia (Butterfield) Morey, called Gran'ma Morey. George ("Father") Morey had died December 14, 1875, though Mollie had never been told [See Letter #100, par. 4].

Pleasanton, [Ia.]                     October 13th, 1880

Dear Cousin Mollie,

[1]     I often think of you, and as often neglect writing to you, but I thought today I would write, and I guess you will be surprised to hear from me. I have started two or three letters and then wouldn't get them finished, and I am ashamed to write, and won't blame you if you don't answer, but want you should all the same, and forgive this once, and I shall do better in future, I think.

[2]     Well, Cousin, you have heard that I am an invalid. Grace [Gurley] said you wanted to know the cause. It was pain in my back causing weakness on the spine and bringing paralysis from my waist down. I have been unable to walk for near two years and am no better, but worse. Though I fail gradually, what the end will be, time will tell, and I can only watch, hope, and wait, and pray for better days which may never come. At least there is no indications to cause me to hope. But I trust, through the mercies of God, to stay with my family until they are better prepared to do without me than they are at present. That is all I can do.

[3]     I am glad to hear that you are getting along so well. I feared when you were here that you would have poor health. And now, take my advice and take care not to work too hard, for I am satisfied that is what brought me here where I am.

[4]  I have a family of nine children, and you know I could find work all the time and kept going and working till I had to stop, and now life is a burden. Only for my children do I desire to stay. But I try to make the best of my troubles and bear in patience, for our rest is not in this world. The time is not far away when we shall all pass away, and the places that know us now shall know us no more.

[5]  I guess I will try and change the subject lest you tire of my gloomy thoughts. I don't give way to such thoughts very often, but am generally cheerful.

[6]  I wish you could come and see me and bring your family with you. Wouldn't you enjoy the trip!

[7]  Eliza [Morey] is 17 and gets along with the work pretty well. Elsie [Morey] is 14 and is a great help to her. I don't know what I would do without them. The baby [Evangeline] is three years old and don't make them much trouble now. I named her after Aunt [Angeline] Robinson.

[8]  Cousin Amulek [Boothe] and wife [Maryann] were here about three week ago. They are well and doing well.

[9]  Cousin Ad [Dennis]'s folks live in Davis City. Their children are all married but the four youngest. Annett [Daily] has six children. Caroline has two.

[10]  Brother George [Rockwell]'s wife [Helen] lives with her mother on the old place. The old lady [Sylvia Morey] is very poorly.

[11]  Sister Adliza [Palmer]'s youngest son [Herbert] made us a visit this fall. She has only two children. They live in Hamilton Co. in this state. I enjoyed the visit very much. I expect the oldest one will come to see me before winter. Adliza is still in Greenesville. They talk of moving to Iowa.

[12]  Ad[a]line [Perry] is in Connecticut [and] is not very healthy. She has three children.

[13]    How is Perry [Works] getting along? And Cousin Joseph
        [Bonney]? Write me all the news. Give my love to George
        [McNutt] and the children.

        From Cousin Deborah

        Write soon and oblige.

[14]    Ada [Adrianna Rockwell Scott] lives near Decatur City. She
        hasn't been down since June. The children see her at the
        fair. She is getting along pretty well.

[15]    George [Rockwell]'s other girl (by his first marriage), Clare, is
        staying with Grace [Gurley]. She will teach our school this
        winter. I am lying in bed writing. Do you wonder that I am
        tired?

[16]    I will send you Elsie [Morey]'s picture. It ain't a good one. I
        think she looks like you used to. I will send Eliza [Morey]'s
        some time.

[17]    This letter was written last week and dated today. Gran'ma
        [Sylvia Morey] died this morning. She was 74 years old. Was
        anxious to go and be at rest.

## 🌺 Letter #100

Now that Deborah has forgiven Mollie for being "converted to
sectarianism," she writes regularly about the Morey family, especially
her sons Charlie and David Ebenezer, called "Eben." In the next letter,
she also asks Mollie to tell her about the Bonneys, whom she has lost
track of. And she reports on Zenas, Grace (Robinson) Gurley's
husband.

After a second mission into the heart of "Brighamite" land during
1878, Zenas Gurley, has returned to Iowa to preach, as Deborah
writes. While he was in Utah, Zenas received word that the RLDS in
General Conference had adopted, not only the writings of Joseph
Smith, Jr., as a rule of faith and practice, but also the past and future
revelations of his son, the present leader of the RLDS, Joseph Smith
III. Zenas immediately resigned from the Church, but when the

church revoked the law requiring belief in the revelations of Joseph Smith III, Zenas rejoined in 1879.

His wife, Gracie, took their first son, two-month-old Zenas Robinson Gurley, into the pleasant spring weather on Good Saturday for a walk next door to the Moreys. There they visited Deborah and may have seen Clara Rockwell, George's daughter. As a schoolteacher, Clara had stayed with the Gurleys in 1880, but now she was staying with the Moreys. Just as it was in an earlier day, part of a schoolteacher's pay was room and board, and the extra burden of boarding a schoolteacher was shared each year by a different family.

Pleasanton, [la.]                    Easter Sunday, April 17, 1881

Dear Cousin Miriam,

[1]     It has been some time since I received your letter, but I have been so poorly that I didn't feel able to answer it, and I guess I won't write a very interesting one now, but you must make allowances for sick folks, for sometimes I fancy my mind is weak as well as my body.

[2]     Well, Miriam, I have some more sad news to write you. Our oldest boy Charlie was married on the sixth of February and lost his wife [Miss Trembly] on the twenty-third of March, and, dear cousin, you may know it has been a severe trial to us all when I tell you she was taken away in 48 hours time. Her disease was congestion of the stomach, and she told us she was getting better. The doctor said that he couldn't have the heart to tell us what he thought, knowing it would distress her. She was so full of hope. They had been keeping house about two weeks. We all loved her so much. It was like losing a daughter.

[3]     Such is life. Full of disappointments, with only here and there a sunny spot peeping through to light our way, only to look more dark as the clouds gather to hide its beauty. But as the poet says: "'Tis only for a moment. It will all be over soon." I try to be patient, knowing there remaineth a rest for those who endure.

[4]     Grace [Gurley] was over yesterday. It was the first time she had taken her babe [Zenas] outdoors. She is looking pretty well. Her children are large and healthy looking. She said you wanted to know about Father [George] Morey. He has been dead five years ago last December. David [Morey] bought the old place for the two oldest boys, Charlie and George [Myron Morey].

[5]     Well, many of the old folks are almost all gone. Mr. and Mrs. [Robert and Phebe] Booth are still living, but are quite feeble.

[6]     You never said whether you thought of coming to see us. You spoke of Cousin Joseph [Bonney]'s children. I thought that the oldest was called Effa Josephine. Was I mistaken?

[7]     Does Perry [Works] live near you? Give my love to him.

[8]     Well, I am getting tired. Will have to say good-bye. Tell George [McNutt] we have not forgotten him and would be ever so glad to see him. My love to all and yourself especially.

        Debbie Morey

[9]     Yesterday was the first pleasant day of the season. Our folks are all at church to hear Zenas [Gurley, Jr.] preach. They think him a great speaker.

[10]    George [Rockwell]'s daughter [Clara] is staying with us. She keeps school in our district this summer.

[11]    Elsie [Morey] would [not] send her picture as she thought it too poor a one. Will send you one as soon as she gets some taken.

## ✿ Letter #101

Amulek's 1881 letter confirms much of what Deborah Morey has written in hers, though he naturally concentrates on the Dennis and Boothe families. The Dennises are now depending on the Lamoni hotel that Caroline started, but Lamoni, Iowa, has become the headquarters of the RLDS. After Illinois proved unsuitable, RLDS leaders came west to Iowa to relocate the church headquarters. Among the prospective towns were Davis City, which the Clark enterprises had helped make prosperous; and Pleasanton (formerly, Pleasant Plains). The church leaders chose to plat a new city four miles west of Davis City in 1879 as their headquarters, calling it Lamoni. A railroad coming from Missouri through the territory helped make their decision. [See Letter #93, par. 7.] The faithful were encouraged to relocate, just as they were encouraged to settle Kirtland, Nauvoo, and earlier Mormon towns, but there was resistance to proclaiming Lamoni a "Zion," which would mean that relocation would be more than encouraged, it would be required. The RLDS later relocated its headquarters to Independence, Missouri.

> Eagle[ville, Mo.]                    May 1st, [1881]
>
> Dear Cousin Miriam,

[1]     As I have no one to talk at, I will write to you and George. This is Sabbath day, and a fine day it is. This leaves us all well, hoping the same with you.

[2]     It is more of a task for me to write than it used to be, as I don't write much.

[3]     We have had a long steady winter as I ever seen, but the spring has now come with its warm sunshine. Times is good and money plenty, but I hain't got any.

[4]     I have just written to brother Mosiah [Boothe]'s wife [Mary] in Idaho. Mosiah has gone to Europe to preach. He passed through Iowa last fall on his way, but didn't stop. He said he would call as he went back home. He will be gone 2 years.

[5]     I was up to Ad [Dennis]'s yesterday. They was well. They keep hotel in Lamoni.

[6]     Grace Gurley has another boy [Zenas Robinson]. They have bought Uncle [Ebenezer Robinson]'s home place, and they live there. Uncle is building some houses in Davis City for the purpose of renting out.

[7]     Deborah [Morey] don't get any better. Charley Morey was married and lost his wife soon after. Old Mrs. [Sylvia] Morey is dead.

[8]     I stayed night before last with Mr. [Robert] Booth. The old lady [Phebe] keeps trotting around yet, but they are both getting very feeble. Still, they keep house alone. The old man is getting tottery so he can't hardly stand still. They live west of Davis City, 2 miles.

[9]     Charley Potter's oldest boy is married. He lives on Booth's old place. Bob Booth is married again. Caroline lives on John Booth's place this year.

[10]    Net [Daily] lives in Independence. Her husband [David] was up here last week, but didn't only just call and went on. They were well.

[11]    Tell George [McNutt] I am trying to build a house this spring. So, good-bye. Write soon. My respects to George.

        Amulek Boothe

        Miriam McNutt

## 🌼 Letter #102

Grace and Zenas Gurley are now living on the Robinson family farm, and with this letter Grace finally tells Mollie about the birth of Zenas Robinson Gurley, their first son. Grace's wishes for Mollie will come true soon, since Mollie is pregnant with Myrtle Dell McNutt.

The first mention of the Boothe's little girl, Louisa, is in this letter. Though she was Amulek's second oldest girl (not his oldest as Grace has it) Louisa died August 24, 1876, one of the few years during this period that no letter from Amulek survives.

Zenas' mother, Margaret Bell (Hickey) Gurley, had been living with her son George in Sandwich, Illinois [See Letter #105, par. 3], but she may have been in Lamoni with a relative when Zenas got the message mentioned in this letter.

In this same year, Zenas went to Washington, D. C., with RLDS Church Elder E. L. Kelly in order to lobby the Forty-seventh Congress and convince President Chester A. Arthur that Utah should not be admitted to the Union until the Edmunds Bill passed. Passage of the Edmunds Bill would outlaw polygamy in the United States. Zenas would work very hard during the next few months to get the bill passed [See letter #103].

Cousin Joe Bonney's daughter Jessie Katie Belle ("Katie") married George Larkin ("Lark") Loudermilk on March 1, 1881, as Gracie supposed.

| | |
|---|---|
| Pleasanton, Iowa | Sunday, August 14th, 1881 |

Dear Mollie,

[1]      I received your kind missive "long long ago" and have neglected answering until I am almost ashamed to write, but please do forgive me, won't you? I have not written a letter this year, so thought I would begin by writing to you.

[2]      In the first place we have bought the old home and have moved here, and we are working the farm this year, which you know is hard work. The weather has been very hot and dry for a month past, until the past two days. We have had a couple of light showers, and the atmosphere is cooler.

[3]      Now for the news! Have you heard that a "young man" has taken up his board with us? It will be six months the 20th of this month since he came; and for short, Zenie calls him "Zenas Robinson Gurley." Of course we feel quite rich. Hope you may be as fortunate in finding a daughter.

[4]      I would be so glad if you could visit us this fall. Deborah [Morey] would also be delighted to see you. Two weeks ago yesterday I spent the day with her in company with Mrs.

Martha Shafer (Cowles) who is here in the neighborhood on a visit from California. Some three or four years ago, Martha married a rich old bachelor and moved to California where they are engaged in fruit raising (oranges, lemons, and grapes) for the market. She will go back in a few weeks. She seems to be very happy and contented.

[5]    You asked about Father [George] Morey. He died several years ago. There has a great many changes taken place among old neighbors. Father [Robert] Booth and wife [Phebe] are still living. I heard when I was at David [Morey]'s that Cousin Amulek [Boothe] had buried his eldest girl. This must be a great sorrow for them. I have not seen them for a year.

[6]    Yesterday a message came for Zenie [Gurley] stating that his mother [Margaret] was very sick and wanted to see him immediately, so he went & has not yet returned. It is 15 miles over there. I could not go with him very well as there is so much to see to. Mother Gurley is in her 75th year, and we feel anxious about her.

[7]    A great many are dying now. I think the excessive heat is the cause of so much sickness. Our baby [Zenas Robinson] has not been very well for a few days.

[8]    Pa [Ebenezer Robinson] is quite well. He makes home with us a part of the time. He has bought property in Davis City & built a number of houses which he rents, so his business keeps him there much of his time. He is gone now. I keep a girl, as I cannot do my work alone.

[9]    Please remember me to your husband and write soon to yours affectionately,

Gracie

[10]    When you write, tell me all the news about Cousins Joseph [Bonney] and Perry [Works]. I suppose Katie [Loudermilk] is married, as a friend of mine who lives in Pleasanton visited LaGrange last winter & saw Katie & said she was to be

married last spring. The lady is well-acquainted with the young man and says he [Larkin] is all right.

[11]    Zenas sent you a Davis City paper containing his oration. Did you receive it?

## ✿ Letter #103

This letter, not to Mollie but to Grace (Robinson) Gurley from her husband Zenas Hovey Gurley, Jr., shows how hard Zenas worked lobbying to prevent Utah from entering the Union. The Reorganized Church sent him, E.L. Kelly, and, eventually, Joseph Smith III to Washington to convince government officials that, unlike the Brighamites in Utah, members of the RLDS did not believe in establishing a Zion, which blurs the separation of church and state, and that the Mormons in Utah not only practiced polygamy, it was a doctrine of their faith. Zenas, like his father before him, who had ordained Joseph Smith III as the head of the RLDS, despised religious polygamy.

The people of Utah Territory had been trying to join the Union since 1849 as the State of Deseret, but the Mormon polygamy doctrine had repulsed officials. The State of Deseret representative was denied a seat in the House of Representatives, despite the efforts of Democratic senator Stephen A. Douglas, chairman of the Committee on Territories, whom the Mormons had asked to help them. Although President Millard Fillmore signed a bill providing for the organization of a Utah Territory in 1850, six years later Senator Douglas advised Mormon representatives who had come to Washington carrying a new constitution for the state not to press for statehood at that time. He apparently wanted them to wait until his principles of popular sovereignty were firmly in place. These same principles, which would have allowed each state—by referendum—to determine whether slavery was allowed within its borders, became one of Douglas' arguing points in his debates with Abraham Lincoln in 1858. Democrats were generally for slavery and polygamy, if they agreed with Douglas' popular sovereignty principles, and Republicans were against them. Indeed, the Republican Party Platform during the election of 1856 had demanded that Congress prohibit in the territories both slavery and polygamy. They were called "...those twin relics of barbarism."

On July 8, 1862, President Lincoln signed the Morrill Anti-Bigamy Act, prohibiting polygamy in the territories. The law also nullified any law "pertaining to polygamy and spiritual marriage" that the legislature in Utah had enacted. When asked, after he had signed the bill into law, what he was going to do about the Mormons, Lincoln was said to have replied with a story about clearing timber for a farm field. "Occasionally we would come to a log which had fallen down," he recalled. "It was too hard to split, too wet to burn, and too heavy to move, so we plowed around it. That's what I intend to do with the Mormons. Tell Brigham Young that if he will let me alone, I will let him alone."[1] To Lincoln in 1862, saving the Union was obviously more important than vigorously enforcing the Morrill Anti-Bigamy Act.

To Zenas Gurley in 1882, however, making the Edmunds Act the law of the land was of utmost importance because it would strengthen the 1862 law and put an end to the detestable practice of church-sanctioned polygamy. Although both acts would punish polygamists with a $500 fine and up to five years in prison, the Edmunds Act disenfranchised polygamists and made them ineligible for public office. It also vacated all registration and elective offices and called for the creation of a five-member Utah Commission, appointed by the President, to oversee elections. The Commission even had the power to deprive citizens of civil rights without a trial. Like the Morrill Act before it, the Edmunds Act would be tested and approved by the U. S. Supreme Court. These are the details, reprinted in the newspaper article, that Zenas includes with his letter. Two days before he writes this letter, the Senate had passed the Act. A little more than a month later, March 22, 1882, President Chester A. Arthur signed it into law.

Despite the emotional demands his lobbying work must have made on him, in his letter, Zenas is careful to instruct Gracie on how to supervise the building of a barn to be built on the farm that they have purchased from her father Ebenezer Robinson. Gracie is busy with Zenas Robinson, their son whose first birthday is two days after the date of the letter. Her husband's fervor for his work in Washington does not stop him from lovingly writing to his three girls. And he and the other RLDS lobbyists were successful. It was not until the president of LDS advised all Mormons to refrain from unlawful marriages and a final Utah Constitution provided penalties for polygamy did Utah become a state in 1896, a full 37 years after its first petition to do so.

825 13th St. N.E.
Washington, D.C.

Feb 18/[18]82

My Darling Gracie:

[1]      Yours, Pa's & the children's letters came yesterday after I had sealed mine to Pa [Ebenezer Robinson]. As I wrote Pa yesterday, will omit answering his of the 13th enclosed with yours of the 12th—

[2]      If Pa has the Bill made out for barn, he can give to Quirt. & let them saw it out and pile the lumber in good shape. After the barn pattern is fully out, saw the balance of 14 foot elm into fencing. And all will be well—If we lack a little for barn, we can get it sawed afterward; however, the Bill can be filled or even a little over as there is generally an extra demand for such stuff, as it's always convenient.

[3]      I am very glad that the sick are improving & hope they may recover. Mr. Bicknell's folks will feel their loss very much. We are constantly assured that "life is a span" & soon passes away. May we also be ready.

[4]      Your views of my mission here are like mine, although I must visit Phil[adelphia] & N.J. [New Jersey]. I wrote Pa of our work before Judiciary Com[mittee], and next week we propose to lay upon the desk of each member of C.[ongress] a copy of the Polygamic Rev.[elation?] together with our argument (which I have sent Pa) and then we shall feel that the responsibility of tolerating or extirpating shall be with Congress.

[5]      Then I expect to go to Phil. Bro[ther] E. L. [Kelly] may go with me, but will return shortly, as we do not feel at liberty to abandon this city while this measure is pending and our presence might aid materially, as we are known to be here to fight it. I would like to see the work we love relieved from this reproach.

[6]     Utah Legislature has just passed [a] resolution asking
        Congress to send out a Com.[mittee] to investigate and see
        whether it is as bad as told. The anti-polygamists there also
        met & passed resolutions at once asking Congress to go on
        with this matter, and was telegraphed here yesterday. You
        see, Utah is getting anxious. I send you N.Y. Herald with text
        of Edmunds Bill against polygamy.

[7]     Be thorough in treatment for colds & may God bless &
        protect you all is the prayer of your loving husband,
        Z. H. Gurley

[8]     Love to Mother [Margaret Bell Hickey Gurley] and Pa & all
        friends. Kiss the babies all for me, dear souls.

        My Darling Children, Angie, Eva, and Julia,

[9]     Your very pleasant letters came to hand yesterday and was
        read with interest and pleasure. I am much pleased with
        progress you are making in letter writing. I am very thankful
        that my little girls can write to me and tell me the news.
        And how they are getting along—

[10]    Yes, Angie, Mr. Kelly & I board together & get along nicely.
        And so, Eva, your little brother [Zenas Robinson] is a "sweet
        man;" good for your brother; hope he may grow sweeter.
        And dear little Julia. You want Papa to "come home
        tomorrow." Well, we shall hope that the "morrow" will soon
        come when he will, and see all his loved ones at home.

        Kiss Grandma for me, & your mother & each other. God
        bless you my dear children.

        As ever, your loving father,
        Z.H. Gurley

## ❧ Letter #104

Nearly six full years after the last one, a letter from Deborah Morey survives. Though she is forty-six, only three years older than Mollie, the illness which has paralyzed her is draining her spirit as well as her body. She spends much of her time in bed, knitting and mending. From there she conducts the family business out of a black satchel full of important papers under her bed. Children needing discipline are sent to her room, and one of her sons, David Ebenezer ("Eben"), whose eyes are bad, often stays with her on sunny days with the shade drawn. In the darkened room, she tells him many family stories and makes him promise to keep them secret. But her worry about his health is mistaken, for though he is not very "stout," it is his younger brother, William Supply, who dies in 1889, many years before Eben [See Letter #106, par. 6]. A year and a half after this letter, on December 3, 1888, Deborah herself dies.

She comments on the importance of education because Mollie has written to her about her son Irvin Perry's graduation from college, something that made Mollie proud [See Letter #105, par. 2].

Zenas Gurley's final break with the RLDS came a year before this letter, but it is still fresh in Deborah's mind. During 1885, Zenas, a Church elder, was attacked in the pages of the *True Latter Day Saints Herald*, the church's official newspaper, because he denied tithing, the gathering to Zion, and the words of Joseph Smith "as if [coming] from God's own mouth."[2] The RLDS had moved its headquarters for the last time to Independence, Missouri. Having to believe in all the revelations of Joseph Smith, Jr., in order to be faithful was abhorrent to Zenas. He had proof that the Mormon Prophet himself had started the practice called "spiritual wifery"—polygamy.

Two days before 1874 began, Zenas, as a notary public, attested to the sworn statement of Ebenezer and Angeline Robinson, that Hyrum Smith, brother of Joseph Smith, had met with the Robinsons in Nauvoo and taught them the doctrine of spiritual wifery that had been revealed to the Prophet. By this doctrine, a woman could only receive the full benefits of heaven if she were "sealed" on earth to a high church official. Many of these sealings were truly spiritual, like the one between Mollie's sixty-five-year-old grandmother Abigail (Marks) Works and Brigham Young in 1846.[3] Abigail, the mother of Miriam (Works) Young, had once been Brigham's mother-in-law. A widow and suffering from breast cancer, she may have been one of the many who were sealed in the newly completed Nauvoo Temple to prepare her way into the afterlife. She died six and a half months after the ceremony.

However, some of the sealings were considerably more earthly. A second affidavit by Ebenezer alone in 1885 attested that Hyrum Smith had detailed a way for Ebenezer to be sealed to a young wife and that if a child resulted from the sealing, Hyrum would swear it was by the young woman's husband who was away on a mission. The affidavit noted that Hyrum was perturbed when Ebenezer refused the offer.[4] Years later, Ebenezer wrote about his moral struggle with the doctrine of spiritual wives, a doctrine that was tearing the Mormons apart:

> I prayed almost constantly to my heavenly Father to know what I should do. I did not trouble myself about others, what they should do but the burden of my soul and the intense agony of my heart was to know what my individual duty was in this matter. I did not wish to embrace anything that was not of the Lord, nor reject anything that was from him.
>
> About ten o'clock, on the morning of the third day, my heavenly Father, in his loving kindness, answered my prayer. As I was walking by myself, down Parley Street, just before entering Main Street, he spake to me, clear and distinct, and said: 'I have not placed you to set in order the affairs of my church. Stand still and see the result of all things, but keep yourself unspotted from the world.' 'Amen, Father,' was my glad response. I knew from that day to this, that if others could have more wives than one, and have the spirit of the Lord, I could not, and there I let the matter rest. It troubled me no more.[5]

Ebenezer had made Zenas promise never to reveal the affidavits while Ebenezer lived, but the attacks on his faith prompted Zenas to have them published in a local history.[6] Zenas defended his stance. He pointed out that when Joseph Smith III spoke with the United States' Secretary of State, outlining the official legal differences between the RLDS and the Utah Church, one of those differences was that the RLDS did not believe in "the gathering to Zion." Assuring Federal officials that the Reorganized Church did not believe in gathering to Zion helped "make prestige and friends for the church," according to Zenas. "Concentrating [the church's] power for religious and political purposes had, from its inception down till today, proven abortive of good, and highly detrimental to the Government," Zenas wrote.[7] The history of resentment against the Mormons who voted in a block, who acted as one, in Ohio, in Missouri, and in Illinois was certainly proof enough for Zenas.

None of his arguments succeeded, however. In 1885 he was not sustained as an officer of the RLDS Church, and the next year Zenas, his wife Grace, his seventy-eight-year-old mother Margaret, and his brother Edwin's family all resigned from the church. So did Jason W. Briggs, who, with Zenas' father, was one of the founders of the Reorganized Church.

In that same year, Ebenezer was talking with RLDS Leader Joseph Smith III as both rode to Independence for the April church conference. Suddenly Ebenezer broke away from the group, cantering off to Richmond, Missouri. There he met with David Whitmer, one of the original founders of Mormonism who had long since been disfellowshipped. With that action, Ebenezer, too, resigned from the Reorganized Church of Jesus Christ of Latter Day Saints. He and David Whitmer, together with David's nephew, John, began a new church.[8]

All this is behind Deborah Morey's simple statements to Mollie about the beliefs of Zenas Gurley and his father-in-law, Ebenezer Robinson.

Pleasanton, [Ia.]                          July 15, [18]87

Dear Cousin Miriam,

[1]    I rec. your long looked-for letter some time ago. Was real glad to hear from you, for I get anxious waiting. Well, I know how time passes when one has so many steps to take, and then letter writing isn't very pleasant when the feet are tired. And sometimes the brain needs rest.

[2]    This is a busy world, and no mistake about that part of it, and sometimes I think 'tis a cruel one, and no mistake. I get weary of it. Sometimes think I have enough of it. Am satisfied to leave it for others to make the same experience, but yet I stay, and perhaps 'tis for the best, for as long as mother is here 'tis home, and without me 'twould never be the same. So I try to be patient and cheerful and, at times, thankful that 'tis as well with us all as it is.

[3]    I am glad you are so pleasantly situated and hope you will all live to enjoy your home for years to come. I wish I could come and see you but 'tis not likely I shall ever be able. But you must come and see me if you can, and I should think you could. Your boys [Irvin and James] could keep house awhile and let you and George [McNutt] rest.

[4]    You are doing better than we are, I think. Well, I suppose that country will always be better than this is. 'Tis one good crop, and two half, and one failure. That is just about how 'tis here. A great many have their farms all in grass. Stock-running will pay the best, I guess. Zenas [Gurley] don't raise any grain. Keeps mostly horses. He tried cattle but has sold most of them now.

[5]    We are elected for hard work, I think. Well, so the world goes round and round, and we wouldn't be missed if we wasn't in it.

[6]    We had an awful dry time last summer, and the ground is dry yet. Corn looks nice but needs rain bad. The grass is dry. Pasture isn't good. Oats are short.

[7]    I am glad you are giving your children such a good education. 'Tis what everyone needs, and something that my children haven't got. How old is your girl [Myrtle]? My youngest [Evangeline] is nine years old. She rides the horses, helps milk, and likes the outdoors pretty well. The children have a swing under the old elm tree. The oak is mostly dead.

[8]    Well, you must come and see how nice we are. I guess you would know the place. The old log house is gone, though.

[9]    Well, Charley [Morey] was home to see us last winter. His wife [Mary] and baby came with him. George [Myron Morey] is in Nebraska farming with Charley. David [Morey] still makes a hand on the farm. We have two boys, one 18, the other [James] 15, but the oldest one [William] isn't very stout. They are tending 35 [acres] of corn and harvesting 25 [acres] of oats. The rest is in grass pasture and brush that don't forget to grow.

[10]    Well, I don't think of anything more to write. Our folks are all well, as usual. I am about the same as last summer.

[11]    Grace [Gurley] and family are well and prospering. Zenas won't never join the church again, I don't think, though he believes what Mormonism was in the beginning, but thinks and knows they done wrong and introduced bad doctrine and are still making mistakes.

[12]    Uncle [Ebenezer Robinson] thinks very much as Zenas does, I think, but haven't had a chance to talk with him lately. He don't come over often. Was here about four weeks ago, just a few minutes. He looked feeble.

[13]    Well, I will close. I have written to Adaline [Perry], and I am getting very tired. Write soon and tell me if you think of coming up this fall. Love to you and yours, as ever.

Your loving cousin,
Debbie M.

[14]    I would like your picture ever so well. Good-bye. I have a photograph of myself, but it is ugly. Worse-looking than I am. So I shan't send any away unless I can get some better ones, and there isn't an artist nearer than Leon [Iowa], and I would have to have them come to the house.

## ❧ Letter #105

By now the formal openings to letters that were so common twenty-five years ago [See Letters #13, #16, and #19 especially] have given way to terse telegraphic prose sprinkled with ampersands, as in this letter of Grace Gurley's.

While attending college in LaGrange, Mollie's oldest son Irvin Perry stayed with Joe Bonney and his daughters. As a college graduate, he would later teach in Liberty and Camp Point, Illinois.

Grace is careful to point out the result of her father Ebenezer Robinson's recent marriage. At sixty-nine he married his second wife, Miss Martha Ann "Mattie" Cunnington. (The title "Miss" was important to let it be known that she had not been married before.) Joseph Smith III, the son of the Prophet who had married Ebenezer and his first wife, Angeline, years before, performed the ceremony on February 5, 1885, just two months before Ebenezer quit the RLDS Church.

Mollie has written to Grace asking about the Gurleys' religious convictions, and Grace explains them in this letter.

Pleasanton, Iowa                        Oct. 2nd, [1887]

Dear Mollie,

[1].    I suppose you are nöt offended because I have been paying you back in a little of your own coin? I am always glad to hear from you & hope you will write more promptly in the future, & I will try & do better if you will.

[2]     I am pleased to hear of Irvin [McNutt] graduating. Suppose you attended commencement exercises at LaGrange. The Institution is a Baptist one, is it not? I read of it in the "Baptist Flag," a paper which is published in St. Louis, & which we are now taking.

[3]     Why haven't you visited us ere this? We have had several visitors this fall or latter part of summer. In the first place, a friend from Des Moines came & stayed nearly a week in July & the latter part of August. Brother George Gurley, wife, & daughter from Sandwich, Ill., visited us & also my husband's mother [Margaret Gurely] was with them. They returned home the 17th of September.

[4]     Do you know that my father [Ebenezer Robinson] has a little daughter [Mary]? It was a year old in June. We have a little boy [Gladstone] three weeks older than it is. They were over to see us in June, and I was there about two weeks ago. They are well.

[5]     Cousin Deborah [Morey] is about the same. Has not been to see me for about a year. Hardly ever goes away from home. She would be very glad to see you. I go to see her quite often. Have not been for some time now, on account of company, but intend to go before long.

[6]     How is your fruit crop this fall? We have a very few apples & other fruit scarce. The drouth caused short crops & hard times for money.

[7]     You ask what church we belong to. We have not united with any as yet. Zenas preaches every Sunday to full houses in different localities. He occupies an "independent pulpit," tells people what he believes & his reasons etc. We accept the Gospel as taught in the New Testament & believe the words of Christ will save us if we follow his teachings.

[8]     Come & see us when you can. Remember me to your family & all the relatives.

Your loving cousin,
Gracie

## NOTES

1. As quoted in *The "Americanization" of Utah for Statehood* by Gustive O. Larson. (San Marino Press) Huntington Library: 1971. p. 60

2. *Record of Ringgold & Decatur County,* p. 542.

3. Stanley P. Hirshson, *The Lion of the Lord, a Biography of Brigham Young,* (New York: Alfred A. Knopf, 1969), pp. 201-202.

4. *Record of Ringgold & Decatur County,* p. 543.

5. Robinson, "Personal History," *The Return,* Vol. 3, No. 2 February 1891, p. 29.

6. Heman C. Smith, ed., *Journal of History,* (Lamoni, Ia.: Board of Publication RLDS, 1917), pp. 366-367.

7. *Record of Ringgold & Decatur County,* p. 542.

8. Joseph Smith III remembers: "To our surprise, he switched off at St. Joseph, and went to Richmond... where...he was baptized and ordained by David Whitmer. Whatever may have been his purpose in leaving us in that manner, I could never determine..." *The Saints' Herald,* February 1936, p. 176.

# BLESS THE CHILDREN, BLESS ALL
## 1890s & 1912

### ✿ Letter #106

Mollie would be forty-six in the year that she receives this letter from Amulek's oldest girl, Olive, already twenty-two. The years have flown. Besides Louisa, Olive's other sister, Viola, has died, leaving the three girls that Olive mentions: Nora Angeline ("Norey"), Luella ("Elly"), and Harriet Naomi ("Oma").

The McNutts had made a visit to the Pleasanton and Eagleville area in the late 1880s, and this might have prompted Olive to believe they were going to visit this year.

Eagleville, Mo.                          [April 1,] 1890
Mrs. Mollie McNutt

Dear Friend,

[1]     I seat myself to write a few lines to you as we hadn't heard from you for so long. Pa [Amulek Boothe] wrote a letter and never received any answer. I wrote one and directed to Quincy, and it came back, so I suppose I directed it wrong. I received a letter from Angie Gurley. She told me to direct to Payson.

[2]     Well, we are all in tolerable good health at this writing. Hoping these few lines will find you enjoying the best of health.

[3]     We have been looking for you folks out here for a year, but failed to see you. I think you might come out this spring. We would be glad to see you all.

[4]     How old is your daughter [Myrtle McNutt]? I saw her picture up to Cousin Gracie's [Robinson Gurley]. I will be 22 the 22nd of April. I am the oldest girl. I have three sisters. My brother [Hiram Ebenezer] is older than I am.

[5]     Well, we have a little cold weather yet. It snowed some last night, but it didn't stay on long. Our folks has sown some oats. I think they will have to sow over if it doesn't turn warm soon.

[6]     Cousin Dave Moreys have gone to Nebraska. They thought they would go out there and see if they wouldn't have better health. I suppose you have heard that their Willie was dead. He died this winter with the fever.

[7]     Angie and Eva Gurley [Grace's daughters] have been going to school at Davis City this winter. I think Angie intends teaching this spring, if she can get a school.

[8]     Everything is awful cheap here. It seems like a person can't get anything for what they sell hardly. Cattle is cheap. Corn, 20 cts bu; oats 12 $1/2$ cts; butter 10 cts pound, and eggs 10 cts doz. We get four or five dozen eggs a day. I expect we will get six & seven doz when it gets a little warmer.

[9]     Well, I guess I had better bring my scribbling to a close. You must excuse this writing as my pen is very poor and I am not a good writer anyhow. Hoping you will all come out and see us soon.

[10]    I would like to have your pictures if you have any to send. I would send you one of mine, but they are taken so poorly, I'll wait and get some better ones taken.

[11]    Hoping to hear from you soon,

from Olive Boothe                    to Mrs. Mollie McNutt
Direct to Eagleville
Harrison Co., Mo.

## ❧ Letter #107

The important news in Grace Gurley's letter of 1892 is about her father Ebenezer Robinson. Many years of searching for the true faith started with his being baptized by the Mormon Prophet, Joseph Smith. Soon afterwards Ebenezer began doubting—not so much the Mormon faith as its leaders and its direction. Especially he hated the monstrosity of polygamy called "spiritual wifery." The abuses of the spiritual wife doctrine was the subject of the first and only publication of the *Nauvoo Expositor,* a newspaper that angered Joseph Smith so much he ordered it and its publishers extirpated. This provoked Smith's arrest and jailing in Carthage, Illinois, where he was killed.

After Smith's death, Sidney Rigdon, who helped frame some Mormon theology, was an obvious choice for leader, though many chose Brigham Young. Rigdon offered a settled Mormonism, without outlandish revelations or a "Prophet," and without the doctrine of spiritual wifery. Ebenezer became a Rigdonite. But establishing the Rigdonite gatheringplace bankrupted the sect, and in 1859 Ebenezer came to Iowa, for yet another stop in his quest for a faith.

Always he brought his special knowledge of printing, publishing, and writing with him. In Iowa, he embraced "the new organization" (RLDS) only after he was sure there were to be no special favors to a special few. He had been a victim of that kind of injustice in Nauvoo when his printing business and his home were commandeered by the church. When he thought "the new organization" was taking on some of the evils that had corrupted the original faith (though not spiritual wifery), he revolted. With early Mormon leader, David Whitmer, he founded a new religion, The Church of Christ. Confident in this new faith, he had recently begun his own private history of Mormonism, called "Items of Personal History, Including Some Items of Church History not Generally Known." This was serialized in another newspaper he founded, *The Return,* so named because he hoped believers would return to the true Mormon church, the one, like the first, that had David Whitmer as one of its founders.

He and his young family were living in one of the rental houses he had built in Davis City, Iowa. His granddaughter, Angie, had become ill while at college in Humeston, Iowa, and his son-in-law, Zenas, had gone there to bring her home. They stopped off to see Ebenezer on the way back. Ebenezer had been very upset with Zenas for publishing the Robinson affidavits about spiritual wifery, affidavits which were his proof that the doctrine had been introduced by Joseph

Smith in Nauvoo. But now the two religious zealots, father and son-in-law, were reconciled. It was in the morning of March 11 of this year that Zenas held the old man in his arms.

Pleasanton, Iowa                    February 14, 1892

Dear Mollie,

[1]    I am very positive that I do not owe you any letter; nevertheless, I am so anxious to hear from you that I am going to write anyhow, and I hope you will be most prompt and let me hear from you.

[2]    There is so much sickness in the country now, and so many deaths. I hope you have all escaped and are enjoying good health. The most of us have been afflicted with "la grippe" but are all improving now.

[3]    Our baby is quite poorly, but she is teething and has a bad cold so think that is the cause. She is a year old the first of December. We had a great time trying to find a name for her. Finally Zenas called her "Gracie" and that settled it.

[4]    Do you know that my dear father [Ebenezer Robinson] has gone to "the land beyond"? He died the eleventh of last March. I was sick at the time and could not visit him, so it seemed doubly hard. He was not sick but a few days. My husband [Zenas] was with him and held him up as he breathed his last. It was as peaceful as a child falling asleep. A good man has gone to rest.

[5]    David Morey and family live in Nebraska, excepting Eliza who is married and lives at her father's old home. They like it there much better than here, and are doing well. Charlie and George [Myron Morey] are both married.

[6]    We have not heard from Amulek [Boothe]'s folks lately. The girls hear from Olive [Boothe] occasionally. Angie Dennis has moved back near Davis City. Her children are nearly all married. One daughter lives in British Columbia. I have not seen her since she came back.

[7]     Olive Clark (Booth) has lost her only daughter, Minnie. She
        was married and lived in Kansas, left a husband and two
        little boys. She was brought to Davis City for burial, died the
        latter part of December.

[8]     Our children are all at home now. Angie has a small class in
        music which she teaches at home. She attended college at
        Humeston last winter, and the latter part of the term she
        was taken sick with catarrhal fever and nearly died, and we
        were afraid to send her away this winter.

[9]     Eva went to Davis City to school for some time, and
        boarded with Pa's wife [Mattie Cunnington Robinson], who
        lived alone with her two children and widowed mother, but
        the mother [Sarah] died last month, and Mattie (Pa's wife)
        broke up housekeeping and went to Des Moines to stay
        with her sister (Mrs. John Sherman). So Eva came home,
        thinks some of teaching this summer.

[10]    Where are your children, and how are they doing? I wish
        you would send us the picture of yourself and the husband
        and the children (I only have Zenas and Myrtle), and we will
        return the compliment when we have some taken.

[11]    How is Cousin Joe [Bonney] and his daughters this winter?

[12]    Mr. Aldens[?] still lives here. Sara is not married. She teaches
        most of the time.

[13]    We took dinner at Mr. [Alfred] Moffet's last Tuesday. It was
        his birthday (68 years). His children are all married.

[14]    Now please write soon, and a long letter. We all send
        regards to you all, not forgetting Cousin Perry [Works].
        When can you visit us?

        Your affectionate cousin,
        G[race] Gurley

[15]    I received a letter a few months ago from E. A. Wolford
        (cousin Ursula Worden's husband). He says Aunt Jerusha

[Worden] lives in Throopsville [New York] all alone. Her children are all married. Lawson [Worden] died a year ago. He was her youngest child. If you want to hear from them, write to cousin Wolford's folks, Weedsport, New York, and they will answer. I never hear from Uncle James [Works].

[16]    I suppose you will all attend the World's Fair at Chicago?

[17]    I am getting grey and losing my teeth. How is it with you?

## ❧ Letter #108

After many years comes a letter from Emma (Johnson) Coulten. Now a mother of adult sons, she suffers from an unknown illness, but she is still anxious about seeing Mollie. She wants Mollie to travel to Shenandoah, Iowa, on either the Wabash or the Burlington Quincy ("the Q") railroad.

Shenandoah, Iowa              Aug. 9, 1892

My dear friend Mrs. McNutt,

[1]    I will try to write a few lines to you this afternoon. We are as well as usual, but I was sick all spring and am not able to do much work now, but I can wear my clothes now. I haven't been able to wear a dress and corset since I was first taken sick till Friday of last week. I had to have wrappers made. I could not wear any wrappers I had. I was a sight, the way I was bloated.

[2]    You must excuse such a delay in answering. When I received your letter, I was getting the boys ready to keep house. They are keeping "bach." They are running a dairy. They are milking 30 cows. Mr. Blake, that is the man where we first lived, furnishes everything, and they do the work and get two-fifths for their work.

[3]    Are you going to visit me this fall? It is almost a year since I was to see you.

[4]     Do you have good crops and fruit this year?

[5]     Come to Shenandoah on the Wabash or Q. Either. If you will
        let us know when you are coming, we will meet you at
        depot. Have Joe [Bonney] to come with you, if you can, and
        bring Myrtle and (I have forgotten your baby's name)
        [Erma].

[6]     We haven't heard from LaGrange since last winter. They (my
        folks) wrote while I was sick but got no answer. I hardly
        know what to think.

[7]     Does Sallie Conly live near you yet? Write and tell me, and I
        will write to her and Em, too.

[8]     Now Mollie, please forgive me for not writing sooner, and
        write me a long letter, and come and see me.

        From your old friend,
        Emma L. Coulten

## 🌸 Letter #109

In 1892, Gracie's husband, Zenas Hovey Gurley, Jr., ran and was
elected—eventually, twice—to the Iowa legislature, a representative
from his Decatur county district. By this time, the family was living in
Lamoni, Iowa. On November 12, 1895, he was one of four featured
speakers—including Joseph Smith III—at the opening of Graceland
College, the RLDS college in Lamoni; this despite the fact that he had
not been a member of the Reorganized Church for several years (See
Letter #105). Some whispered to Zenas that he should run for
governor. Instead, he would later accept a job as deputy warden of
the prison in Anamosa, Iowa.

It is clear from Gracie's letter that Zenas is in his second term as an
Iowa state assemblyman. Though Gracie seems a bit jaded by politics,
she reverts to her girlish practice (See Letter #55) of italicizing certain
words to emphasize her sense of excitement about the official
inauguration pageantry.

Gracie mentions Eva, her second child, who had married J.
Franklin Kane in 1894. Their boy, Cecil Kane, would grow up to
enlist in the army during World War I, despite his mother's efforts,

through her political contacts, to keep him away from danger. Eva gained some fame as a reader of dramatic literature. Under the stage name, Evelyn Gurley Kane, she was sometimes the entertainment at formal parties for government officials in Washington, D.C. Gracie's eldest child, Angie, was married to J.W. Waterman in 1893. Their child's name was Lenore. Both Mollie and Gracie were entering the latest stage of their lives, becoming grandmothers.

Later in the year that this letter was written, Mollie's second son, James Ernest McNutt, would begin his adventurous trip west, stopping at the Gurley home in Lamoni. It was during his stayover with the Gurleys that he met Gracie's third child, Julia Louisa. Although the reserved—some would say "stuffy"—James could not be accused of falling in love at first sight, in a letter to his mother, he commented that Julia was "...a girl with lots of hard sense and does not look at outward appearances." On the last day of May 1899, Julia and James were married. Two cousins who grew up together, Gracie and Mollie, were united even more by two of their children marrying.

> Lamoni, Iowa,
> Jan 21st 1896
> Dear Mollie,

[1]    It is too bad that your good kind letter should remain unanswered so long, but sickness and various other things have caused the delay. We spent Thanksgiving with Eva; was gone about ten days, had a pleasant time. They are getting along quite well, have a fine boy. Of course they are proud of him.

[2]    We "took in" the sights of Des Moines, climbed to the top of the Capitol, the building cost the modest or moderate sum of three million dollars. Iowa is a proud State and getting more so every day. Our new governor was inaugurated last Thursday; we are now under the rule of a Drake and a Parrott. I wanted to attend the ceremonies, but as the fever robbed me of my hair, and my teeth are nearly gone, thought I was not in very good plight to be presented to His Excellency.

[3]    Zenas has been gone two weeks; I see from the late paper that the Assembly will adjourn to-morrow, for a few days, so

think Zenas may come home for a visit. I rec'd a letter from him Friday, but he did not know then that they were going to adjourn.

[4]    Angie [Waterman] lives close to us now; her husband is teaching some distance from here, comes home every Friday; they have bought here and will likely stay for some time.

[5]    There is an epidemic of bad colds just now, and some cases of Diphtheria among children.

[6]    Hiram Booth[e] was here on a visit last fall. He had not seen Angeline [Dennis] for forty seven years; is a fine looking man, and I think quite well off. I did not talk with him on religion, but think he is a Brighamite all right.

[7]    I wish you could visit me next fall; why can't you? We have a good dentist here who extracts teeth "without pain." I know, for I have tried him—better come here and have him pull yours, and we will both get new teeth. It will improve our looks so much, you know.

[8]    Give my kind regards to Cousin George and the boys, kiss the little girls for me, and tell them I would like to see them. Write soon. Don't wait as long as I have.

[9]    Grandma [Margaret Bell Hickey] Gurley is with us and I have to look after her just as I would a child, does not know how to dress herself—and is crazy half the time. It is a great task. I think sometimes I have more than my share, but it will be all right in a hundred years, I suppose.

[10]    We are having lovely weather. I must write to Katie [Bonney Loudermilk] soon. Have you been to visit all of them this winter?

Good bye, your loving cousin,
Grace R. Gurley

## ❧ Letter #110

Amulek is sixty as he writes this nostalgic letter to Mollie. Hard work and old age has made his penmanship poor, but he still has a knack for the poetic phrase, and politics can put a twinkle in his eye, as he tweaks George McNutt about being "a silver man."

This is a reference to the presidential campaign just ended, during which successive Republican administrations were strongly challenged by William Jennings Bryan. Bryan called for a change in the backing of U.S. currency from gold to both silver and gold. Adopting the cheaper silver would allow for the printing of more paper dollars and make it easier for debt-ridden Western farmers to pay off long-standing debts. That is why many of Amulek's relatives and guests were for Bryan.

Mollie's second son, James, began a trek west in 1896 at the age of twenty-six. On the way, he met many of Mollie's Mormon relatives and friends, including Amulek [See par. 4 of this letter]. James also met his future bride, Julia Louisa Gurley, Zenas and Grace's nineteen-year-old daughter. James' western adventures ended in Utah. There he taught school, but the financial burdens that everyone hoped would be lifted became worse. With Bryan's loss, the bimetal backing of U.S. currency was delayed, and James was forced to return home. There was too little money for his wages.

Eagleville, [Mo.]                    Nov. 14, [18]96

Cousin Miriam,

[1]    After so long a time, I got answer to the last letter I wrote. You thought you wrote last, but I think not. I wrote, but it failed to get to you, or else you have forgotten. Let that go. I write again.

[2]    Your letter came last night. We were truly glad to hear from you again. We are all well at this time. Hope the same with you all.

[3]    We have nice weather now after the election. All is quiet now, and people has settled down to business. I take no offense in regards to cheering McKinley, as I vote that way, and if I did not, it would make no difference. I can't go back

on the Republican Party—not at all. They may be wrong in some things, but where and when was it ever bettered, I fail to see. Our county elected every Republican officer was.

[4]     Mary, your son [James McNutt] was here and made us a visit. Quite a genteel young man. I think him a very good boy. Proud I am of your family, from what I hear of them. Let them be good, true, truthful, and honest to home and abroad.

[5]     Our three youngest is at home yet. Olive [Boothe] is married and lives in sight. Hiram lives one mile from us. You see, they can come home every day or two, and they do.

[6]     I still live where I did when you and George were here. I have no help—only the girls. We make molasses every fall, commence the first of September and finish in October, from four to six weeks. I still farm, but [not] so much as I did when I was younger.

[7]     My brother Hyrum [Boothe] was out to see us last October a year ago. From Utah. First time he has ever been to see us. We had quite a time. Angeline [Dennis] was here. She had not seen him for 40 years. Don't that look hard for children.

[8]     Mosiah [Boothe] has never been here. They are both large and I am small.

[9]     Mary[ann Boothe] had a brother and sister to visit us this fall which had not been here for 17 years. We had a family reunion. I tell you we had a pleasant gathering. Still, all was [William Jennings] Bryan—me but three. There was 64 here for dinner outside of our own household. They started for their home next morning, south of here, 150 miles.

[10]    George keeps dreadful still. He may be a silver man. Still, it don't make no difference. I have them all round me. It would not do for all to be of the same opinion.

[11]    George, write if you will. I will try and answer. I will leave space for the children. Mary says she can't write you

enough. The girls make so much noise on the organ, I can't hardly write. Now they have quit.

[12]    Write more often. It seems a long time since we have written before. Tell the children I would be glad to have them write.

[13]    My hand trembles, you see.

[14]    I would be glad to see you all. Come out some time. You won't regret it. My love to all. Bless the children. Bless all.

From your cousin,
A[mulek] Boothe

## 🌺 Letter #111

Though he lives three more years, this is Amulek's last letter and the last letter to Mollie reprinted here. From Civil War soldier to seeing automobiles scurrying back and forth, he is full of memories as he knows Mollie must be. News of the children and grandchildren excite him, as does the steam thresher George McNutt saved so long to buy. Again, he promises to visit George and Mollie, but he never did.

Eagleville, Mo.                    Dec. 22, 1912

Dear Cousin Miriam,

[1]    You will no doubt be surprised to get a letter from me. We are only tolerable well—able to be on foot. This is fine winter weather. Roads are fine. Autos running every day, which are many.

[2]    Mary[ann Boothe] and I are at home alone, and I thought I would write to you and George. Christmas will soon be here. The children will most all be at home that day to a turkey dinner. Better come up and help eat it. I would like it the best kind. Would like to see your face again.

[3]     How is George and the children all? Where is Julie and
        James [McNutt]? Our children are well as far as I know. Olive
        [Boothe] is in Denver, yet. She was here this summer. Her
        oldest girl is married. We expect her here through Holy
        Days. They live at St. Joseph, Mo., 84 miles from here. Sister
        Angeline [Dennis] is still living in Independence, Mo.

[4]     We had a houseful last Sunday. Today, nobody.

[5]     Hiram [Boothe]'s oldest boy is teaching school this winter.
        Norey, our second girl, lives at Blythedale, nine miles from
        here. Oma and Elly [Boothe] live closer. Hiram lives where
        he did when you were here.

[6]     One [of] Angeline's girls lives in the mountains, one boy in
        Kans., one in Iowa, one in Nebraska, one in south Mo., two
        girls in Independence, Mo. Three are dead: Feelia [Amelia?],
        Susan, and Ida [Dennis].

[7]     I wrote to Joseph Bonney, and his girl [Kate Bonney
        Loudermilk] answered.

[8]     Hope you will have a Merry Xmas. Write if you will.
        Goodbye.

        Amulek Boothe

        To George
        Hello George,

[9]     A line to you. How are you? Still able to work with the
        thrasher? Do you farm? How was crops out there? They
        were good here, only potatoes, they were scarce. Wheat
        was good. Our apples was not very heavy here. Hogs and
        cattle are out of sight. Times is fairly good.

[10]    Come up and help eat the turkey next Wednesday. I would
        like to come and see you folks if I could. Hope I will some
        day. I am bothered with the asthma a good deal of the
        time. Some nights I have to sit up in a chair. Am some
        better now.

[11]     I will be 77 next May. You see, I am getting old. Not many years left. Hope this will find you all well.

[12]     This is all. Wishing you a Merry Christmas and Happy New Year for 1913.

[13]     Write when you will. Goodbye from,

         Amulek Boothe                    To George I. McNutt

**Julia Louisa Gurley** *(1877 – 1955) and* **James Ernest McNutt** *(1870 – 1953) taken most likely on their wedding day, 30 May 1899. Julia was the third of Grace and Zenas Hovey Gurley's children. James was the second of Miriam "Mollie" and George Irvin McNutt's children. When James travelled west to teach in Utah during 1896, he stopped at the Gurleys in Iowa, and met Julia, his first cousin once removed. At least two of his letters to his mother, Mollie, that year mention how much he approved of Julia's serious demeanor. He would eventually inherit the McNutt family farm, although he worked as an Adams County, Illinois, court reporter for 43 years. Julia and James had six children: Miriam Eda, Genevieve, Marjorie, James, George Albert, and Robert Gurley.*

# Epilogue

Mollie's life was simple, if hard. She supported her husband George in the few ventures he tried, like their investment in cousin Joe Bonney's planing mill operation in LaGrange. The failure of this business, despite Joe's hard work, may have prompted Mollie, in the spring of 1870, to sue her uncle Samuel Stewart for the rest of her father's estate. Mollie vividly remembered her aunt Rachel "stealing" the Works' household goods and winter provisions after her father and mother died. Mollie always believed there was much more to the Works' estate than her uncle spent supporting her and her brother Perry. But she lost the suit.

Like other farm housewives, she had ways of earning "pin money." She raised chickens and regularly sold them and their eggs. But her efforts to raise money depended on others. In a letter to her son, James, she complained that her husband would not take some chickens into Quincy, "...and I don't like to ask anyone else to take them...Wilmer [Stewart] offered to take a coop of chickens for me...and he took a coopful for himself, and I didn't like to ask him to take any more, but I have plenty more you can have if I can get them up there...I just couldn't get Papa to take them."

Other people regularly crowded into Mollie's life. George's sisters were often her guests for long periods of time, especially when their husbands were unemployed. The sisters may have felt George owed them something because he alone, as the sole surviving male, inherited the farm. Other relatives borrowed money from George. Even Mollie's brother, Perry, had George co-sign a note on which Perry defaulted. The McNutt farm was a refuge, a place to go when all else failed. In a letter to her son, James, on March 14, 1911, Mollie revealed what it was like for her:

> Erma has got settled for a while. Don't know how long they will stay. Till the bees swarm, I guess. Albert had to move, and he let them have a good many of his things to use till

> he calls for them. I don't know when that will be. They are
> here now and brought nearly all their clothes. They occupy
> the front rooms upstairs. The way Mabel talks, they intend
> to stay all summer. I suppose I am in for it again...Erma and
> Frank had been gone just two weeks when Albert and
> Mabel come, and Aunt Lina was gone five days, so you see
> they don't want me to get lonesome. Roy has been here
> about three months. I tell you, I am getting tired of having
> so many around. It keeps me so nervous and worried I can't
> hardly sleep or eat.

But it is certain that the others ate and slept well enough.

Hers was the home to visit during the summer, or on school holidays, for Joe Bonney's daughters, Katie and Ola, especially after their mother, Sallie, died in 1871. Later, even Katie's children stayed with Mollie. Going to the McNutt farm for the summer was a treat for children. When the mail hack finally arrived with guests, Mollie would come onto the front porch and call out, "Well, mercy on us. You got here, didya?"

When, in the late 1890s, it was obvious that Mollie's son, James, would marry her cousin Grace's daughter, Julia, Mollie invited the young woman to the farm. She was careful, however, to send her own daughters, Myrtle and Erma, to stay with friends, because she feared her daughter-in-law-to-be, Julia, who had been raised in the Mormon Church tradition of hierarchy, might look down on mere farmer's daughters. She feared Myrtle and Erma would be waiting on Julia as if they were servants. But young Julia was not such a snob. The marriage between Mollie's son and Grace's daughter further strengthened the ties between the two cousins. Now the two girls who had grown up together would have the same grandchildren.

Once, in 1916, Mollie again visited her friends in Decatur County, Iowa, and Eagleville, Missouri. But this time she learned that Amulek Boothe had died the year before. Nobody had told her. Heartbroken, she asked George to take her home immediately. He did.

Four years later, at 10:30 p.m. on Saturday, December 18, 1920, Mollie herself died. Besides the references to her parents, her husband, her children, and even her brother, Perry, who had died 10 years before, her obituary in the local Payson, Illinois, newspaper recalled that "her hospitality has been enjoyed by innumerable acquaintances..." that "she was charitable to a fault..." and that she was "a woman frail in body, but of remarkable energy, ambition;

retiring in disposition and devoted to her family and friends." Nothing was written about her learning from Aunt Angeline; about Deborah Morey; about her promises to Eunice and Helen; Tine Alford's teasing; Emma Johnson's complaining; or of whether, as a child, she had been frightened by Uncle Ebenezer's bushy eyebrows; of what she thought of her Mormon heritage; of what it was like to live where everyone believed the end of the world was near and looked on the Civil War as proof. There is never a word, never a string of words, that can pull the full weight of the slightest, frailest human life. So Mollie, as light as she was, rested at last, and the mementos of her life, the letters from her friends and relatives, were put in a trunk and left for the mice in the attic of the farmhouse. Until now.

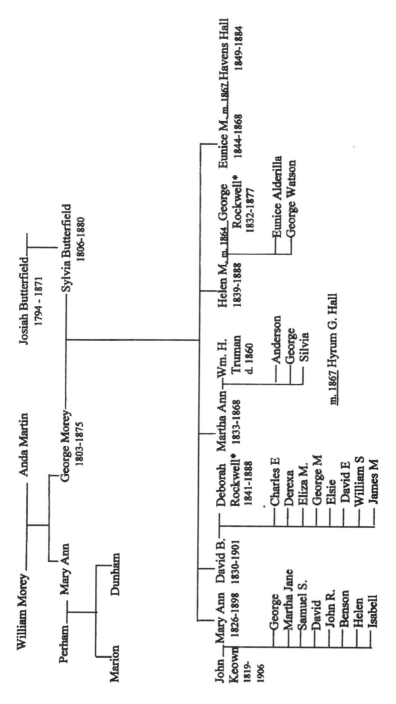

*A partial Morey Family Tree, showing the unusual relationship between the Halls (father and son) and Moreys, and the more usual relationship between the Rockwells (sister and brother) and the Moreys.*

*See Works family tree.

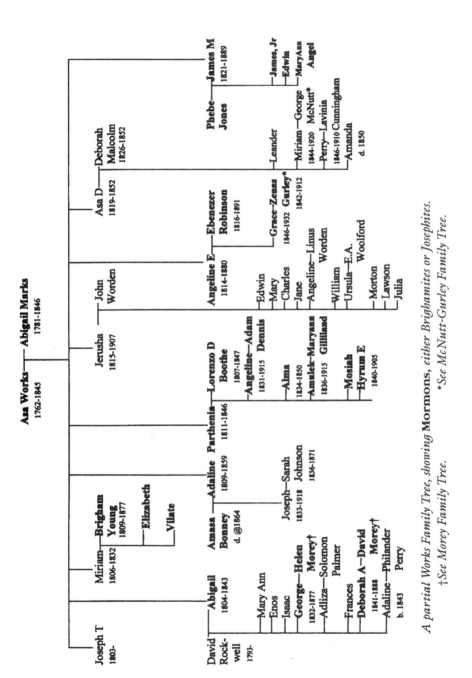

A partial Works Family Tree, showing **Mormons**, either *Brighamites or Josephites.*

†*See Morey Family Tree.*   *See McNutt-Gurley Family Tree.*

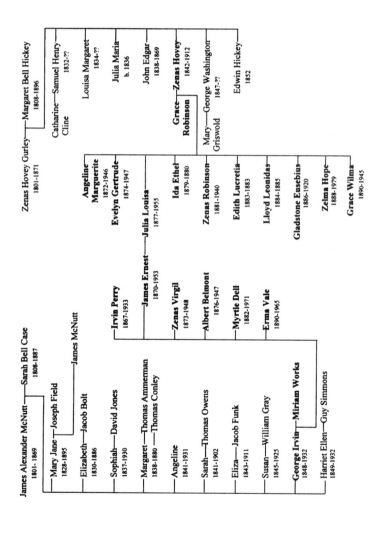

*Partial McNutt and Gurley Family Trees (early infant deaths omitted), showing cousins Mollie and Gracie's children and the marriage of two of them, James and Julia.*

# INDEX

# Partial Bibliography

Andrus, Hiram L. and Richard E. Bennett. *Mormon Mss to 1846: A Guide to Holdings of Harold B. Lee Library.* Provo: Brigham Young University Press, 1977.

*Biographical & Historical Record of Ringgold & Decatur Counties (Ia.).* Chicago: Lewis Publishing Co., 1887.

Bowman, John S., ed., *The Civil War Almanac.* New York City: Bison Books Corp., 1982.

Circuit Court Records of Adams County, Illinois 1852, Box 85. Archives of the State of Illinois. Springfield, Illinois.

Cook, Adrian. *The Armies of the Streets: The New York City Draft Riots of 1863.* Louisville: University Press of Kentucky, 1974.

Estate Records of Asa D. Works, Adams County, Illinois, filed January 21, 1852. Archives of the State of Illinois. Springfield, Illinois.

Ferris, Mrs. B. G. *Mormons At Home, with Some Incidents of Travel from Missouri to California 1852-3.* New York: Dix & Edwards, 1856.

Flanders, Robert Bruce. *Nauvoo: Kingdom on the River.* Urbana: University of Illinois Press, 1965.

Gates, Susa Young. *The Life Story of Brigham Young.* New York: MacMillan Company, 1930.

Hargrove, Catherine Perry. *A History of Playing Cards and a Bibliography of Cards and Gaming.* New York: Dover Publications, 1979.

Harlow, Alvin F. "Old Wires and New Waves," *Dictionary of American History,* New York: Charles Scribner's Sons, 1976.

Hill, Marvin S., C. Keith Rooker, and Larry T. Wimmer. *The Kirtland Economy Revisited: A Market Critique of Sectarian Economics.* Provo: Brigham Young University Press, 1977.

Hicken, Victor. *Illinois in the Civil War.* Urbana: University of Illinois Press, 1966.

Hirshson, Stanley P. *The Lion of the Lord, a Biography of Brigham Young.* New York: Alfred A. Knopf, 1969.

*Historical Encyclopedia of Illinois and History of Fulton County, Vol. 2.* Chicago: Munsell, 1908.

*History of Adams County, Illinois 1879.* Chicago: Murray, Williamson, and Phelps, 1879.

*History of the Church, Vol. 3.* Independence: Herald House Publishing, 1954.

*History of Lewis County, Missouri.* Chicago: Goodspeed Publishing, 1887.

*History of Harrison County, Missouri.* St. Louis: George W. Wanamaker, 1888.

*History of Decatur County, Iowa 1915. Vols. 1 & 2.* Des Moines: Nickleson Publishers, 1915.

Kennedy, James Henry. *Early Days of Mormonism.* Scribner's Sons. New York: 1888.

Keown, Helen Isabell. Family records. Unpublished.

Landrum, Carl. *Quincy in the Civil War.* Quincy, Ill.: Quincy Historical Society, 1966.

—— "'Epizootic' epidemic of 1872 took heavy toll of horses." *Quincy Herald-Whig.* Quincy, Ill.: Whig Publishing, 17 April 1987.

Larson, Gustive O. *The "Americanization" of Utah for Statehood.* San Marino Press. Huntington Library: 1971.

Leach, Jack Franklin. *Conscription in the United States: Historical Background.* Yokohama, Japan: Charles E. Tuttle, 1952.

Long, Everette B. with Barbara Long. *The Civil War Day By Day: An Almanac 1861 - 1865.* Garden City: Doubleday & Co., 1971.

MacLean, Kay. "Publications Series III: Popular History #12: Christmas Celebrations." Springfield, Ill.: Sangamon State University, 1979.

McKiernan, F. Mark and Roger D. Launius, eds. *An Early Latter Day Saint History: The Book of John Whitmer, Kept by Commandment.* Independence, Mo.: Herald House Publishing House, 1980.

McNutt, James Ernest. Personal letters to his mother Miriam "Mollie" Works McNutt 1896-1897. Unpublished.

*Marriage Records of Harrison County Missouri: A-D.* St. Louis: Missouri Genealogical Society, 1972.

Maslowski, Peter. *Treason Must Be Made Odious.* Milwood: KTO Press, 1978.

*Nauvoo Expositor.* William Law, Wilson Law, et al, publishers. Nauvoo: 7 June 1844.

Robinson, Ebenezer. "Items of Personal History of the Editor," *The Return,* Davis City: 1888-1891.

Ohlmert, Michael. "Points of Origin," *Smithsonian,* May 1984.

Parrish, William E. *David Rice Atchison of Missouri: Border Politician.* University of Missouri Studies, Vol. 34, No. 1. Columbia: University of Missouri, 1961.

Quinn, D. Michael. *The King Strang Story.* New York City: MacMillan Co., 1978.

— . *The Mormon Succession Crisis of 1844, Vol. 16, No. 2.* Provo: Brigham Young University Press: 1976.

Smith, Heman C. ed., *Journal of History.* Lamoni, Ia.: Board of Publication Reorganized Church of Jesus Christ of Latter Day Saints, 1917.

Smith Davis, Inez. *The Story of the Church.* Independence: Herald House, 1934.

Smith, Page. *Trial By Fire: A People's History of the Civil War and Reconstruction, Vol. 5.* New York: McGraw-Hill, 1982.

Smucker, Samuel and H. L. Williams. *Life Among the Mormons.* New York: Hurst & Co, 1879.

Steiner, Paul E. *Disease in the Civil War.* Springfield, Ill.: Charles C. Thomas, 1968.

Taylor, Samuel W. *Nightfall at Nauvoo.* New York: Avon Books, 1971.

*True Latter Day Saints Herald.* Isaac Sheen, ed. Plano, Ill.: Reorganized Church of Latter Day Saints, 1860+

*Webster's New International Dictionary of the English Language.* Springfield, Mass.: G & C Merriam Co., 1930.

Works, James Marks. Letter to Jerusha Works Worden, 19 January 1865. Unpublished.